AMERICAN PIE

American Pie

My Search for the Perfect Pizza

Peter Reinhart

TEN SPEED PRESS

Berkeley

Except as otherwise noted, photography © 2003 by Maren Caruso. Shot on location
    at Pizzetta 211, San Francisco.
Photos on pages 16, 17, 22, 26, 27, and 74 by Peter Reinhart.

Library of Congress Cataloging-in-Publication Data
Reinhart, Peter.
  American pie : my search for the perfect pizza / Peter Reinhart.
      p. cm.
1. Pizza. 2. Italy—Description and travel. 3. United States—Description and travel.
I. Title.
TX770.P58 .R45 2003
641.8'248—dc22

                                          2003019597
ISBN-13: 978-1-58008-422-2

Printed in China

Book design by Nancy Austin

16 15 14 13 12 11 10 9 8

First Edition

Contents

v

Introduction

For a long time, I thought the best pizza in the country was from Mama's in Bala Cynwyd, just outside of Philadelphia. And then something happened.

I grew up on Mama's, even worked there briefly as a delivery boy, and found warm comfort in its stringy cheese and crisp, yet floppy crust whenever I'd been rejected for a date, lost a basketball game, or got together with high-school friends for a Saturday-night poker game. My family was equally hooked, and we often picked up a Mama's pizza for dinner when my mom wanted a break from cooking, especially if going out for Chinese food, our other favorite pastime, seemed like too much trouble. We knew the owners of Pagano's Pizzeria in West Philadelphia and often went there when we wanted an actual restaurant experience to go along with our pizza, pasta, and broasted chicken (they were pioneers in this now rarely seen pressurized frying system). But as good as Pagano's pizza was, it never measured up to Mama's for deeply felt satisfaction, a culinary balm of Gilead. More than forty years after eating my first Mama's pizza, almost always made by Paul Castelucci (though I never knew his last name when I worked as a delivery boy), the business is still in the family, and the pizzas are now supervised, but not made, by Paul Jr., Paul's son. Mama's is still extremely popular, with long waiting times not only for pizza, but also for fabulous stromboli, hoagies, and cheese steaks.

My brother Fred, who now lives forty-five minutes from Mama's instead of the five minutes of our childhood, continues to make the pilgrimage whenever he needs a fix. He brought us a Mama's pizza when my wife, Susan, and I were in Philadelphia for a big food event. Susan had sprained her ankle at the airport just after we landed, forcing us to cancel our dinner plans so she could keep her foot on

1

ice. When I called Fred to explain our plight, he said, "No problem, I'll pick up a pizza and some cheese steaks at Mama's and we'll eat in." I loved the idea. It had been years since my last Mama's pizza.

The pizza arrived ninety minutes later, accompanied by Fred and his wife, Patty. I rushed through the greetings—hug, hug, "great to see you"—while Patty comforted Susan. I was captivated by the aroma of the pizzas and cheese steaks, and my mind floated away to distant times. It was like a long-lost friend, triggering painful and joyful memories that were flashing like a deck of cards rifled in front of my eyes. I'd deal with those later. For now, as far as I was concerned, it was about opening the pizza box, unwrapping the butcher paper from the cheese steaks, and getting everyone to stop talking and start eating. We divvied up the cheese steaks, which tasted even better than I remembered them to be, and then, at last, passed around slices of the pizza. I took a bite and stopped, the pleasant image-streaming of food memories suddenly interrupted by a mental disconnect. I shook it off and took another bite expecting an automatic memory flash to kick in so I could resume my forty-year flavor retrospective. Instead, I got a blast of "Whoa!"

There was definitely something amiss. The words just came out without forethought. "Fred, they've changed the crust."

"No they haven't."

"Yes they have."

"No, they haven't. Maybe it's you."

"I don't think so. The crust is thicker and there are no air bubbles in the lip. Definitely not the Mama's I grew up with."

"I think it's you."

"No, it isn't."

Fred took another bite. "Well, it does seem a little thicker than usual. I heard they were breaking in a new pizza guy. But, I gotta tell you, it's still pretty close to usual."

"Maybe it is me," I thought. It wasn't just that the crust was a little different. The cheese and sauce certainly still resonated with old memories, and even if it wasn't the best Mama's, it was close enough that it should have elicited, within my usually tolerant margin-for-error forgiveness code, at least a sigh of pleasure. But something had changed within me. My expectations, an internal bar of standards that is both conscious and subconscious, had been violated. A slow wave of realization set in, one that I couldn't suppress even though I tried.

"Maybe," I said to myself, "it was never as good as I thought it was, just the best I'd been exposed to during my sheltered youth." I knew it was something I couldn't say out loud because Fred and Patty still lived here, while I was going back to Providence and might not have another Mama's pizza for years. Yet I couldn't shake the thought.

Since 1990, when I left the communal setting of a religious order in which everyone lived a vow of poverty and thus had limited restaurant experience, I have had the privilege of teaching and writing about food, especially bread. I've traveled around the country and beyond, belatedly pursuing knowledge about my taste passions. These passions are simple, not of the great gourmand type. I have learned that one of my inherent gifts is the ability to recognize flavors and textures of universal appeal and show people how to reproduce them. As a result of this gift, I have carved out a career as an educator, writer, and product developer. Which brings me back to pizza.

I have had a steady stream of students who have their own sets of childhood food associations that have driven them to the gates of learning. Food memories, as James Beard and M.F.K. Fisher have shown us, are powerful and compelling forces. Wherever I teach, if I want to get a lively conversation going, I need only ask, "Where do I find the best pizza around here?" Nearly everyone has a pizza story and a strong opinion. Pizza, it seems, lives in everyone's hall of fame.

In 1976, I worked in Raleigh, North Carolina, as a houseparent in a home for what we euphemistically called undisciplined teenagers; in other words, juvenile delinquents. There was a pizzeria on Hillsborough Street called Brothers Pizza, and although I barely remember the details of the place, I do remember the experience of it. I took the kids there whenever we needed to decompress from the latest dramatic event in our house, and there were always, always dramas. That pizza, and only that pizza among all the pizza shops in town, was a panacea, our emotional salve. It had a crispy, crackly crust, like hot buttered toast, comforting and satisfying. It was perfect. The cheese was stringy and slightly salty. Was it the best pizza I'd ever had? No, but it was "perfect" pizza, a peerless match of textures and flavors that fed more than our stomachs and palates. But if I had it now, all these years later, I imagine it would be like having a Mama's now. It would be good, perhaps the same as it always was, but it wouldn't be the pizza of 1976, when teenage boys and girls from shattered families, with broken hearts and raging hormones, felt safe enough to confess their fears to me and to one another as they ate their pizza. That pizza, out of that context, could never be that perfect again.

So here I was, years after Raleigh, in Philadelphia, realizing that I was caught in a nature versus nurture situation. Was it me or was it the pizza that had changed, or was it a little bit of both? I'm pretty sure that when I asked myself that question, I set this whole pizza quest in motion.

Pizzeria Bianco

A few years before what I now refer to as my "Mama's awakening," a student of mine at the California Culinary Academy in San Francisco told me about a guy named Chris Bianco, who owned Pizzeria Bianco, in Phoenix, Arizona. She had worked at his restaurant prior to coming to school and raved about his pizza. By a happy coincidence, I was headed to Phoenix for the annual conference of the International Association of Culinary Professionals, which is always held in a different city. Most of us went to Phoenix expecting to experience a blitz of great Southwest cuisine, and we weren't disappointed. But the restaurant that had the biggest buzz of all was Pizzeria Bianco, located just a short walk from the convention center in downtown Phoenix.

I was scheduled to make a presentation on bread-baking techniques at one of the conference workshops, so prior to leaving San Francisco, I asked my Phoenix student to recommend a bakery that I could partner with for making my workshop breads. She said there weren't any good bread bakeries, but that Chris Bianco made his own bread for his pizzeria, and it was easily the best in town. I called him and we arranged to bake bread together.

When I got to town, I walked over to Pizzeria Bianco with Steve Garner, a friend of mine who hosts a radio food show in Santa Rosa, California, and John Ash, one of the great chefs of America who also cohosts the show with Steve. It was three o'clock in the afternoon and the restaurant wasn't scheduled to open for another two hours. My idea was that we'd talk and plan out our bread baking, but Chris insisted on making us a couple of pizzas first.

"Okay," I said without resistance, hoping, but doubtful, that they would live up to their reputation. A few minutes later, two perfect, I mean *perfect*, pizzas landed on our table, a classic *Margherita* and a white pizza with arugula and onions, and all thought of bread baking vanished for the moment. Steve and John immediately kicked into their radio-interview mode and began grilling Chris about his pizzas. We learned that as a young man with cooking talent he had gone to Naples from the Bronx, his hometown, to learn how to make true Neapolitan pizza. When his family moved to Phoenix, he decided to make his culinary statement by trying to create the best pizza in the world. He made his own mozzarella cheese and grew his own basil and lettuce behind the restaurant. He and his brother, Marco, made their own rustic Italian bread (similar to *ciabatta*) from the pizza dough, and their mother came in to make the three desserts on the menu. Chris served five types of pizza (no substitutes, please), house salad, an appetizer course, beverages, and dessert. There was no pasta course on the menu, nor any other entrée. It was just a pizzeria, but with haute cuisine attitude. I asked him why no pasta.

"I think I actually could make the best pasta in town, and if we served it people would love it," he explained. "But then I'd have my attention divided and the pizzas might suffer. So I decided my true goal is to make the best pizza in the world. If I ever want to do pasta, I'll open a different restaurant and do it there."

Did he have plans to do just that? He smiled sheepishly and said, "No, not really. You've got to understand, I love making pizza."

We talked for quite awhile and I realized it was almost five o'clock. A crowd had been gathering outside the front door for over an hour—hot, anxious people hoping to be in the first wave to grab one of the forty-two seats and not have to wait for the second seating. (I soon learned that this is a daily ritual at Bianco.)

Chris anticipated my question and said, "I don't do takeout. Can't keep up. Besides, I want them to eat the pizza the way it's meant to be eaten, right out of the oven. It's just not the same out of the box. But even so, a wood-fired oven can only handle so many pies and that's that." He excused himself to get ready for dinner.

Now we were getting dirty looks from some of the people peering through the window, wondering why we were on the inside, eating pizza, while they had to wait until the doors opened at five. More to the point, probably, they were worried our three precious seats might not be available when the doors opened. So, we made our exit, and a collective sigh of relief rose from the line.

The next morning I returned to make my bread dough and watched Chris make his pizza dough. "I don't use a mixer, just a big bowl and my hands," he said. Sure enough, he combined about fifty pounds of flour (specially flown in from the Giusto's mill in San Francisco) with salt, yeast, and water. Unlike most American pizza makers, he used no oil, true to the Neapolitan rule.

"It's really all about feel," he explained. "I have to make it by hand because it's the only way to really know when it's right. I can just feel what adjustments are needed and when it's ready."

Twenty minutes later we had finished mixing our respective doughs. Mine, using a new technique I had just learned in France, had to be chilled, but Chris's dough stayed out, covered in the bowl, to ferment slowly. Hours later he divided it into smaller pieces for either pizza or bread, shaped his loaves, and again allowed the dough to ferment, chilling the evening pizza dough in the refrigerator and leaving the bread pieces out for Marco to bake off later. The rest of the time he and his crew did all the prep, making the sauces, picking lettuce and basil from the garden, and readying themselves for the rush of people gathered at the still-locked door.

Watching Chris work helped me to realize how much I still had to learn about that simple yet complex substance called dough and, more importantly, about how dough is transformed, in the hands of a skilled *pizzaiolo* (pizza maker) into pizza. A few years passed and I got deeper and deeper into the intricacies of bread making, trying to figure out how, as I described it, to evoke the full potential of flavor from the grain. In developing pizza dough for several companies, I gradually came to understand what causes some dough to be better than others. I ate a lot of pizza along the way and tasted many toppings and, more important, heard many pizza philosophies. Whenever the subject of great pizza came up, I mentioned Bianco. At first I was met with laughter and disbelief. The idea of great pizza in Phoenix just didn't compute. But then I ran into people who knew about Pizzeria Bianco, either from experience or from reading or hearing about it.

It had been a while since I'd tasted the pizza at Pizzeria Bianco, so I began to doubt my memory. Shortly after the "Mama's awakening," I ran into one of my favorite food writers, Jeffrey Steingarten, and he asked me who I thought made the best pizza. "I used to think it was Mama's in Bala Cynwyd, Pennsylvania," I told him, "but now I think it might be Pizzeria Bianco in Phoenix."

He hadn't been there but had heard of it. "How can you call it the best if you haven't tried Frank Pepe's or Sally's in New Haven, or John's or Grimaldi's in New York City?" he asked.

Of course he was right. Pizzeria Bianco might have been the best I'd ever had, but there were so many other legendary places still to try. So I did go to Pepe's, Sally's, Grimaldi's, John's, and many other places. I went to Genoa and then to Naples, into the belly of the beast, to the source, and then returned to America to immerse myself in pizza of all types: classic, modern, avant-garde, you name it. I was searching for the perfect slice. That meant I had to discover what perfection, at least pizza perfection, really is. Along the way I went back to Pizzeria Bianco in Phoenix to find out if my memory held true, or if it was to be another Mama's moment, surpassed by even better pizza found elsewhere.

In the pages that follow, I recount the journey that took place between my two visits to Phoenix, plus some trips that followed it. (This is a journey with no clear endpoint; it doesn't begin or end with Pizzeria Bianco or Mama's, but is merely signposted by them.) I had become a hunter of sorts, a pizza hunter, and I enlisted others to join me on the hunts. With Mama's no longer the benchmark, and with the memory of Pizzeria Bianco serving as a temporary beacon and standard, I sought out great pizza everywhere I traveled, and I traveled to seek out great pizza.

Some of the numerous pizza excursions I choreographed were thwarted by circumstances: trip cancellations, a restaurant Closed sign, logistical mix-ups. But almost every time something went wrong, something else occurred to make it all right. In fact, Plan B was often better than Plan A could ever have been. As result I came up with the Reinhart Pizza Hunter's Credo, a sound axiom for anyone who decides to adopt it: It's all about the adventure, not the pizza. The pizza is just grace.

Sometimes my fellow pizza hunters made the hunt itself a more memorable adventure than the pizza did. I had so many interesting conversations around a pizza, on the way to get a pizza, or in anticipation of a pizza, that the pizza itself became the excuse for the hunt. But every now and then, the quality of the pizza transcended the hunt, stopped all conversation and refocused everything on itself, the object and subject, and the thrill of the hunt fulfilled itself in the quarry. When that happened it was magical, and all that mattered again was pizza.

So, I followed the trail wherever it led. And where it inevitably led, to no one's surprise, was Italy.

[PART 1]

THE HUNT

Those who have traveled to Naples, or to Genoa and its surrounding Ligurian coast, know that American pizza and focaccia (the northern Italian version of pizza) are not always the same as what we call Neapolitan, or *Napoletana*, pizza or Ligurian focaccia. There are a number of reasons for this difference, and it is not necessarily a bad thing that ours are different from theirs. Pizza is, and has always been, a work in progress.

My Greek friends insist that pizza isn't even originally Italian, but Greek, brought to Naples by Peloponnesians escaping the Ottomon Turks or, much earlier, by Trojans fleeing the builders of that famous horse. Indeed, most Greeks are happy to take credit for contributions from both eras and like to connect nearly everything in Italy to their famous ancestors, Odysseus and Aeneas. In relation to pizza, their reasoning may be accurate. Naples, originally called Neapolis, was founded in the sixth century B.C. by Greek colonists from the even earlier nearby settlement of Cumae. We also know that the ancient Greeks made a flatbread with toppings called *placenta*.

But here's the pith of it: Pizza evolved from one of the most basic food concepts—bread and topping, specifically dough cooked over or in a fire, finished off with sauce, oil, cheese, whatever was at hand. Did the Greeks invent it? Why not the Egyptians? Or the Indians? Forget about who invented pizza. The real question is where was it perfected, where was it elevated from a simple peasant food to the craft, to the art form we appreciate today? You do not have to be an Italian or even an Italian American to know the answer to that one. When Gennaro Lombardi brought pizza to New York City's Lower East Side in 1905, he brought it from Italy; his influence was the pie of Naples. But the fuel in New York was coal, not the wood of southern Italy, so from the moment pizza hit the shores of America, modification and adaptability were inevitable. Thus began the evolution (some would say the devolution) of pizza as we now know it.

I knew I would have to visit the surviving great early pizzerias of America, not only for the pleasure of their pies, but also to back my response to the inescapable challenge, "How can you say Pizzeria Bianco is the best if you haven't been to — ?" But even more important, I knew I would have to (would want to, would love to) visit the original role models, the pizzerias of Naples and the *focaccerie* of Liguria, to understand what they had fostered on this side of the Atlantic. In other words, I would have to go to Italy.

LIGURIA

I began my search for the roots of pizza in the port city of Genoa, the commercial heart of the northwest region of Liguria. Susan and I settled into a hotel room just around the corner from the statue of Christopher Columbus near the central train station, and then set out to explore this hardworking harbor town known as the epicenter of *focaccia alla genovese*. The people of Genoa are as proud of their focaccia as the Neapolitans are of their pizza. Some variation of it is served at most meals. *Focaccerie*, similar to the pizza-by-the-slice shops of New York City, are found every few blocks in this colorful, maritime town, which meant that freshly baked focaccia was never more than a few minutes away, no matter where we found ourselves.

In my brief sampling, I came to the following conclusion: focaccia is not automatically extraordinary just because it is made in Genoa. Like pizzas everywhere, focaccia can be great, good, or forgettable. Whether topped with cheese, onions, potatoes, cured meats, or pesto or another sauce, the bread itself is usually good but seldom outstanding, mind-numbing, conversation stopping, or otherwise memorable.

One thing I learned during two previous trips to Italy is that while Italians love bread, you won't find great bread everywhere in the country. The ratio of world-class bread to average bread is about the same as in the United States. Even so, Italians are loyal to their local bread products, regardless of outside opinion. For instance, while visiting Bologna, I encountered the *manino*, a roll shaped to look like a hand. The locals raved to me about how special this bread was, and I found I had to hide my disappointment when I finally tried some. What was special was that the

Bolognans had grown up with this unusually shaped bread. What was a bit perplexing was how these food-savvy people could be so deluded about their dry, overly starchy bread that had no discernible special property other than its shape. This is not an unusual circumstance. People are notoriously—and naturally—chauvinistic to the point of delusion about many of the things they have known since childhood. I myself am that way—or once was—about Mama's pizza.

The focaccia of Genoa was certainly better than the *manino* of Bologna. But would I make a return trip for it? No. The focaccia in San Francisco's North Beach, from the aptly named Liguria Bakery, is as good. The focaccia-like pizza at Sullivan Street Bakery in Manhattan is substantially better. The focaccia my culinary students make is actually as good or better than anything I had in Genoa.

"Well, do you think we should still go to Recco?" Susan asked.

"We've got nothing to lose," I replied, trying to remain hopeful that something new and different awaited us there.

We bought train tickets for the forty-five-minute ride to Recco, a small town just south of Genoa. Carol Field, author of *The Italian Baker* among other classics, and Johanne Killeen and George Germon, owners of the Al Forno Restaurant in Providence (see page 64), had all said we must go to try the local *focaccia col formaggio di Recco*. Once on the train, Susan asked me what I thought about the focaccia in Genoa. Our conversation went something like this:

"Well, focaccia is just bread with something on it or in it. So if it's going to be memorable, the bread has to be really, really good. The breakfast focaccia at the hotel, plain with just a little salt and aniseed on top, was good. It was flavorful, the bread was moist and not dry—I liked it. But will I dream about it? Will I crave it when we get home and regret not being able to find anything like it? I doubt it. The pesto focaccia from the shop near our hotel was good. The sauce was wonderful, which I would expect here in Genoa since pesto, focaccia, and Christopher Columbus are the three things for which the city is famous."

"So what's the big deal then about focaccia?" Susan asked.

"The potential for greatness is always there, but I think focaccia is like most things that have been around for a while: bakers settle into a routine until someone comes along and pushes the envelope. As long as people buy it at this level, most bakers have no incentive to take it to another level. I'm sure there are *focaccerie* that do it better than what we've sampled, and bakers who know there are ways to make the bread better. That said, I do appreciate one thing about all Genoa focaccia: the thickness. In the States, focaccia is usually too thick—more than an inch and sometimes even two inches tall—so that it becomes too much about the bread and not enough about the topping. Here, it's just right, about a half inch thick, and even though it looks like it's going to be dry, it stays moist and creamy. That's the most valuable thing I saw in Genoa."

As we pulled into our stop, Susan sighed, "Well I hope this Recco focaccia is better than what we've had so far." We would soon discover that she had just uttered the understatement of the trip.

The train station stood at the top of a hill, and the street that led away from it spiraled down to sea level and the Via Roma, the main street of Recco. According to Ed Behr, who reported on Recco in his wonderful journal, *The Art of Eating*, the town had been heavily bombed during World War II and then rebuilt. That explains its rather modern feel, which is reminiscent of a small East Coast beach community in America. As we wound our way down to the town, its charm began to grow on us.

We were in search of the most famous restaurant in Recco, Manuelina, the purported early-twentieth-century birthplace of the legendary *focaccia col formaggio di Recco*. Ed Behr's research seemed to suggest that it was probably Manuelina Capurra's marketing skills that earned her the credit for inventing something that was already being served in many towns along the coast (and in similar permutations in Greece under the generic category "pita"). The civic fathers of Recco realized well before their neighbors the value in "owning" a celebrated product. The town had once been known for its watch factory, but that was long gone. So it latched onto dough and cheese, established an annual *focaccia col formaggio* festival, and pulled off a coup that would make any chamber of commerce proud. Recco claimed *focaccia col formaggio* as its own, and the town had the franchise by fiat.

Almost every restaurant we passed proudly listed this item in its window display, but only a select few have become renowned for it. We had been given a street address for Manuelina on Via Roma, so we kept walking until we came to it, about a mile down the road. It was closed.

"This can't be happening," I moaned.

Susan responded more philosophically, proposing "Maybe this is one of those times when, you know, if a door closes, a window opens."

I groaned as I knocked on the door. Amazingly, it was unlocked and opened slowly. We went in, hoping that our American audaciousness would result in us finding someone who would tell us that even though the restaurant was closed on Wednesdays, and this was Wednesday, the staff would cook for us. The restaurant was beautiful and I wanted to eat there. We heard someone walking toward us. It was the cleaning woman, and even though she did not speak English, a series of desperate hand gestures prompted her to lead us across the alley into a pleasant hotel and to a woman who seemed to be in charge. I explained that we had come all the way from the United States to experience the *focaccia col formaggio di Recco* at Manuelina and how distressed we were to find the restaurant closed.

"Ah yes," she said in good English, "It is our restaurant, but it is closed every Wednesday. I am so sorry."

I put on my saddest face and asked, "Are any of the cooks around? Is there any chance?"

"Ah no," she said. "But I have an idea. About sixty meters down the road is another restaurant, Da Vittorio. They also make the focaccia and theirs is," and at this point she whispered, "as good as ours."

"Really?"

"Well, almost as good. But it is very good and they are open and we are not."

She pointed us back toward the train station and we walked until we came to Da Vittorio. It looked like a Swiss chalet, less fancy than Manuelina, but charming in its own way. Like Manuelina, it seemed to be a combination hotel and restaurant. The doors were open and we saw movement inside, so we went in. Two men were at work in the room, setting things up for the lunch hour. They both looked up and smiled as we entered. They were identical twins. We approached one of them and explained our plight. He nodded, gestured with the international wait-a-second motion, and then returned with the other twin.

"I am Giovanni, and this is my twin brother, Vittorio. We are the Bisso brothers. I speak English but he does not."

So I again explained our mission, how we discovered that Manuelina was closed after traveling all the way from the United States to eat there, but that we had heard

A *focaccia col formaggio di Recco*, just out of the oven, made by *focacciaiolo* Fabio, and Da Vittorio co-owner Giovanni Bisso.

that their restaurant was equally good. He especially liked the last point and translated it for his brother, who smiled and nodded.

"Yes, there are three such famous places in Recco, and we are one of them. We will take good care of you."

Those were the magic words I had been waiting all day to hear.

Giovanni, whose nickname is Gian, guided us into the kitchen where we were surrounded by bubbling pots of fish stock and an active little community of three cooks calmly but busily making sauces, fresh pasta, and, in its own little corner of the kitchen, *focaccia col formaggio*. We moved to the very back of the room where we met the *focacciaiolo*, Fabio, who generously demonstrated for us the simple art of Recco's gift to the culinary lexicon.

I had never had *focaccia col formaggio di Recco*, so I had no idea that it was unlike all the other focaccia I had seen in Genoa. It is made from unyeasted dough—just flour, water, and a bit of salt. Fabio first rolled it out and then stretched it by hand into a larger and larger disk that was so paper-thin that it was almost translucent, much like strudel or phyllo dough. He draped the disk over a large copper pan about twenty-four inches in diameter with a half-inch lip around the edge, and then tucked it in to eliminate any air pockets. Next, he topped it with dollops of creamy *stracchino*, a fresh cheese that looked like a rich ricotta but was more like mascarpone or soft cream cheese. He then shaped a second piece of the dough just like the first one, used it to cover the top of the "pie" (for that was what it had now become), and

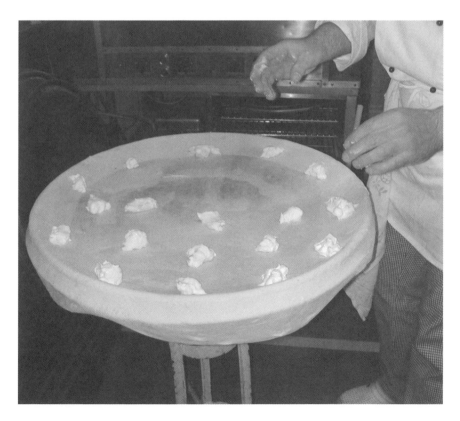

This is what a *focaccia col formaggio di Recco* looks like just before the top crust covers all that luscious *stracchino* cheese.

crimped the edges of the two disks together. Finally, he poked four or five holes in the top, pulled them out slightly to create vents, drizzled the entire surface with olive oil, sprinkled on a little salt, and slid the pan into the oven (after a little awkward translation, we decided it was heated to the equivalent of 500 degrees). Fabio told us to come back in about eight minutes.

Gian then took us up a short flight of stairs to his pasta shop, where we met Renato, who was making *trofie* (or *troffie*) and *pansotti* from a simple dough of flour, water, and salt—no eggs, no oil. To make the *trofie*, Renato cut off small snippets of dough and rolled them into little corkscrewed twigs with the edge of his hand. He showed me how to do it and was a little surprised, and pleased, that I was able to pick up the technique fairly quickly. Within a few minutes he had, with the addition of my few pieces, created a large pile of *trofie*, ready to be boiled. Some of the remaining dough was rolled into small disks, about the size of a silver dollar, and then pressed with a small wooden stamp that imprinted a design. These decorative, delicate pastas were called *corzetti stampati*. Gian explained that the stamps came in many patterns, some personal and some of general interest, ranging from abstract lines and geometric shapes to more representational pastoral scenes and figures.

By this time the *focaccia col formaggio* was ready to be pulled from the oven. It had turned a deep golden color with caramelized splotches that were dark brown. Gian quickly escorted us to our table in the dining room. A couple at the table across the aisle from us were sipping some white wine. We were brought a bottle of the same local wine, and the pan of focaccia that we had watched Fabio make was placed next to our table. The waiter sliced it into squares, not wedges as with pizza, and lifted a few pieces onto each of our plates. He did the same for the couple across the aisle. It looked like a lot of pie, larger than what we think of as an extra-large pizza, but because the dough was so thin, it was not a lot of food. As soon as we finished our servings, Susan and I realized that we could have easily devoured the entire pie without the help of the other couple. I even felt pangs of resentment toward them. I wanted more.

But we didn't get more. Gian had taken charge of our dining experience, and it was time for the definitive Genoese pasta experience, *trofie col pesto*. Those toothsome little pasta twigs that we had twisted in the kitchen had been boiled for just a few minutes and were now served in a sauce of fresh basil, garlic, pine nuts, olive oil, and Parmesan. We had had pasta with pesto before, of course, but there is something to be said for being served this dish by people who are proud of what they do and of what their region has contributed to the culinary vocabulary. Gian and Vittorio both had the appearance of hosts content with fulfilling their appointed purpose in life. They were bringing us pleasure and they were doing it through total immersion in their heritage. The Bisso brothers' pesto was excellent, brightly colored and flavored. It was perhaps not the best I had ever eaten, but given the context, it was certainly the most memorable.

The *trofie* was followed by the *pansotti* served in *salsa di noce*, a rich béchamel-like cream sauce with walnuts, garlic, marjoram, pine nuts, and some kind of fresh, creamy cheese which Gian casually referred to as *formagita*. What remains in my memory about both the *trofie* and the *pansotti* is not the sauce, but the texture of the pasta, one of slightly chewy resistance that just gave way under the tooth, complemented by the sauce but not really dependent on it.

By the time the fish stew was served, we were so sated we were practically hanging onto our chairs. I have no idea what we had for dessert, though I remember that it was very good; my mind was still rapt with thoughts, cravings, for *focaccia col formaggio di Recco*. Gian sat with us as we collected ourselves, telling us nostalgic stories of his region. I remember little bits of what he said, like how the term *blue jeans* was named after the blue trousers of Genoese sailors; that the flag of London was based on the flag of Genoa; that the patron saints of the area are Mary the Suffering, Saint John the Baptist, and Saint George (of dragon fame); and that Vitturin, Manuelina, and La Barachetta di Biagio were other restaurants where you can find excellent *focaccia col formaggio di Recco*. Some places, he told us, don't bake it in copper pans but directly on the stone hearth. Opinion is divided on the matter of which method is best, and we didn't have another day to stick around to find out, but I wondered, "How could it get any better than this?"

As we prepared to leave, Vittorio, who is named after his grandfather, the original owner of Da Vittorio, took us to a large urn and indicated that we should choose something from it. Gian explained, "He wants you to take a wooden pasta stamp as a souvenir of your time here."

We pulled one of the stamps from the bowl. It had a simple design on it, but the pattern did not matter. It was a touching moment. We had been treated to true

Ligurian hospitality, and even though this scene may have been repeated countless times with other visitors, we felt that for a few hours we had been adopted, maybe even initiated, into a special private society.

As we walked back to the train station, I said, "You know, even if nothing else remarkable happens on this trip, it will all have been worth it just for this experience."

Then I remembered Susan's optimistic comment about serendipity, and officially adopted the credo that informed the next few months of pizza discovery: it's all about the adventure.

FLORENCE

The bookends of our Italian pizza hunting were Genoa and Naples, but there were two important stops between them, Florence and Rome. Faith Willinger lives in Florence. A New Yorker married to an Italian businessman, her heart now belongs to Italy. She has carved out an important niche in the city, taking people on market and vineyard tours and teaching them how to cook in her home kitchen with the things they bring back. Faith is a star among the chefs in Italy; everyone knows her and she, in turn, seems to know everyone. When I told her we were coming to town, she invited us over for lunch, choreographed our visit to Florence, and also helped us plan out our time for Rome and Naples.

Faith even recommended our hotel, Palazzo Castiglione, which was only a ten-minute walk from her house and was located in a wonderful old palazzo, with a different hotel occupying each floor. Indeed, everything in Florence seemed like a ten-minute walk from everything else. We spent much of our time doing the typical first-time-in-Florence things, such as being overwhelmed by Michelangelo's *David*, visiting various museums, buying jewelry on the Ponte Vecchio, and exploring the many narrow streets and alleys in search of the best *gelateria*. Faith arranged for us to have lunch at Cibrèo, one of the finest restaurants in Florence, where the flavors were so fresh and perfectly balanced that we just sighed and, as in Recco, let go. All of these things would have been enough to make our stay perfectly satisfying. We were not expecting to find great pizza in Florence. After all, the city is not known for it. But we got lucky on our final evening.

Just up the block from our sweet little hotel was a pizzeria we had walked past a number of times. It took the recommendation of an Australian chap, a handyman at our hotel, to give us the nudge we needed to check out the place.

"If it's pizza you want, you won't do any better than that Antica place just a few doors up the street," he said. That was enough for us.

We were greeted at Antica Pizzeria dell'Arte by the first of two Salvatores. This one was the headwaiter and he would turn out to be the only employee we met who was not one of the three sons of the owners, Ciro Urbano and his wife, Palma (who was also the pastry chef). It was a warm, not-too-muggy night, so we decided to eat outside. In a scene that was to repeat itself many times, sometimes in English and sometimes through a fractured, though practiced, Italian phrase, Susan explained to the waiter that I was a writer of cookbooks ("Buongiorno. Mi chiamo Susan Reinhart. Mio marito Peter Reinhart è un autore dei libri della cucina."), that I was doing a book on pizza, and that we'd heard that the pizza here was very good (that part was always in English).

"Not just good but the best," Salvatore, the proud waiter, told us. "Come, I will show you."

He beckoned us inside where the *pizzaiolo*, the other Salvatore (son of Ciro), was happily stationed in front of the *forno*, a beehivelike brick oven fueled by hardwood logs that we could see glowing through the oven's open mouth. As I held up my camera to show that I wanted to take pictures of him making a pizza, Salvatore I explained to Salvatore II who we were. He smiled and nodded. I asked Salvatore II what his best pizza was, and Salvatore I translated his response. He thought that we should order a *Margherita*, the most famous style, but that we should also try a special pizza that he had invented. As Salvatore I repeated that advice, I saw a proud smile appear on the second Salvatore's face, and then he said something else in Italian.

"He says he has, how do you say, marked this, registered this pizza."

"You mean trademarked it?" I asked.

Big smile, nods all around, "Yes, like that. He calls it his Vesuvio pizza. It is very good, you will see."

He explained that it was made with the famed *mozzarella di bufala*, and also black truffles and tomatoes, to which I reprised my usual, "Bring it on."

More nods, more smiles. I took pictures of Salvatore II making the pizzas as Salvatore I filled in more of the story. He asked if we had been to Naples, and I explained that we were headed there in a few days. He said we should go to Pizzeria Brandi, where the *pizza Margherita* was invented and also where Salvatore II had learned to make authentic DOC pizza.

"You know DOC?" he asked, pronouncing the word "dock," not as three initials.

"Yes, I know DOC," I replied. DOC, which stands for Denominazione di Origine Controllata, is a government system that regulates the standards for some Italian foods and beverages, primarily cheeses and wines. But in this instance the designation means that a pizza is made according to strict guidelines established by the Associazione della Vera Pizza Napoletana.

"We're DOC here," he told me.

So I watched Salvatore II make our first official *pizza napoletana*. It was not a flashy process—there was no tossing of a disk into the air—but rather a brisk working of the dough into a circle on a floured counter, followed by a swift knuckling of it by

A *pizza marinara* about to go in the *forno* for its 60-second bake at about 800 degrees.

one hand to stretch it a bit further, about ten inches across. He placed it on a floured wooden peel, spread it with a small amount of sauce made from fresh-looking crushed tomatoes, arranged four large basil leaves on top, and then scattered shredded fresh cow's milk mozzarella, known as *fior di latte*, over the surface. Salvatore II told us that *mozzarella di bufala*, the prized fresh cheese made from the milk of the water buffalo, was saved for special pizzas, while most of the fresh mozzarella used on everyday pizzas, like the *Margherita* he was making, was *fior di latte* because it was less expensive and not as puddly when melted. (This is actually stretching the DOC rules, but we did not know that at the time.) He finished off the pizza with a small dusting of grated Parmesan cheese, and slid it into the oven. Then he put a small amount of what looked like sawdust or fine wood shavings on the peel and flicked them over the hot coals. They flared like a swarm of lightning bugs and created a burst of smoke. Salvatore II looked over at us with a satisfied smile.

Next, he began to work on the *pizza Vesuvio*, stretching the dough and then laying it on the wooden peel as he had just done for the *Margherita*, stopping his work after exactly sixty seconds to remove the first pizza from the oven. He returned to the dough, laying a bed of chopped fresh tomatoes on it, and then placing a small ball of *mozzarella di bufala* in the center, but only after first cradling it in his hands with a gentle, affectionate rocking motion. My heart leapt as he opened a jar of black paste that released an earthy pungency into the air. It was, of course, chopped black truffle, and he spooned out a healthy dollop of it, balancing it on top of the ball of cheese. He quickly flattened a second ball of dough, cut off strips, and then laid them on top of the pizza from the rim to the center, like spokes on a wheel. He pinched the ends of the strips together on top of the now thoroughly truffled mozzarella ball, and slid the pizza into the oven. He suggested we go back to the table, where our first pizza was waiting for us.

The *Margherita* was truly wonderful, especially since it was the first supposedly official DOC pizza we had eaten, and we didn't really have anything with which to compare it. The dough puffed around the edge, creating what Salvatore I called the *cornicione*. The edge had the texture of *ciabatta*, but the pie was thin toward the center. At first the slice seemed crisp, but it quickly softened. Somewhere along the journey we had been told to eat Neapolitan-style pizzas with a knife and fork and not to try to pick up the slices as you would an American-style pizza. I cut a wedge and rolled it back from the pointy nose to the *cornicione*, like a jelly roll. Then I sliced off a portion and ate it with my fork, working confidently as if I knew what I was doing.

The *pizza Vesuvio* soon arrived, and it was a fantastic sight. The strips of dough running across the top and rising toward the center gave it its namesake look. The ball of fresh mozzarella had melted into a semiliquid state, and the black truffle paste running through it in rivulets was reminiscent of molten lava. The chopped tomatoes brought some acidity and liveliness to the flavors, while the top crust, although not solid, gave the pizza the quality of a calzone. In the end, I thought the dough strips took away from the overall flavor of the pie, diluting the impact of the amazing truffled flavor that flowed from the "volcano." I'm ashamed to admit I had the terribly vain thought, "This is really good, but I think I can make it even better."

As our meal wound down, I became lost in my own musings. I was thinking about the tweaks I might make to the Vesuvio, until I suddenly shook myself free of such thoughts, aware that I was beginning to step on sacred pizza turf. I quickly tempered my irreverence by adding the thought, "Well, maybe it will be more perfect when we get to Naples." But first we had to go through Rome.

ROME

An American we met on the train to Rome told us we should go to Da Baffetto for the best Roman-style pizza, and since it was a mere ten-minute walk from our hotel we did, passing numerous other pizzerias along the way. There is something liberating about having a recommended place, even if it comes from a stranger. It fit the spirit of the hunt, and it didn't hurt that it was also on a published list of best pizzerias in Rome that someone else had given us.

Da Baffetto had a tiny interior, but it had a lot of picnic tables along the side of the building, and the tables were full, always a good sign. We sat at the only empty bench. Almost immediately another couple was assigned to the two vacant seats next to us by the rough-and-tumble-but-heart-of-gold-looking host. I almost always, automatically, impulsively, imagine a backstory for interesting-looking waiters or restaurant workers. At Da Baffetto, the entire crew was backstory worthy; they all looked like motley sailors, pirates really, who, without warning, could break into

"Blow the Man Down," or its Italian equivalent. They were all smiling, especially the two *pizzaioli*, who were working as a team. One guy shaped the dough, stretching it thin and flat, into a circle larger than the Neapolitan-style pizza we had had in Florence. He laid it out on a large wooden peel, and then the other man sauced it, topped it, and slid it into a brick oven, where it baked for two or three minutes. It emerged as a thin pizza with a nice char around the edge and even on the cheese. The crust was nearly cracker crisp with very little air in it, and without the puffed edge of a Naples pizza.

The young couple seated next to us were Americans, and they seemed familiar with the menu. I asked them if they'd been to Da Baffetto before.

"We discovered this place on our first night here, three days ago, and have eaten here every night since," the husband said. "I don't know if it's just because were are in Rome, or maybe because we haven't had great pizza before, or maybe even because this is our honeymoon, but this is the best pizza I've ever had in my life."

I would never discount the "aah Roma" factor in falling in love with a place, but whenever I hear the words, "The best I've ever had," I take them seriously. So I asked, "Well, do you have any good pizza where you live?"

They looked at each other, trying to recall, and then he said, "Well, actually, we do have a couple of places we like. We used to think they were good, but now . . . ," and they drifted off into the kind of semiswoon that happens only when lovers are caught in the thrall of finding their own special place. Our dining companions definitely had a contented "we'll always have Da Baffetto" look. It's nice to be around that look.

Susan and I were hoping to have our own bonding moment, but when our *Margherita* and prosciutto pizzas came, we knew by the first bite that as good as they were, and they were good, this was not going to be an "our place" moment. The sauce of crushed tomatoes, the fresh and dry cheeses, the char—they were all great. Both pizzas were executed, in their style, about as well as I could imagine they could be done. But there was something about the ultrathin crust that didn't work for either of us. It was as if it was too slight when matched up against the bold flavors of the toppings.

Would I go back to Da Baffetto? Absolutely. We had other pizzas in this same style while in Rome and none was as tasty. But is it one of my favorites of all time?

I can only say that the style itself precludes it from making my hall of fame. I am, after all, a bread baker and love an undulating, holey *cornicione*. So I learned this much: the Roman crackerlike crust is not my favorite style, but within that style, there are some excellent versions.

I thought that would end my Roman pizza tasting, but then I remembered a place that Faith Willinger had told us was a must-see. Called Antico Forno, it was a bakery located in Campo dei Fiori, a large square in central Rome that is the site of a farmers' market each morning. Only two kinds of pizza are made there: *bianca*, topped only with olive oil and salt, and *rossa*, brushed with a red sauce. Similar versions in other places are called by at least two names, *pizza al taglio* (by the slice) and *pizza al metro* (by the meter). Basically this is a long pizza, over two meters, and it's fun to watch it being made, which they let you do at Antico Forno. In a room adjacent to the sales shop, with its own door open to the outside, a team of bakers rolls out balls of dough into lengths of about seven feet and about one-quarter inch

Don't be fooled by the unassuming exterior of Antico Forno. Inside, treasures abound for the long line of customers waiting to indicate how big a piece of *pizza bianca* or *pizza rossa* they would like sliced from the 7-foot "plank."

Three pieces of dough ready to be transformed into seven-foot-long pizzas at Antico Forno in the Campo dei Fiori section of Rome.

thick. This is done in a couple of stages, as the dough must relax a few times along the way before it will yield to the baker's final push to its full length. But it would be difficult to slide a seven-foot banner of dough into the oven, so the bakers (and this is the part that Faith enthused over) scrunch the dough back accordion style until it is about three feet long and then jiggle it off the peel, carefully extending it to its full length on the oven deck. It bakes for five to seven minutes and comes out of the oven golden brown and crisp. The bakers transfer the pizzas to a rack, from which the man at the cash register retrieves them for sale.

Early one morning while Susan slept in, I visited Antico Forno and watched the bakers create plank after plank, snapping pictures with my camera, much to their delight. I couldn't wait to try some. When it was time to place my order, I imitated those who had gone before me and held my hands out to indicate a piece about eighteen inches long. Pretending to know what I was saying, I said, "Uno rouge et uno bianca."

The cash register guy asked, "One red and one white?"

I smiled, nodded, and, I think, blushed.

When I returned to the hotel, I had only six inches of each type left, which I vowed to save for Susan. She finally woke up and I gave her what remained of the two pizzas, now just four inches of each. She devoured them.

"This is really good. I like it much better than the focaccia in Genoa. Is that all you got?" she asked.

"Afraid so," I replied quietly. "But we could go back and get some more."

NAPLES

When hearing about the pizza of Naples from a person who has just been there, one can easily be convinced that real pizza doesn't exist in the United States. Send an American to Naples and it is as if he or she has seen the burning bush—that person's pizza world has been rocked and will never be the same again, or so it seems. The once-hallowed *pizza americana* (my catchall term for mainstream American pizza) is suddenly perceived as an abomination; even the neighborhood Naples-style pizzeria back home, no matter how authentic, is seen as a pretender. It was clear I had to go to Naples myself to find out if I too would become a *pizza napoletana* zealot.

The next day we took the train from Rome to Naples. Friends had warned us to the point of paranoia about the seedy side of the city, so we did our best impression of seasoned travelers, brushing off the many drivers offering us cheap taxi rates and heading for the first car that had a visible meter. Our driver, Ciro, was a nice young man who proudly told us that he took Naples's bad reputation personally. It wasn't long before we let down our guard, seduced by the rhythms and charms of the bustling coastal city.

We checked into the Hotel Majestic, took a walk around the neighborhood, and then decided to go to Mattozzi for our first authentic Naples pizza. Recommended by Ciro and seconded by the hotel clerk, it proved to be the perfect introduction to the joyous Neapolitan spirit. After some antipasti and a salad, Susan ordered her usual, a *pizza Margherita*, and I ordered a *caprese*, which is like a *Margherita* except that it uses small grape-sized tomatoes from Capri instead of crushed San Marzano tomatoes. The pizzas were very good, a little puffier than the DOC version we had in Florence and clearly made with *fior di latte* (cow's milk mozzarella) and not the *mozzarella di bufala* of a DOC *vera pizza napoletana*. I didn't mind and they didn't apologize. I learned that you must ask for the DOC version, and be prepared to pay a little more for it. This stop turned out to be a good way to tiptoe up to the real-deal Neapolitan pizza, especially since Mattozzi was not considered the best pizzeria in town.

The waiter took Susan and me back to meet Maurizio, the *pizzaiolo*, who gave me a quick shaping lesson, pressing out the *petola*, or disk, of dough in a circular motion, but not lifting or spinning it, which, as was becoming apparent, is an American technique. The *cornicione* was fairly thick, and the disk itself was not stretched as far or as thin as Salvatore's in Florence. By keeping the dough a little smaller and thicker, Maurizio was also able to apply more sauce than Salvatore had. I soon realized Maurizio was making a *pizza alla marinara*, not a *pizza Margherita*, as it had no cheese and the sauce was topped with a sprinkle of oregano and a few basil leaves. It took exactly sixty seconds to bake in the beautiful ceramic-tiled *forno*.

As we watched the pizza show, owner Alfonso Mattozzi came into the kitchen to see the cause of all the hubbub. Since he didn't speak English, our waiter, Gennaro, acted as translator, explaining who I was based on Susan's usual icebreaker: "Buongiorno, mi chiamo Susan Reinhart. Mio marito Peter Reinhart è un autore dei libri della cucina." Everyone seemed fascinated by my background as a teacher of bread making, and Alfonso asked if I knew some of his friends in America, especially one at Café Milano in Washington. I gave him my Johnson & Wales card, and he added it to a large pile of American contacts.

Then I learned the reason behind his excitement about my bread background. He asked Maurizio to slide a pizza disk without any toppings on it into the oven. In less than a minute, it rose dramatically, ballooning and then splitting through the center into two even-sided bread walls. When it charred to the same degree as a pizza, Maurizio pulled it from the deck and Alfonso split it open, revealing long strands of gluten dangling like stalactites and stalagmites. Then he stuffed the center with what looked like prosciutto, a slice of mozzarella, and a handful of arugula. He sliced it into wedges and gave one piece to Susan and another one to me.

"Do you think this would be well received in America?" he asked.

"Yes, would you like to come over and make them?" I answered quickly.

"Oh yes," he responded just as quickly, and his eyes took on a wistful look as he stared into the distance for, maybe, three seconds, and then he quickly came back to the present. He smiled and nodded at his sandwich creation, pleased that we liked it.

When we returned to our table, shots of ice-cold *limoncello*, the wondrous, sweet lemon liqueur from the Amalfi coast, were waiting for us. We were very content and very full.

The next day I was hungry again, but first we took a tour to the volcanic ruins of Pompeii, just a few dozen miles southeast of Naples. There I posed for a scrapbook picture in the town bakery, and kept an eye on nearby Vesuvius to make sure it was docile. I flashed back to Florence and that truffled *pizza Vesuvio* that I couldn't wait to try to make.

As the tour bus returned us to town, we asked our guide, Maria, if we would pass near Da Michele, probably the most recommended pizzeria on our list. When we explained our interest, Maria and the bus driver got excited for us and assumed the roles of co-conspirators, detouring the bus to Via Cesare Sersale and our destination. Maria jumped off first, ran inside, and came out with a piece of paper with a number on it. She explained to us that everyone had to wait outside until their numbers were called, but that she had told the man inside who we were and he promised to watch out for us. Then she pointed to an intersection about two blocks away and said we could catch a taxi home there.

"If you go there, it is very safe," she said, "but not so much there," as she pointed to just about everywhere else. "So go there when you are ready to return to your hotel. It will be okay. Ciao." And she jumped back on the bus and waved good-bye.

We waited for about twenty minutes in the middle of a wildly diverse crowd. There were nicely dressed men and women, some shadier-looking characters, young lovers, older folks—all types really. We were the only Americans, but nobody seemed to notice or care. Then our number was called and we were escorted inside, past an old poster with a love poem to the noble pizza printed on it. I took a photo and everyone looked up at once, smiled, and then returned to their conversations and their pizzas.

What I loved about Da Michele is that only two kinds of pizza are made, the *Margherita* and the *marinara* (though you can ask for extra cheese on the *Margherita* and also for a special larger size), yet the place is always busy. We ordered one of each type. On the way to the table I noticed the *pizzaiolo* cranking out his wares, and I could see that he spread his dough into a circle larger than what we had seen elsewhere. The dough overhung the peel as it was maneuvered into the *forno*, requiring great dexterity on the part of the *pizzaiolo* to avoid getting it stuck. The pizzas came out of the oven puffy at first, and then immediately settled down to beautiful, flat disks nearly twelve inches in diameter. They were perfect.

We struck up a conversation with the people at the next table. They were two brothers, one of whom lived and worked in Sardinia as a merchant marine. Anytime he came to visit Naples, the brothers would meet at Da Michele to catch up on family news. I asked what kind of pizza they liked and one answered *Margherita*, the other *marinara*. When I asked what was the best place to eat a true Neapolitan pizza, I was told that we were sitting in it.

"But where else do you go?" I pressed.

"Only here. We go nowhere else but here."

Two girls sitting at a nearby table started giggling and said something to one of the brothers. He explained, "She says my English is very funny."

So I asked the girls if this was true. "Oh yes, he speaks bad English, but it is also cute, or, maybe, funny."

By now everyone in the room, about thirty people, was aware of us, all of them wanting to be in my pictures as I snapped away at the walls and the oven and shot close-ups of the pies. Then, as if on cue, an older fellow entered the room playing "Sorrento," a Neapolitan classic, on the accordion. The place had turned into a festival and the pizzas were among the best I had ever eaten, and still among the best I have had since. There was not one thing that could be done to them to make them better. The crust had all the properties I crave—the snap, the sweetness, the smoky char—the cheese and the sauce were impeccable, and I even found I appreciated the *pizza alla marinara*, despite the absence of cheese. I didn't realize it at the time, but this was to be the summer I learned to like pizza without cheese.

Meanwhile, the two brothers had shifted their conversation to the girls next to them. But we hardly noticed. Our pizzas took all our attention.

When we tried to leave, the owner, Michele Condurro (descendant of Michele Gargivolo, who opened the original Da Michele in 1900) embraced us and brought us over to the oven to meet Luigi, the *pizzaiolo*. I took pictures of Luigi making pizzas and promised to stay in touch.

We walked to the intersection that Maria had pointed out and waited for a taxi. One appeared within seconds and we were whisked back to our hotel, amazed at how perfectly the day was going. We took a long walk around the neighborhood and then down to the marina, trying to work off lunch so that we could keep our appointment at Ciro a Santa Brigida for dinner. We still had research to do.

The restaurant was also only a short walk from the hotel, and we were becoming accustomed to the narrow, winding, bustling streets peopled mainly by young, nicely dressed Neapolitans. The reason we needed to go to Ciro a Santa Brigida is because the owner, Antonio Pace, is the president of the Associazione della Vera Pizza Napoletana and has become the point man, the grand protector, of the DOC status. I wanted to meet him and to see if his pizzas were as good as his marketing skills. The answer: almost but not quite. Perhaps it was because we felt we had touched the top of the Neapolitan pizza pyramid at lunch, or maybe because we spent too much time enjoying the antipasti, but the pizza was not as satisfying as I'd hoped. Antonio Pace is as genuinely committed to the purity of his city's pizza as anyone on earth, but I realized that I was now forming a set of criteria that, right or wrong, was beginning to narrow my focus. Even within the rules, subtle shadings of quality and execution exist, and my preference had definitely shifted to the Da Michele style: larger, thinner, cheesier.

Signore Pace was very kind to us, however, and through Mauro, our waiter and translator, he explained the brief history of the *associazione* and how he and others felt it was important to establish the key principles that set *la vera pizza napoletana* apart from all other pizzas before the phrase lost its meaning. For instance, when you order a DOC pizza, he explained, it should always be made with *mozzarella di bufala*, not *fior di latte*. The dough should always be of a high standard, following preordained mixing and fermentation rules. He noted that although American pizza is influenced by Neapolitan pizza, it has become its own kind of pie and should not be called *Napoletana*, or Neapolitan, but, maybe, "in the style of *pizza napoletana*."

The next day we took a trip to Capri, and while on a small, motorized shuttle boat to visit the Blue Grotto—the single most touristy, yet obligatory, destination in southern Italy—we met a young American couple from Massachusetts, Susanna and Mark. As soon as they heard about my pizza research, they told me about a place called Tony's Pizza in Springfield. "But there are a few Tony's," Mark called out after

Susan and I transferred to a little gondolier-propelled rowboat for our entrance into the grotto. Just as I was ducking to prevent my head from getting bashed on the low-hanging rock at the cave door, I heard Mark yell, "So be sure it's the one in Springfield."

Later that same day, on the ferry back to the mainland, we met another American couple, this time from San Jose, California. At the mention of pizza research, they told us about a place called Dante's in State Park, Pennsylvania, where they had gone to college. "Or check out Highway Pizza—it's owned by the same guy. They have the best sauce, plus a double-crusted, two-level pie."

Pizza hunters, they're everywhere.

That evening we got all dressed up, not because the restaurant was fancy, but to celebrate our last Naples pizza. We were headed the next day to Positano, a little slice of paradise farther down the Amalfi coast, just past Sorrento, for three days of, well, nothing. While the whole trip was an adventure, these three days were our official vacation, and the only food I really wanted to see at Positano was one of my other passions—sweet, little Mediterranean clams and, maybe, some mussels.

Pizzeria Brandi had very good pizza, almost as good as the pizza at Da Michele. It was my second favorite pizza on the trip. The reason we went there was because Brandi owns the bragging rights to the invention of the *pizza Margherita*. The story of how Raffaele Esposito made three types of pizza for King Umberto and Queen Margherita of Savoy is well documented. Apparently, the pair had once lived in Naples and, upon returning to their palace, wanted some pizza. Esposito was invited to prepare the pizza and made, or so it goes, a *marinara* pizza with anchovies; a *bianca*, or white pizza, with lard, provolone or creamy *caciocavallo* cheese, and basil; and a pizza with tomatoes, mozzarella, and basil—red, white, and green in honor of the Italian flag. The queen flipped for the latter, and when Esposito received a note of thanks from the monarch, he dedicated the pizza to her, calling it *pizza Margherita*. In her book *Pizza Napoletana!*, author Pamela Sheldon Johns explains that Esposito's pizzeria was called Pietro il Pizzaiolo when he prepared pizzas for Queen Margherita, but was later renamed Pizzeria Brandi. Just as Antonio Pace and his *associazione* grabbed the *vera pizza napoletana* franchise and the town of Recco grabbed the *focaccia col formaggio* franchise, Brandi grabbed the *Margherita* franchise. Based on our visit, I'd say the tradition is in good hands.

As we sat on the balcony of the pizzeria, with the sun slowly setting on the Mediterranean, we ate a *pizza Margherita* and watched the evening street activity below. Franco, our waiter, had responded in the usual helpful fashion to our routine ("Buongiorno, mi chiamo Susan Reinhart . . ."), which added to an already wonderful night. We laughed our way through dinner and then raised our glasses in a final toast to *pizza napoletana* and to a series of indelible memories.

We returned to the United States, where we slowly emerged from the glow of our Italian pilgrimage. Then, gradually feeling the tug of the hunt, I embarked on an intensive summer of pizza hunting, which turned into twelve months. I ate at dozens of New York City pizzerias; trekked through the streets of New Haven in search of coal-fired pizza; picked up knife and fork to compare deep-dish pizzas in Chicago; consumed across the spectrum of so-called California-style pizza in the San Francisco Bay Area and Los Angeles; gobbled up dozens of slices of conventional college town–style pizza around universities in five cities; tracked down American attempts at duplicating the DOC pizzas of Naples in Washington, D.C., and Manhasset, New York (where the restaurant Naples 22 actually imports its water from Naples); tasted pizza from over thirty pizzerias in the Providence area; stumbled upon Sardinian pizza in Dallas, Texas, and Croatian pizza in Bellevue, Washington; fell in love again and again with grilled pizza in Providence; tested many brands of frozen pizza; read numerous books and scoured countless websites containing pizza facts and emotional opinions (including www.pizzatherapy.com, my favorite); interviewed the editors of three pizza publications; and went on dozens of pizza hunts with chefs, writers, childhood friends, colleagues from work, total strangers, and pretty much anyone who said, "Let's get some pizza." I ate more pizza in that single year than I had eaten in my entire life, and even though I often got sick of it, I found myself craving it within a week. So I would set out again.

NEW YORK CITY

Jeffrey Steingarten warned me that he was not a pizza ecumenist when we went on our hunt. "You need to know," he told me, "that I judge pizzas this way: the crust I judge on a scale of one to ten, the sauce and toppings on a scale of one to two."

"So you're telling me that the crust is at least five times more important than the sauce and toppings?" I asked.

"At least, but probably more."

"I have no problem with that," I said. I too consider myself a crust guy first and foremost. But I saw the problem this can cause when we shared a pizza in Brooklyn at DiFara's Pizzeria on Avenue J. We had gone there on the recommendation of my boyhood friend Joel Kostman, who is a writer and, more important, also a locksmith. Because of the latter profession, Joel knows the fastest way to get anywhere in New York City. He is also a great storyteller, so I asked him if he would join us on the hunt as a sort of urban safari guide. We left Jeffrey's apartment in Manhattan's Flatiron District at about two o'clock in the afternoon, and Joel got us to Brooklyn's Midwood neighborhood in less than thirty minutes, narrating the rationale behind his road choices and providing some historical perspective on pizza as we traveled (". . . and over to the left, there's the Original Ray's that a lot of people think is the actual Original Ray's, but it really isn't; at least it's not worth going into, not like the one on Prince Street, which is much better . . .").

I loved the sauce and cheese pizza we had at DiFara's. On the wall is a photo of owner Domenico DeMarco taken forty years ago, picturing him standing in the exact position where he stood making our pizza. He imports his fresh mozzarella from the town where he grew up, and he has a window box where he grows thyme, oregano, and hot peppers. This is his world and has been for a long time. I made a sentimental connection within seconds of arriving, giving the place strong emotional perfection points before even tasting the pizza. DiFara's is a classic neighborhood pizzeria, the kind of place that would be there in your childhood and then follow you into adulthood. This kind of emotional hit, plus my admiration for Domenico's longevity and soulfulness, may have clouded my judgment, but I simply loved the pizza, even though the crust was not as crisp as I like it. I was willing to overlook this shortcoming because the tomato sauce was about the best I'd tasted outside of Naples.

It was slightly acidic, but sweet at the same time, and herbed modestly, with no one flavor dominating another. Domenico's sauce has probably been this good from day one, and it will hopefully continue to be this good.

I learned that the sauce is a combination of canned San Marzano tomatoes, the pride and joy of Campania, and chopped fresh tomatoes, and includes snippets of herbs from the pizzeria's window box, among other seasonings. It was one of the few times—Da Michele was another—that I noticed the sauce as an equal player with the cheese and crust. In this case it was the best part, though I also liked the hand-shredded full-fat mozzarella from the Grande Cheese Company (one of the better domestic brands, from Wisconsin) mixed with ample amounts of fresh mozzarella. (Domenico said the blend was 75 percent *mozzarella di bufala* from Casapulla, near Caserta, just outside Naples, and 25 percent Grande mozzarella.) Then he topped the whole thing off with some grated *grana padano* to salt things up a bit. The flavors were so fresh and balanced that I was willing to overlook the tender but slightly underbaked crust. (The tenderness, which I liked, is a result of Domenico's choice of flour. Unlike most American pizzerias, which use all high-gluten flour, DiFara's uses a mix of 75 percent Italian "00" flour and 25 percent American high-gluten flour. As for the underbaked crust, I learned of a solution two weeks later when I came across a website that recommended always buying DiFara's pizza by the slice, not the whole pie, because the crust crisps up perfectly when it is reheated to serve.)

Jeffrey was not so forgiving. On the ride home, he went into great depth on how and why the crust was not to his liking: too limp, too thick, not the proper snap, and so on. When I asked him how he liked the sauce, he said, "The crust bothered me so much that I can barely remember the sauce." And then, in a moment of conciliation, he added, "Since you liked it so much, maybe I should have paid more attention to the sauce, but I just couldn't get past that crust."

I can respect that kind of honesty. There are very few rules while on the hunt other than respecting each other's criteria. I knew that Jeffrey's included a five-to-one focus on the crust, and I learned that, on rare occasions like at DiFara's, I am capable of loosening up my own crust-to-sauce bias, but the sauce had better be exceptional. I'm actually kind of proud of the flexibility I discovered and displayed on that particular hunt, even though I also discovered what a sentimental pushover I am.

★ ★ ★

Pizza in New York is not Neapolitan, but a hybrid of the Naples influence and the coal-fired reality of late-nineteenth-century New York. Like an Abrahamic patriarch, Gennaro Lombardi gets due credit for establishing the first formal pizzeria in 1905. It in turn begat Totonno's on Coney Island and then John's in the Village, which begat Patsy's in Harlem, Grimaldi's in Brooklyn, Angelo's in Midtown, and Nick's in Queens. Unlike Naples, which founded its pizza heritage on hardwood-fired ovens, New York City fueled its first pizzerias with bituminous coal, a soft, tarry substance rich in hydrocarbons that burns with an intense, bright yellow flame and heats up ovens to 1,200 degrees. Coal changed everything about pizzas; it made it possible to heat large, brick bread ovens efficiently and bake many pizzas at one time. These made-in-America pies, though assembled with similar ingredients, were also much larger than the individual pizzas of Naples. Coal eventually gave way to gas and electric heat, but the style of the pies remained the same. Now the predominant pizza genre in the world, this style is generally called neo-Neapolitan, with subsets such as Newyorkapolitan, coined by food writer David Rosengarten, and, on a national level, what I call *pizza americana.*

One day, I took a train to Manhattan from Providence and had lunch with my nephew Rudy and good friend Hal Robinson, an actor who was understudying for Hal Linden in *Cabaret* at the time. We went to two different Ray's Pizzerias on the Upper West Side, both of which said "Famous" and "Original," but neither of which is. Nor are they related to each other. We ordered a variety of slices at each place; Hal told us some backstage stories about life on Broadway; and Rudy summed up the pizza for all of us: "Pretty typical New York style, but definitely not the best." All Ray's outlets are not created equal, but it's still possible to get a serviceable slice of pizza at most of them. Of course, the one on Prince Street, as Joel the locksmith pointed out, is clearly better.

The next night I went to Joel's apartment in Park Slope and watched a video with him; his wife, Becca; their oldest daughter, Quinn; and my goddaughter, Rose Cahn, and her boyfriend, Jonathan Ossler. The film was called *Original Original* and was made by two of Rose's friends, Paul Malouf and Paul Starkman. It was about the search for the one true Original Ray's Pizzeria. If the film is to be believed, and why not, the first Ray's, the original, was at 1073 First Avenue and opened in 1961, but has long been closed. The Ray's at Eleventh Street and Sixth Avenue, the one most people think is the actual original Ray's, is really the third Ray's (after the one on Seventy-Sixth Street), and was never owned by Ray, but instead by one of his friends, a protégé. The film at last tracks down Rosalino Mangano, a native of Sicily, who is in fact the original Ray and now hangs out at an Original Ray's on East Houston. The film is entertaining and has made the rounds of the rooftop and garage festivals of New York City. I was just glad to know that someone had taken responsibility for getting to the bottom of the Ray's mystery, and also to know that I wasn't the only one obsessed with such matters.

Joel brought pizzas from Grimaldi's to eat while we watched the film. They are made in the former Patsy's just under the Brooklyn Bridge, and are great to eat in the restaurant, right out of the coal-fired oven. But as we learned that night, they don't travel well. That's one thing about pizzas with superthin crusts—they are not as good after they cool down, especially when the fresh mozzarella gets rubbery.

These are the kinds of lessons I learned during my many visits to New York City, thanks to Joel and to my many other fellow hunters. It isn't difficult to find people interested in joining the search. When I first told Joel about my pizza hunts, he offered to drive me around New York City to his favorite places. As I noted earlier, Joel is a locksmith and knows the city extremely well because of that. But once we had visited his top pizza spots, he didn't want to stop. He liked the idea of the hunt, of seeing what new places we could uncover. Indeed, everybody, it seems, likes the idea, and I have never had trouble finding recruits.

Joel has a friend named Howie Buten who lives most of the year in Paris, but who also keeps an apartment in Manhattan. Howie is, among many other things, a clown, a real clown, trained at the Ringling Brothers clown school. His character is named Buffo and is quite famous in France. Howie is also a psychologist who uses his Buffo performance piece, which he has taken all over the world, to raise money in support of a clinic he runs for severely autistic adults and teenagers in Paris. He is like the Jerry Lewis of clown psychologists: the French love him, even if he is unappreciated in his own country. Among the many things that I like about Howie is that although he only comes back to the United States for a few weeks each year, he seems always to be in New York City when I am in town for a pizza hunt. This tells me that in addition to being an interesting person, he is also an instinctual pizza hunter.

Years ago, Howie was part of the locksmith business with Joel, so he and Joel have certain beloved pizza haunts that they share. One of these is Ray's, but as we all now know, there are many Ray's in New York City. There is Ray's, Original Ray's, Famous Ray's, Famous Original Ray's, Original Famous Ray's, and even one called Not Ray's (I learned this from watching *Original Original*). There is, in one form or another, a Ray's within a short walk of almost anywhere in Manhattan, yet they do not seem to be connected to one another. No one seems to know if anyone owns the name Ray's, or if anyone who owns a Ray's pays someone else to use that name. In fact, every Ray's seems to be an independent operation, not a franchise but a freestanding Ray's with some kind of Ray's format that has established itself as the quintessential model for New York–style pizza by the slice. When you go into a Ray's, you find a few variations of already baked large pizzas. A slice will set you back about two bucks. In some Ray's, you will also find calzone (folded pizza) and *stromboli* (rolled pizza).

What I learned from Joel and Howie is that all Ray's are definitely not equal. They took me to their favorite Ray's, on Prince Street in Little Italy on the Lower East Side. In fact, this is not only their favorite Ray's, but rather the only Ray's that they now patronize, having determined that every other Ray's has either inferior sauce or inferior crust. Usually it's the sauce, but sometimes it's because there is too much cheese, they claim. But the Prince Street Ray's has the best sauce of any Ray's and also uses less cheese—the perfect amount of cheese according to Joel, Howie, and Joel's sixteen-year-old daughter, Quinn, a born pizza hunter. We ordered a few slices, including plain cheese and sauce, pesto, white with spinach and ricotta, and pepperoni. Pepperoni, by the way, is clearly the most popular pizza topping in the nation. I'm pretty sure it's because pepperoni can save an otherwise mediocre pizza, distracting the consumer from noticing how blah the dough and sauce are. At Ray's on Prince Street, pepperoni was not needed to save the day. The pizza was terrific with or without it.

A few months later I asked Joel to go with me to an Original Ray's near my hotel on the Upper West Side, just off Broadway. He scoffed and said, "I know that Ray's, and I'll never go in there again. It's not worthy of the name Ray's." When I mentioned that particular Ray's to Quinn and asked if she concurred, she made a pained face. It was as if I had asked her to eat live worms. So I went there on my own and then, on a subsequent visit, went to three more Ray's, all in Midtown, in the Times Square area. They were similar, the layouts were nearly identical, yet the pizzas were all slightly different, even though they looked the same. The crust was always, as is the New York style, medium thick and breadlike at the edge (the fabled *cornicione*) and then thinner as it moved toward the point, or nose, of the slice, where it ultimately became too thin to hold itself up and instead flopped downward. The cheese and sauce toppings were nearly alike, too, but none was as balanced in flavor as in the Prince Street shop, which was also a much smaller space than any of its colleagues in Midtown. It was as if the Prince Street guys had their own special touch, a pride, as if they took their pizza a little more seriously, a little more personally than the others. The Ray's on Eighth Avenue, between Fifty-fifth and Fifty-sixth, had a better crust than either the Ray's on Seventh Avenue or the one on Broadway, but my sense was that this is a day-to-day thing, based on the skill of the pizza maker at work. All the pizzas could be labeled as "in the Ray's mode," and anyone in need of a quick slice—except Joel, Howie, and Quinn, of course—should feel confident that his or her craving would be adequately sated by a stop in any Ray's.

But pizza in Manhattan is not only about Ray's. Indeed, the problem with pizza hunting in New York City is that there are so many places to try that, unless you live there, it is a futile pursuit. There is no way I could get to all the great by-the-slice pizzerias, like Joe's in Greenwich Village, Louie & Ernie's in the Bronx, Patsy's in East Harlem (according to writer Ed Levine, the only by-the-slice pizzeria that still uses a coal-fired oven), and Nunzio's and Joe & Pat's in Staten Island. For whole pies I would have gladly visited Candido, Angelo's, Sofia, Da Ciro, and Orso in Manhattan; Goodfella's on Staten Island; Lento's in Brooklyn; and (my favorite pizzeria name) L&B Spumoni Gardens, also in Brooklyn. I managed to slip into Mario Batali's Otto Enoteca, which had a novel griddle crust, and I also visited Jim Lahey at his Sullivan Street Bakery, where I tried a variety of his amazing neo-Roman-style pizzas (they looked like focaccia but had a crust more like the pizza at Antico Forno in the Campo dei Fiori). But I was unable to try the pizza at Apizz and Pie, two Manhattan pizzerias that have created quite a buzz. I read Internet reports from chowhounds and pizza heads who seem to have eaten at hundreds of pizzerias throughout the five boroughs. The best I could do was skim through the reviews, pick out the places that were consensus winners, and try to get to as many as possible.

Of course, I visited the three arguably most famous and venerable pizzerias in New York: Lombardi's, John's, and Totonno's. I liked Totonno's best because the crust was fantastic and the sauce and cheese were flawless. But I know from personal experience that the performance at any of the great pizzerias, especially the busy ones where the pizzas are no longer baked by a *pizzaiolo* who is a family member, can vary from day to day. When you read the online diaries of pizza fanatics, it's apparent how strong the divergent feelings run. While one very credible, professional food writer lists Totonno's in Coney Island as still the greatest of them all, another writer of equal stature says that Totonno's has not even been top-ten caliber for over twenty years. John's now has three locations, with the original in Greenwich Village, yet many people, including me, think the newest John's on Forty-sixth Street, located in a former Episcopal Church in the theater district, is the best of the trio. Lombardi's, the true *original* original—though no longer in its original location— still has fanatical devotees, and I have to say that one of the pizzas I had there, with just sauce and cheese, ranks among the best I've ever eaten. But at the same meal I had a clam pizza that was awful.

Howie, Joel, Quinn, and I once trekked to Forest Hills in Queens to hunt out Nick's, a relatively new pizzeria (it opened in the early 1990s) that proved it is possible to make a world-class pizza in New York without a coal-fired brick oven. The crust was perfectly crisp, the cheese nicely caramelized, the edge slightly charred, and the sauce nice and tangy. It was a beautiful pizza, and we had that rare experience of table consensus.

There is so much pizza history in the Big Apple that it warrants its own book. But as good as the pizza is there and as much as New Yorkers like to insist that their city is home to the world's most perfect pizzerias, I had to go one hundred miles north of New York City to find the neo-Neapolitan pizza of my dreams.

NEW HAVEN

To put my relationship with New Haven pizza in its proper context requires some background. I grew up loving clams. Steamers, clams casino, clam chowder, smoked clams—any way you made them I was there. My dad was my mentor. In love with clams drenched in garlic butter and herbs, topped with toasted bread crumbs, and baked on the half shell (aka clams casino), he was also not averse to a bucketful of long-neck steamers served with two bowls, one of broth and the other of drawn butter. He started me on what has now been a nearly fifty-year love affair with this noble bivalve. Shortly after moving to Providence, I heard about the famous white clam pizza at Frank Pepe Pizzeria Napoletana on Wooster Street in New Haven, so I quickly manipulated my schedule to allow for a visit, despite the hour and a half drive each way. I was hoping for a satisfying clam fete, but also worried about the disappointment that so often piggybacks onto too much hype.

The plan was to take Susan to see a Sheridan play at the Yale Drama Theater, to be followed (ah, the real motive) by pizza with friends at Frank Pepe's. Our friends Peter and Robin Friedman and their two boys, Joe and Steve, live about an hour south of New Haven, so they too had a bit of a drive. They arrived thirty minutes before us to secure a place in line. This was followed by another thirty-minute wait after we arrived to join the painfully slow-moving sidewalk line in frigid, drizzly February weather. The boys' lips were blue and it was obvious they would have been happier at their favorite neighborhood pizza place, the Watch Box. I was feeling guilty to have subjected everyone to such an ordeal just for a pizza, but when we finally got in and ordered, it was as if the sun had returned.

Pepe's is the whole pizza package: long lines to get in, large, plastic pitchers of soda, a huge bituminous coal oven in plain view, a focused team of *pizzaioli* busily loading and unloading large, gorgeous pizza pies covered with creamy full-fat mozzarella, and, of course, a funky, no-frills atmosphere. It is perfect on so many levels that even its flaws, like the hour-long lines that spill out onto the sidewalk for up to a block, winter or summer, are part of the gestalt.

There were no tomatoes or sauce on our white clam pizza, just a bed of melted mozzarella and Parmesan cheese crowned with a generous portion of tender, whole, freshly shucked clams seasoned with garlic and oregano. This was not a clam tease—

a fear I had had during the long drive to Pepe's—but a serious clam festival celebrated on top of one luscious pie with a crispy, properly charred, very thin crust. I thought about how much my late father would have enjoyed Pepe's. It was, in that moment, a perfect pizza.

During the months that followed, I returned to Pepe's often, bringing along friends and acquaintances, finding any excuse to arrange a meeting. In time, I met Gary Bimonte, the grandson of Frank and Filomena Pepe. He now manages the place and is the co-owner with the six other grandkids. His grandfather arrived in America in 1919 and became a bread baker, eventually making anchovy-topped pizzas that he sold out of a cart. In 1925, he opened a small pizzeria in a building next to the current location. The original place is still operated by the family under the name the Spot and catches the overflow from the larger Pepe's.

After my first visit, I started reading about Frank Pepe Pizzeria Napoletana in magazines and on the Internet. Some writers complained that it was not as good as in the past, that the dough seemed too oily, that standards had slipped. These people were having the same experience that I had had with Mama's: Pepe's just wasn't the same place they remembered. Being a latecomer to the Pepe's world, I cannot say if this is true. Pizza at this level is not an automatic process, and a lot of pizzas are cranked out at Pepe's every day. The oven temperature can fluctuate, the *pizzaioli* can have off days, and memory can play tricks.

But one day I brought five British visitors to Pepe's as part of a pizza trends tour. They were product developers looking for new ideas to take back home, where chilled, ready-to-bake pizzas have cornered a huge market. Some of these folks had been to pizzerias all over the world, including Naples, and we had just spent two days tasting pizza at a number of the best places in New York City. We arrived shortly after the restaurant opened, thus reducing the wait for a table to about twenty minutes. No clams were available that day because of inclement weather, so we ordered four other pizzas, including Pepe's equally legendary Italian sausage pizza. At the end of the meal one of the product developers turned to me and said very matter-of-factly, "This is the best pizza I've ever tasted, anywhere."

On another occasion, Susan and I went pizza hunting in New Haven with our friends Bill and Suzie Van Wyck. This time we went to Sally's Apizza, New Haven's other famous pizzeria, also on Wooster Street. It was our first time there, after numerous visits to Pepe's, and I liked it better than Susan did, who by now had become a die-hard Pepe's loyalist. ("I'm pretty sure I'll never have pizza better than this at any place else I'll ever go, ever," was one of her comments after a particularly magical cheese and sauce with garlic pie we had one night.) We got to Sally's before it opened, figuring that we would not have to wait for a table. Instead, we stood in line for forty minutes, which, we quickly learned, was preferable to the usual wait of up to two hours.

While we were waiting, I ran across the street to a place called Nick's Apizza to use the men's room. Nick's was a combination bar and pizza place and had only a few customers. But I saw one of the pizzas and it was gorgeous. When I asked the waitress where everyone was, she said that Nick's was a new place, or at least had new owners, and people hadn't yet discovered it. As I returned to the line, I thought, "Being across the street from Sally's is probably tough, but that was one good-looking pizza." Nick's Apizza (Apizza, a slang throwback to Neapolitan influence, is pronounced "Aa beetz") looked like it could be a potential rival to Sally's once the word got out, so I made a mental note to come back and try it another time. Six months later, when I finally returned to try a Nick's pizza, it was out of business.

When we were finally seated at Sally's, one of the waiters brought around a *pizza bianca* with potato and onion for everyone in the restaurant to try. Susan, who didn't think Sally's regular sauce and cheese pizza was as good as Pepe's, said that she would be willing to come back just for that potato and onion pizza.

On the other hand, I loved the regular sauce and mozzarella (called "mutz"— pronounced "mootz"—by the locals) pizza at Sally's better than the one at Frank Pepe's. The crust was thinner, very rustic looking, and irregularly shaped, a Sally's trademark. It was not round, yet not quite rectangular or oblong either, just amorphous. The sauce was as enjoyable as at DiFara's in Brooklyn, with the sweetness of the tomatoes shining through.

I spoke with Flo Consiglio, whose husband, Sal, left his job at Frank Pepe's to open Sally's in 1938. He died in 1989, but, as Flo explained, everyone else working there is either family or "like family." The oven is smaller than the one at Pepe's, and not as visible to the customers, but the drama of watching lifelong *pizzaioli* assembling and baking their odd-shaped pies was like a theater experience. While in the waiting line, I had engaged some of the assembled in conversation and a strong family theme emerged. Most of them were regulars who felt they were part of the Sally's community. At Pepe's, where a similar community spirit existed, some regulars told me they preferred Pepe's simply because they didn't feel like they were part of the Sally's family. "If they don't know you, they treat you rudely," was a comment I heard more than once. The Sally's regulars said the same thing about Pepe's. I suddenly realized we were dealing with the Coke and Pepsi of the pizza world.

Fortunately, Susan and I didn't feel unwelcome at either Sally's or Pepe's. Maybe it was because we were out-of-towners and just happy to be there, or because we told people in line about our search for the perfect pizza and they took us under their wings, telling us about their favorite pizza, or why they preferred Pepe's over Sally's, or Sally's over Pepe's. We felt we were witnessing almost tribal alliances—passionate loyalties that made the New Haven pizza experience special. It was like we had crashed a party and had immediately become familiar friends.

But I wasn't finished with the pizza of New Haven yet. I recruited my friend Bonnie Tandy Leblang for a local pizza hunt. Among her many other activities, Bonnie writes about food trends for *Parade* magazine. She wanted to take me to Naples, a popular pizzeria just off the Yale campus, so we went there first. It is the kind of place that encourages you to carve your initials in a booth, and Bonnie showed me hers from a long time ago. The pizza was good, though not quite Wooster Street level. But for Bonnie, and I'm sure for many other regulars at Naples over the years, this was *the* place to go for a pizza fix. As we sat there sharing a small cheese and sauce pizza, I could see that the Naples experience was slowly becoming bittersweet for Bonnie. She was realizing that much of what the pizzeria represented for her had to do with another time in her life, and that it wasn't quite the same now because she's not the same now. I recognized that look—another Mama's moment.

So we headed over to Modern's Famous Brick Oven Apizza on State Street, where the two ovens are oil fired, rather than coal fired like the Wooster Street ovens. Whatever the fuel, the pizza was extraordinary. The white clam pizza was not as good as Pepe's because the clams were too few and not of the same high quality, but the sauce and mutz with garlic pizza was as good as any I can remember having anywhere, including Sally's.

After a few bites, Bonnie said, "You know, it's been so long since I've been here that I'd forgotten how good this pizza is. This wasn't my 'place' back then."

She paused for a second, took another bite, and continued, "I can't believe how amazingly good this is."

Neither Bill nor Mary Pustari, the owners, were around, so all I was allowed to see were the two pizza ovens, which are large enough to bake up to 150 pizzas per hour. I've used German-made oil-fired bread ovens, and there is no doubt that they can generate and sustain even more intense heat than coal. This was the first time I'd seen one used for pizza, but it makes sense. I'm sure the heat recovery is better than with wood or coal, and maintaining heat is the name of the game. Whether it was due to the oven or to something in the dough itself, a distinctive feature of Modern's pizzas was the beautiful edge, the *cornicione*. It maintained a little bigger puff than I found at either Sally's or Pepe's, giving the pizza a more *Napoletana* look without sacrificing any crispness in the bottom. In a city that prides itself on being the pizza center of America, it is important that every pizzeria offer something distinguishing while still working within local customs. Modern's Apizza had its own identity distinct from Pepe's or Sally's, yet I found it comparable, as do many locals. (I also believe that Modern's owes some of its popularity to the fact that it is open all day, rather than only for dinner like Pepe's or Sally's, making it easier to get in.)

"They really take their pizza seriously around here, don't they?" I asked Bonnie.

"Oh yeah," she said.

Pizza in America was not born in New Haven, although many New Haven residents fervently believe that it was. Yet the neo-Neopolitan style has unquestionably reached new levels of expression on Wooster Street, and at Modern's just a few blocks away. There are many other pizzerias in the New Haven area, each with its own enthusiasts, but they are always compared against the gold standard of either Pepe's, Sally's, or Modern's. I haven't yet tried DePalma's Apizza and Tolli's in East Haven; Zuppardi's, Paul's, or Mike's in West Haven; or the dozens of other neighborhood legends. They are all in the New Haven tradition, which means a brick oven, a thin crispy crust, and full-fat mozzarella—mutz, that is. The sauce is often, but not always, made from 6 in 1 brand tomatoes, the cheese is either all full-fat low-moisture mozzarella or a blend of full-fat and low-fat mutz, and everyone claims to have their own special recipe or source for Italian sausage. The subtle shadings and battles among the pizzerias only add to the legendary luster of New Haven. It is, dare I say it, pizza Mecca.

Having discovered such a rich vein of pizza gems, I could have been happy confining my hunts to New Haven alone. But I had a hunch that I'd have some pretty interesting pizza adventures if I headed west, so I got on a plane and flew to San Francisco.

SAN FRANCISCO BAY AREA

As I sat in the linen-tabled dining room of one of the finest Italian restaurants in the country, Paul Bertolli's Oliveto restaurant in Oakland, California, dining with two of the best cooks in America, I suddenly knew I had gone over the edge of pizza obsession. We were eating some amazing house-made *salumi*, and would soon be served such classy dishes as spit-roasted saddle of rabbit and *maltagliate* with spicy lamb *sugo* (meat sauce), yet all I could think about was that the pizzas are only served downstairs, in the café part of the restaurant.

This was my dilemma as I dined with Margaret Fox, who used to own one of my all-time favorite restaurants, Café Beaujolais in Mendocino (where Susan and I honeymooned), and Linda Carucci, who had just received the International Association of Culinary Professionals Cooking School Teacher of the Year Award. Linda had been the dean of students at the California Culinary Academy (CCA) when I first started teaching there in the early 1990s, and Margaret had served Susan and me breakfast the first morning after our marriage. As we ate at Oliveto, we were engaged in a lively discussion about how our culinary careers had taken unforeseen detours, about how we were now finding more fulfillment through mentoring others than through cooking in restaurants. There were periodic pauses in the discussion when the various courses arrived because the flavors were so vibrant that each of us insisted that the others have a taste. Between sighs of delight, we managed to cover a lot of ground.

Yet despite the serious bonding over careers and food, I was still thinking about the pizzas downstairs. I had to find out if Paul Bertolli's renowned attention to authentic techniques and flavors extended to his pizzas. So after Margaret, Linda, and I said our good-nights and the restaurant started closing down, I slipped back into the downstairs café, went right to where the pizzas are made, and hung out with the *pizzaiolo* while he broke down his station. He was a student at the CCA, working his way through school, but he was new to pizza making. I told him about my quest. He wanted to know what I thought of his technique, so he made me three pizzas, a *Margherita*, another with smoked prosciutto and dandelion greens, and the third one with potato and Gorgonzola cheese. The only problem was that the wood-fired oven was beginning to cool, so the pizzas took twice as long to bake as they normally would, which dried out the crusts somewhat. Even so, the combination of smoked prosciutto and dandelion greens was a great idea, and the pizza was better than some I'd had in Italy, at least outside of Naples.

I sensed that the potential for great pizza was there, but excellent ingredients alone are not enough. It was not a fair test, I know, but it highlighted a dilemma that I saw repeatedly during my travels: the lack of a *pizzaiolo* tradition. Making pizzas in many restaurants is just one of the station stops; the pieces are in place for greatness, but without a particular type of fervor and vision—a sense of mission— greatness yields to goodness. After enjoying a slice from each pizza, while also wondering how they might have tasted if the oven had been at full strength, I brought the rest back to my friends John and Paige, with whom I was staying. Eaten cold, the pizzas made a first-rate late-night snack.

I owed John and Paige at least that much because on the previous night they had taken me to the wonderful Pizzetta 211, in San Francisco's Richmond District. It's a tiny hole-in-the-wall café run by two women with a vision, Tamar Peltz and Ria Ramsey. They make their pizzas in a little electric pizza oven, but somehow the pies come out closer to real Naples-style pizza than any I'd tried except for those at Pizzeria Bianco. Clearly, they love what they are doing and have the skill and knowledge to deliver a *Napoletana* spirit without adhering to the strict rules of the *associazione*.

Our group of six squeezed into a corner table, and since there were five pizzas on the menu, I said, "Bring us one of each." Later we ordered a few more. We ate pizza and nibbled from a platter of marinated olives for about three hours. The pizzas were creative, yet anchored in sensible Italian flavor traditions. That evening's choices were tomato, mozzarella, basil, and white anchovies; rosemary, *fiore sardo* (a sheep's milk cheese), and pine nuts; roasted peppers, lamb sausage, and *ricotta salata* (salted ricotta); heirloom tomatoes and a variety of basils topped with an egg; and shiitake mushrooms, *crescenza* cheese, prosciutto, and arugula.

While we were there, a fellow came in with some sardines he had marinated and traded them for dinner. He turned out to be Robert Steinberg, a cofounder of the highly praised Scharffen Berger chocolate company; someone at our table said that he does stuff like that all the time. The whole neighborhood seems to have adopted Pizzetta 211, making it the kind of community gathering place more often found in Europe than in the States.

While Tamar was assembling pizzas for the never-ending crowd, I asked her how she and Ria had managed to create such a special spot. She said, "It's hard work, but we wanted to have a place where people of all ages would want to come together. This place used to be a bakery, which gave us the idea to serve pizza because it's something that just about everyone appreciates. It seems like our regulars love the smallness and intimacy of the restaurant."

I asked Tamar about the other menu items: the soups, salads, and specials, which seemed a cut far above a typical pizzeria. "The other thing we had in mind was to support local growers and products, especially organic farmers and, hopefully, to serve as a model for others who want to use organic products at their restaurants. We like to turn some of our cooks loose to be creative since we have such great ingredients to work with."

Orders were starting to stack up, so Tamar returned to making pizzas. She was clearly exhausted. Ria was out recuperating from an accident, and Tamar was holding down the fort with the help of a loyal team of friends. The place was only two years old, but the troops were weary.

Frankie Whitman, who had actually organized this particular hunt, introduced me to her daughter Sarah, who was also our waitress. "She just came in here one day and decided she didn't want to leave. She's going off to college in a few weeks and her sister, Leah, is going to take her place." It brought back memories of where I had learned to cook, the Root One Café, a Boston hippie restaurant I stumbled into in 1971 and didn't leave for three years.

There were nitpicky things I found that kept the pizza at Pizzetta 211 from being technically perfect, most of them due to the oven. But they were so minor, and the purity of vision was so genuine, the flavors so good, and the spirit so alive that I didn't care. Even if the pizza itself wasn't perfect, this was as nearly a perfect pizzeria as I had found anywhere. Should it survive its infancy, I had the feeling that

Pizzetta 211 could evolve into something akin to a *Chez Panisse* for the next gen-eration. I thought of Domenico DeMarco at DiFara's in Brooklyn, with the 1964 picture on the wall of himself standing in the same place he now stands while mak-ing his delicious pizzas. Not too many people have that kind of stamina. I told my tablemates about a food salesman, Stan, who used to come into the café Susan and I ran in Forestville, California, in the 1980s. Every week when he made his sales call, he first looked around our small dining area and nodded. He'd say, "Looks like your energy is still good." Finally, after about a year, I asked him what he meant by, "Your energy is still good."

"I look around to see if there are any pictures hanging crooked, or burned-out light bulbs that haven't been changed," he explained. "When I see those kinds of signs, it tells me your energy is running down, and that's a critical time in any restaurant's existence. Everyone comes out of the blocks full of good energy, but not everyone can sustain it."

Pizzetta 211 is a special place, and it has good energy. I plan to visit it every time I am in San Francisco, and I'll be checking the light bulbs, hoping they are all still glowing.

The fact that Pizzetta 211 reminded me of a potential Chez Panisse in the making was probably because my publisher had just thrown a pizza party for me at the legendary Berkeley restaurant. That afternoon I sat next to cookbook author David Lebovitz, who had been pastry chef at Chez Panisse in 1986, the first time I ate there. The pizzas were, as expected, wonderful, especially the wild nettle pizza, which has become a signature dish. But there was something missing from it, and I couldn't put my finger on what it was. The flavors were great, the wild nettle had an almost citrus-fennel quality, the crust was crisp, and the cheese was impeccable—it just didn't connect with me the way the pizza had years before at Chez Panisse.

It wasn't until later, when David took me back to the office to visit with Alice Waters, that I figured it out, thanks to Alice. She asked if I thought the pizzas were okay, especially the crust, and I replied, "Yes, the pizzas were great."

But then she said, "It's been one of the hardest things to do consistently because of the commitment needed from the people making them. Nobody wants to stay at that station." Then she gave me leads on a few other places making pizza in the Bay Area. One of them was Pizzetta 211.

Alice Waters has many talents, not the least of which is the wisdom of staying true to her vision of simplicity, of presenting food in its pure state. In the case of pizza, Chez Panisse's classic rendition is understated by American standards, made up of a modest arrangement of excellent ingredients presented on a crisp crust with a touch of whole grain in it. Yet it is this pizza, so loyal to the pie's peasant roots, that helped change the role of pizza in American fine-dining restaurants. However, with quality control an issue and so many other restaurants now doing pizzas at a high level, I got the feeling that if the pizzas weren't so popular, Alice might drop them from the menu altogether.

When she asked me about the crust, and then admitted that she worried about the day-to-day consistency, I finally realized what had been missing from that potentially great wild nettle pizza. True *pizzaioli* dedicate their lives to the craft, but at restaurants even of the caliber of Chez Panisse or Oliveto, making pizza is only a station that line cooks pass through as they work their way up the ladder. Some days the magic works and some days it doesn't. What usually saves the day is the caliber of the ingredients, the flavors on top. But what once made the pizzas legendary at Chez Panisse was that these great flavors, delivered on a great crust, were made with a level of artistry that had rarely been seen by Americans. Now the field has caught up with the old benchmark. Alice Waters and Chez Panisse accomplished the original mission, to elevate the pizza, but in doing so revealed another mission, one that I hope is now in process: to elevate the *pizzaiolo*, the craftsman.

The next day, I stopped in at the Cheese Board Collective, just across the street from Chez Panisse, and had a few slices of sourdough pizza. The Cheese Board is a unique pizza experience because it doesn't conform to how anybody else does it. The ovens aren't that good, the dough is thicker than I usually like, the toppings are different every day, and there's only one choice: whatever they're making that day. But boy is it good. Of course, when you have access to some of the best cheese in the world, you have a good start, plus the Cheese Board had been making sourdough bread for many years before they opened the pizza side. It's definitely a very Berkeley kind of place. Even the musicians who play to the long line of people waiting to buy slices are, not surprisingly, members of a musician's collective. Ursula Schulz, a longtime member of the Cheese Board Collective, gave me a wonderful tour of the operation, which was like traveling through the past thirty years of Berkeley itself. This is pizza by the slice, Berkeley style, and it is a different creature altogether.

First of all, the sourdough in the San Francisco area really is different than sourdough anywhere else due to a local bacterial strain aptly named *Lactobacillus sanfrancisco*. Bacteria digest the natural sugars in bread dough at the same time wild yeast does. The difference is that yeast creates carbon dioxide and alcohol while bacteria produces acid—lactic acid in this instance. The particular acid produced by *Lactobacillus sanfrancisco* happens to be especially tangy and quite tasty. Because the Cheese Board makes hearty slices of pizza, loaded with cheese and various vegetables (and never tomato sauce or meat), the dough is rolled out thicker than New York pizza (though not so thick as to be out of balance with the toppings). In other words, one or two slices of Cheese Board pizza can be a meal in itself.

Aside from the political and economic realities that govern collective businesses, the best (and maybe worst) thing about them is that they are tribal—every member is a partner and every partner is bonded to every other partner—whether the members like one another or not. I know this because the Root One Café was a collective of sorts (and also a commune), and I have to say it was one of the most exhilarating and challenging times of my life.

At the Cheese Board, there are actually two collectives, the cheese and bread store and the pizza side. While the format of the pizza collective is unconventional when compared to a typical American pizzeria, the underlying structure is actually rooted in the old-world *pizziaolo* tradition in one regard: the people who make the pizzas stay focused on pizza; they do not move around to various stations. It was fun watching the members of the collective work—assembling the pizzas, juggling them in the tall stack of roasting ovens that are not really pizza ovens, getting them out just in time to meet the needs of the seemingly endless customer line—because they were having fun. I know that everything about these pizzas would freak out the Associazione della Vera Pizza Napoletana, but the pizza makers at the Cheese Board are as dedicated to their craft as any I have ever met. Whether I have the three-onion, four-herb, and four-cheese pizza, the equally interesting corn zucchini pizza with lime, cilantro, mozzarella, and feta cheese, or any of their other exotic combinations, I always walk out the door with a smile.

Back across the bridge, in San Francisco, I went pizza hunting with cookbook author and teacher Joanne Weir, who led me to two discoveries. The first was Francis Ford Coppola's sweet, little Café Niebaum-Coppola in North Beach. Coppola invested a lot of money in the café in the hope of replicating the pizza of Naples, including the cost of bringing over a *pizzaiolo* to train his staff on how to use the authentic Italian wood-burning *forno*. But even though the pizza was in the style of Naples, the oven was not hot enough, the dough was not as wet and springy, and the *cornicione* did not pop like it should. This is not unique to Coppola's. No pizzeria I visited that tried to do the authentic Naples style was able to capture it exactly. What places like Pizzetta 211 and Pizzeria Bianco were able to capture was the spirit of *Napoletana*, but only because they had their own artistic vision and were not merely trying to reproduce the Neapolitan prototype.

The other find that Joanne guided me to was absolutely delicious focaccia from North Beach's Liguria Bakery. Because the bakery was closed by the time we arrived, we had to track down its focaccia at Mario's Bohemian Cigar Store Café, about a block away. This quirky luncheonette makes little pizzas in a tiny electric pizza oven and lots of sandwiches on Liguria Bakery's focaccia. We shared a meatball sandwich with Swiss cheese, sliced onions, and Mario's *marinara* sauce. The focaccia melted in my mouth with a flavor burst that any baker would kill to duplicate. It was actually more enjoyable than the focaccia I had in Genoa, partly because it was put to such good use as a sandwich bread—kind of like a northern Italian flatbread meets southern Italian red-sauce-and-meat combo.

What made the focaccia so good? A pleasant, robust olive oil flavor permeated the dough, and the bread was exactly the right thickness, just over a half inch, which was easily split horizontally into two thinner slices for sandwiches. But most important, it tasted moist in the mouth. Mouthfeel and flavor are the final arbiters when it comes to any food, and a cool, creamy quality in bread is an indication of long fermentation and a hot oven. When focaccia dough is fermented too quickly, the interior tends to be dry and starchy, instead of sweet and creamy and with a coolness created by properly gelatinized starches. Good bakers understand this intuitively, or they can be trained to implement proper technique, but when demand for bread products increases, long fermentation is often the first thing to go. Sometimes warmer proofing temperatures are used to speed up the rising of the dough and thus save production time and costs. The trade-off for faster rising is an inferior product, even if subtly inferior or covered up by olive oil or fancy toppings. The Liguria Bakery focaccia was perfectly executed.

I visited a number of other pizza places in northern California, many of them quite good, but two in particular were memorable. I had lunch at Viognier, a restaurant located upstairs in Draeger's in San Mateo. I love the whole idea of this place: a quality restaurant inside a premium supermarket, serving creative dishes based on what the market sells downstairs. The pizzetta with oven-roasted tomatoes, crisp pancetta, and a basil–mascarpone sauce was a treat, especially on the ultrathin and crisp rye crust, but I was completely bowled over by the fresh ahi pizzetta with a spicy sauce on a paper-thin, crisp *masa* (corn flour) crust. The crust was first baked in the *forno* and then topped with the ahi and sauce; it was essentially a sushi pizza, and I knew then that I would have to get to Philly and try the sushi pizza I'd heard about at Morimoto.

Although the pizzette at Viognier were delicious, they were not pizzas in the strictest sense. They were instead pizza derivatives, a fact that raised an important existential question for me: just how far out of the box was I willing to go in my search for perfect pizza? I still don't know the answer to that question, but I do know this: I am willing to go further than I would have imagined.

Sushi pizza would seem to be about as unconventional as pizza gets, but on the final day of my northern California swing, I got so far out of the box that I wondered if I'd ever find my way back in again. Susan and I stopped at Roxanne's in Larkspur, just north of the Golden Gate Bridge. Roxanne Klein has created, quite possibly the most original new restaurant in the country, and the pizza there, I think it is safe to say, is unlike any made anywhere else in the cosmos.

I've never liked the term *California pizza* because it has so many connotations, positive and negative. Sometimes it is used for an unrestrained style of topping pizza crusts with unusual, nontraditional combinations, such as what you find at the numerous California Pizza Kitchens. It can also mean exquisite neo-Neapolitan pizzas with traditional, but creatively modified, toppings, such as the pies served at Chez Panisse and Pizzetta 211. But Roxanne's pizza really deserves to be called California pizza because I cannot imagine it existing elsewhere.

Calling what I had at Roxanne's "pizza" treads on sensitive ground. Roxanne's pizza is, as is everything in her restaurant, purely vegan and totally raw, that is, uncooked. It is made with an almond-flour crust, marinated olives, freshly picked tomatoes, and cheeses made from—are you ready?—cashew milk and shredded turnips. The pizza is, admittedly, in the outer limits of envelope pushing, but because years ago I studied at the Hippocrates Health Institute, a pioneering center for the study of raw-food diets, I was game.

I eat sprouts because I like them and not just because they are good for me. If I did not also like all sorts of other foods, and if I ate the way that I think is best for my health, I would probably eat only raw foods. And if I could eat all the time the way Roxanne "cooks," I might even abandon my beloved cooked foods without looking back. Other people have tried to do raw restaurants with varying degrees of success (we've gotten sick in some of them), but Roxanne's level of creativity puts her in culinary-frontier territory. Her kitchen does not have a stove or oven, just a dehydrator, and nothing is heated above 118 degrees, so as not to destroy the natural enzymes in the ingredients. She does not use regular wheat flour because it is indigestible in a raw state. Instead, she substitutes combinations of nuts ground into flour and then hydrates the mixture with water in which wheat berries have been soaking. This raw "dough" is shaped into a crust and put into a dehydrator to make it crisp. Finally, it is topped with other raw foods, either fresh vegetables or sauces made, again, from nuts or vegetables. Nonetheless, it is a pizza, albeit a strange pizza, and it was fabulous. The nut crust even had the snap of a baked crust.

One thing that my pizza hunts revealed is that pizza is subject to many interpretations. While most pizzas stay within the realm of recognizable Mediterranean influences, the line of demarcation keeps moving outward, animated more powerfully by flavor than by tradition and convention. Much of what is to come could be laughably bad, nothing more than a blip on the screen and then rapidly retired to the culinary graveyard occupied by so many other ill-conceived fusions. But my guess is that we will see more, not less, of sushi pizza, raw pizza, and their descendents.

LOS ANGELES

"Wolfgang asked me to help him make the best pizza in Los Angeles, and I said I'd give him the best pizza in the world. I asked for only one thing from him, to leave me alone and just let me do it."

Ed LaDou told me this when we spoke on the phone. Nancy Silverton, who was the first pastry chef at Spago many years ago and is now the co-owner of La Brea Bakery and Campanile Restaurant, insisted that if I was writing about Spago pizza, I should call Ed LaDou. He was the one who introduced the gourmet pizza concept both at Spago, where he worked as the *pizzaiolo* for the first two years of the restaurant's pizza era, and later at the California Pizza Kitchen, where he was a consultant. In other words, Ed LaDou taught Wolfgang Puck how to do pizza.

I assumed that if Alice Waters was responsible for redefining pizza in the late 1970s, then Wolfgang Puck should get the credit for bringing the concept all the way home to the general public. And to a large degree this is true, for no single restaurant and chef are more influential in the pizza boom of the past twenty years than Spago and Wolfgang Puck. I also have to concede that my own revitalized interest in pizza was in part due to some of the wonderful pizzas I had at Postrio, Wolfgang's San Francisco restaurant based on the Spago model. Postrio was probably my single most favorite restaurant in San Francisco when I lived in the area, and I especially liked going to the upstairs bar café to order whatever crisp pizza du jour was being pulled from the wood-burning oven. For a long time, there was nothing else like it in San Francisco.

When Susan and I planned our Los Angeles pizza hunt, I tried to meet with Wolfgang, but he declined to be interviewed. After hearing about Ed LaDou's contribution to the evolution of what we now call Wolfgang Puck pizza, I was beginning to understand why. But we ate at Spago Beverly Hills anyway, and we ordered the famous smoked salmon with crème fraîche pizza, one of the restaurant's signature

dishes. Like the ahi tuna pizza from Viognier, this is a pie that pushes the pizza envelope. The crust is fully baked and then topped with the uncooked ingredients—
smoked salmon, crème fraîche, capers, dill—to produce a glorified, almost ethereal
lox-and-bagel experience. The pizza was enjoyable, even though the crust was no
match for the last few pizzas I'd had at Postrio. In the end, my Spago meal was an
echo of my Chez Panisse and Oliveto visits: a fancy restaurant with excellent pizzas
made by a talented line cook rather than a dedicated *pizzaiolo*.

Wolfgang Puck, through the venue of Spago and the help of Ed LaDou, long
ago presented to the world a revelatory pizza breakthrough. He stretched the age-
old pizza paradigm into new frontiers, staring the antifusion food police straight in
the eye and boldly declaring pizza a flavor-delivery system with global implications,
rather than the exclusive domain of the Neapolitans. His pizzas have become so
integrated into the American food vernacular that they are almost a cliché, the
gourmet designer pizza. Cliché or not and line cook notwithstanding, the pizza at
Spago was delicious, the flavors of the smoked salmon and dill and caper sauce in
perfect harmony. I'd gladly order it again, though preferably not at Spago's Beverly
Hills prices.

Instead, if I want a designer pizza almost as good but at popular prices, I'd
head to the California Pizza Kitchen (CPK), which we did the next day, choosing
the Santa Monica branch near our hotel. I had to try the famous barbecued chicken
pizza, their biggest seller and the one for which they are best known, as well as the
neo-traditional five cheese and tomato pie and the thin-crusted (which it wasn't)
Margherita. I was disappointed that the smoked salmon pizza was not on the menu
that day since I was dying to compare it with Spago's.

From its inception, CPK's brilliance was in taking the Spago pizza concept
and making it accessible to the masses by charging half the price in a less uptight
setting. Founders Rick Rosenfield and Larry Flax deserve a lot of credit for main-
streaming a gourmet idea and delivering it at a fairly high level, and then replicating it around the country.

The topping ideas and flavors are excellent and also wildly—even at times
recklessly—eclectic. Ed LaDou told me that by the time he left Spago in the mid-
1980s, he had presented over two hundred and fifty different pizza concepts there,
many of which became part of the CPK standard and revolving menu (CPK has

also added many new pizza toppings since Ed left in 1986). Skeptical at first, I was surprised at how attractive, flavorful, and consistent the pizzas were that day in Santa Monica and at the many CPK locations I have tried in other cities since then. With a great crust, they could become legendary, but that's the main thing missing at every CPK. It is the same old dilemma: how do you make great pizza without dedicated *pizzaioli*? The solution seems to be don't even try. Instead, make fun pizza and make it easy for the cooks to knock them out in a consistent fashion.

Ed LaDou personally resolved the problem by opening his own place, Caiote Pizza Café, starting out in Laurel Canyon in 1988 and then moving it to Studio City a few years later. "There were a lot of coyotes in the Laurel Canyon hills, thus the name, but I changed the spelling because I thought *caiote* looked more Italian."

I probed to see if there was lingering bitterness toward Wolfgang Puck, Larry Flax, or Rick Rosenfield. None of them has given Ed much public acknowledgment for his contributions to their success. He took the high road.

"I learned early on that wasn't something I should expect."

Instead, Ed got back into the kitchen, built his own family-style restaurant, and has been doing it his way ever since. A close friend of mine, Philip Goodrich, took his family to Ed's restaurant and wrote me about the experience. He was impressed with the crust and with one topping in particular that combined lamb sausage, chèvre, roasted garlic, and eggplant. "From the sound of it I didn't think the flavors would work together, but they were surprisingly complementary."

When I asked Ed to help me understand what differentiates his pizzas from those of others who have borrowed from his legacy, he said, "To do this right you need a seasoned staff, people who will see their products through from beginning to end and who have pride in their work. Pizza making is part of a transmission; it's almost spiritual. Dough is a living thing; it has a life cycle that goes from birth to consumption, with stages in between like childhood and adulthood. A good pizza maker has to honor this. The process possesses a kind of potential centeredness; it's almost Zen-like."

I'd say he's into it.

There is plenty of good regular pizza in Los Angeles in addition to the so-called designer pies. But just as Chicago will be forever linked to deep-dish pizza, New York City to neo-Neapolitan, and Naples to *Napoletana*, Los Angeles will always be associated with what has now become known as California pizza. Ed LaDou, Wolfgang Puck, and the CPK guys let the genie out of the bottle and, for better or worse, things will never be the same again.

SARDINIA IN DALLAS
AND CROATIA IN BELLEVUE

With the innovations of California-style pizza fresh on my mind, I began to uncover more ways the envelope can be pushed. I went to Dallas to teach a bread class, but I found myself seemingly in Sardinia for a few hours once the class was finished. Francee Garcia, who works at Sur la Table, took me to her favorite restaurant, Arcodoro & Pomodoro, where we were met at the door by Francesco Farris. He is the younger of the two Farris brothers, who together own the restaurant. Francesco told me that their mission is simple: to re-create the Sardinian experience for their customers. What is the Sardinian experience? If my short time there is any indication, it's a sense that daily life, difficult as it may be, is a pure gift and an opportunity for festivity. He and his older brother, Efisio, whom I met a few months later at a Montreal culinary conference where he was teaching a workshop on native Sardinian cooking, rarely work the same shift, which is probably why their partnership has endured the eleven passion-filled years of their restaurant's existence.

Although the island of Sardinia is connected politically to Italy—it is one of the country's twenty governmental regions—it has its own cultural identity, which extends to its cuisine. Most of the food at Arcodoro & Pomodoro is cooked in a wood-fired *forno*. Fish, meat, fowl, pizza—it doesn't matter. They all go into the hearth oven. Fire cooking is king, and the oven is the locus of the restaurant.

But one food not cooked in their oven is the famous Sardinian bread called *pane carasau* in dialect and known more popularly as *carta di musica*, or sheet-music bread. Francesco showed me how it is made, but, to ensure consistency, this is the one product the brothers bring in prebaked. The process is similar to how pita bread is made. You slide a thin disk of bread dough into a hot wood-fired oven, and in about a minute the dough pops, puffing up like a balloon. It reminded me of Alfonso

Mattozzi and his pizza-dough sandwich in Naples. Mattozzi's dough was quickly pulled out of the oven before it turned crisp, but when *carta di musica* is removed from the oven, it is split horizontally into ultrathin halves and then returned to the oven to crisp. The dough becomes cracker bread and takes on a parchmentlike quality that gives it the appearance of a page of old sheet music about to be rolled up into a scroll. It is served in a bread basket as an accompaniment to almost everything.

The pizzas at Arcodoro & Pomodoro were made with standard Neapolitan dough and were excellent, similar to true *Napoletana* pizza. But I couldn't help wondering what a pizza made on *carta di musica* might be like, so I made a mental note that I must try making it that way when I got home. When I asked Francesco if his pizzas were as good as pizzas are in Sardinia, he said, without false modesty, "They're better. But that's because these ingredients are so good and my oven is excellent. It's not always so easy there to get everything."

The pizzas were excellent and I fell in love with Arcodoro & Pomodoro, vowing to return with Susan, who I knew would love it as well. But the most important thing that came of this particular hunt was something else: I asked Francesco if anyone ever made pizza on the thin cracker bread, the *carta di musica*? He said no, not as far as he knew. But I saw his eyes go into a familiar wheels-are-turning mode and he looked off in the distance for a few moments. Then, after a brief wrinkle in time, we resumed our conversation as if nothing had happened. But it had happened, at least for me, and perhaps for Francesco as well. In any case, as things sometimes go in this universe of no original ideas, a few months later I read in the newspaper that chef Mario Batali was opening a pizzeria in Manhattan called Otto Enoteca with a menu built around the "Sardinian thin-crusted pizzas made on the famous *carta di musica*" (an idea he later dropped in favor of a quasi-*Napoletana* style).

"I knew it," I told Susan, rattling the paper dramatically. "There really is a way to do pizza on that crust. I knew it. I knew it the minute I saw that cracker bread and Francesco showed me how to make it!"

Susan merely gave me the look that we all reserve for loved ones who have fallen into a pit of obsession, hopeful they will climb out and return to sanity after a good night's sleep. "That's great, really great," she kept saying, but I knew that this would have to be one of those victory moments celebrated proudly but privately.

Shortly after my Sardinian revelation, still pondering the pizza frontier, I ventured to the Seattle area and hooked up with my close childhood friend Andy Ryan and his wife, Marla. Andy is an investigative reporter, so he was salivating at the idea of choreographing a pizza hunt. I coaxed a few other longtime friends to join in, and we all met up at Pogacha, a restaurant in suburban Bellevue.

We decided on Pogacha because it has an interesting backstory. In 1986, Helen Brocard, a Croatian American who was raised on a farm on Vashon Island in Puget Sound, decided to open a tribute restaurant to her heritage. She called it Pogacha, which in her Croatian vernacular means "soft, chewy flatbread." (Hmmm . . . I'm sure I'm not the first person to notice that *pogacha* rhymes with *focaccia*.) Helen built the restaurant around a family bread recipe that called for high-gluten flour, vegetable oil, eggs, sugar, salt, yeast, and water, and she used the dough to make not only pizza, but also sandwich rolls and loaves. She sold the restaurant a few years ago to Brad and Lisa Cassidy, who, even though not Croatian themselves, loved the place and have now expanded it to three locations. They describe their food as "Pacific Northwest with the added flair of the Adriatic."

At first glance, a *pogacha* pizza looks like a *pizza napoletana*, with a puffy *cornicione* evocative of the pizza we had at Mattozzi in Naples, but without tomato sauce (the menu says tomatoes are included only on special request). The dough is made early in the morning and allowed to ferment slowly all day at cool temperatures before being turned into loaves, rolls, and pizza crusts. The eggs enrich the dough, adding a touch of tenderness that works well in the rolls, but less successfully in the pizza crusts. The Naples connection soon begins to fade with the topping options, which include spinach, goat cheese, eggplant, sun-dried tomatoes, Kalamata olives, and a variety of cheeses, marinated meats, and sausages in many creative combinations. In other words, it may be Northwest and Adriatic, but in the end it is California-fusion-style pizza. Interestingly, we all had different takes on it; as a group we were only partially won over, and I think I know why.

Like Arcodoro & Pomodoro, the intent of Pogacha is to transplant and, perhaps, reinterpret foreign tradition and spirit within a North American setting. The flatbreads of the former Yugoslavia play important roles in their native kitchens, and I love the idea of *pogacha* appearing on this side of the Atlantic, even if its Croatian identity is dominated by Pacific Northwest fusion. But the key to its ongoing success will depend on whether the current staff is as dedicated to the spirit of the cuisine as

Helen Brocard was when she gave her restaurant birth. A restaurant concept, especially one designed to re-create a kind of magical old-world experience, is only as good—as strong—as the connection it builds between the customers and the vision behind the concept. This is the challenge of cultural transmission that Pogacha must meet through its interpretations of the menu items. As I journeyed from pizzeria to pizzeria, I felt that I was beginning to zero in on the subtle, intangible quality that allows that kind of magic to happen.

To round out the trip, Andy and I spent a day in Seattle trying out examples of the college-town pizzeria, a genre unto itself that is usually anchored in the New York pizza-by-the-slice model, with big, cheesy, oozy pies. I love such places, the oozier the better, and nearly everyone I know has a favorite from his or her college days. In Seattle, the king of this style is Pagliacci's, but just down the street is Pizza Brava, so we went to both. They were very much alike in style and flavor, and not unlike many of the Ray's pizzerias of Manhattan. I liked Pagliacci's better, but Andy preferred Pizza Brava. The only reason I can think of that we disagreed is because of past associations. Andy has a history with Pizza Brava. It has long been his go-to place when he needed a pizza fix. Pagliacci's, on the other hand, reminded me of a combination of the Mama's of my childhood and of Ray's on Prince Street. We decided to leave it at that, especially since neither place was what I would call unique or exceptional. However, both were good examples of an important archetype, and, perhaps more importantly, settings where many an indelible food memory has been formed.

PROVIDENCE

I have seen the future and it's called grilled pizza. When Susan and I moved to Providence in 1999, one of the first things on my to-do list was to visit Al Forno, the restaurant credited with inventing grilled pizza. Owners George Germon and Johanne Killeen are now nationally celebrated chefs, and although their renown is not just because of grilled pizza, they are probably better known for that single menu item than any other. I had heard about grilled pizza for years, but until we moved to Providence, I never had experienced it firsthand.

We met Johanne and George on our first visit to Al Forno and became immediate converts to their grilled pizza creations. In time, after watching them and their talented executive chef Brian Kingsford in action, and studying the method in their book, *Cucina Simpatica*, I grew skilled at making backyard grilled pizza and now do it often, both at home and in the backyards of others. We wowed friends on a visit to the West Coast where grilled pizza of this caliber had not yet taken hold. (Even though many restaurants now have grilled pizza on the menu, few, if any, actually have the Al Forno panache.) Whenever out-of-town friends come to visit, I either grill pizza for them or whisk them to Al Forno where they can have the real thing. It's a given.

Grilled pizza has earned its way into the global culinary lexicon, a journey that began in Providence in the early 1980s. Of course, Providence is the birthplace of grilled pizza in the same way that Naples is the birthplace of the *Margherita* pizza: Providence claims it and George Germon gets bragging rights, just as Raffaelle Esposito gets credit for "inventing" the *Margherita* in Naples. But people have been grilling bread over coals and melting cheese and other goodies on it for centuries. In other words, grilled pizza may be as old as pizza itself, which certainly predates Naples and even Greece and, by my calculations, lands somewhere near Egypt about six thousand years ago. But Providence is where the modern paradigm was established, and all subsequent versions are always judged against the Al Forno model. Or as I tell my friends when they claim to have found a great grilled pizza elsewhere, "Fine, but Al Forno is the mother ship."

George Germon grew up loving pizza, but when he and Johanne left the Rhode Island School of Design, where he was a teacher and she was a student, and opened Al Forno in 1979, the last thing he wanted was to be known as a pizza guy. There was no pizza on the menu. Three years later he was buying a large fish for the restaurant, and the fish merchant asked him how he planned to cook it. George said he was thinking of grilling it because he was excited about the new charcoal grill in the restaurant (previously everything was cooked in the wood-fired oven, the *forno*, thus the restaurant's name). The fish guy got excited when he heard the word *grill* and, mistakenly as it turned out, told George about discovering grilled pizza when he was in southern Italy. What he really meant was that the pizza was cooked in a wood-fired oven, but the notion of grilling pizza got George's creative wheels turning. He and Johanne began playing with the idea of using their grill to make something like pizza, that is, a crisp dough with interesting things on top. They quickly perfected a system and have now been serving grilled pizza for over twenty years.

The main reason George never wanted to be known as a pizza guy was because he grew up in a Greek American community in which Greeks and pizza parlors were synonymous. But now he has sort of made peace with it.

"I'm working it out, I guess. When I first told my dad we were opening a restaurant, he complained, 'Now you'll be just like any other Greek, making pizza.' I explained we weren't going to make pizza, but then a couple of years later we figured out how to do these grilled pizzas and, you know, you have to take what life gives you and go with it. . . . There are many things besides pizza that I am very proud of at Al Forno, yet most people talk only about the grilled pizza. But, hey, I can live with that. Pizza has been very good to me."

Johanne is protective of George's legacy, concerned he hasn't received the acknowledgment he deserves for creating and perfecting grilled pizza. "Now that others are doing it, they all act as if they were the ones who came up with it, but we know it began here."

When I asked George about this problem of recognition, he added, "It seems whenever others start making it, they get so drawn into the process that eventually they begin to think it really is their creation, and then they claim it. I guess that's just natural and it's fine. But I think the one thing that distinguishes our pizzas from the others is that we understand how labor-intensive it is to make them and we won't take shortcuts. I mean any kind of pizza is great, but what is it besides dough with something on it? How many ways are there to do that? Yet I could give the same recipe to two hundred people and everyone's pizza would come out different. What we have at Al Forno is a lot of experience with the technique, and there are things that you do, choices that you make, like how to set up the coals properly, or what equipment and wood you use, that make a difference. Not everyone understands that."

I have watched Brian Kingsford make more than a few pizzas on the Al Forno grill. He makes it look surprisingly simple, mainly because he has a well-worked-out system in place. A Neapolitan *pizzaiolo* does all of his assembly before sliding the pizza into the oven, but an Al Forno *pizzaiolo* performs his artistry while the pizza is cooking.

The dough is made, divided into small balls, and then left to sit on a sheet pan in a generous bath of olive oil. "This," George once told me, "is one of the most important tricks. The oil reacts to the intense heat and is seared into the dough, almost like frying it."

Al Forno uses mostly all-purpose flour, so the dough is more tender than most pizzeria dough, more like the dough made in Italy. Because it has been sitting in the oil for at least thirty minutes, and sometimes for up to a few hours, it is very relaxed. When an order for pizza comes into the kitchen, the *pizzaiolo* hand presses a dough ball into a flat disk on the back of an oiled sheet pan, moving it around, lifting it from time to time to pull it out farther, until it is stretched to the proper size. Like the pizza at Sally's in New Haven, the pressed, stretched, and shaped dough is neither round, oval, nor rectangular; it just becomes what it becomes. It is then slid onto the grill over a bed of hardwood lump charcoal, usually but not always from maple.

After a minute or so on the fire, the dough begins to blister, which means it is charring on the underside. This is where grilled pizza takes a different path from traditional pizza. The dough gets flipped over and the charred side is now face up. The cheese goes on, instantly starting to melt as it hits the hot surface. Since the two or three pizza offerings vary from night to night, season to season, sometimes there is sauce, sometimes there isn't. Then drops, dollops, and dabs of whatever toppings are in play that night are applied. Meanwhile, the cook is moving the pizza to different places on the grill, playing the heat like a harp, waiting for everything to meld. When it comes off the grill, it gets a thread of spicy oil and then a splash of garnish, usually frizzy green onion curls. The final presentation glistens; it is strikingly beautiful, more so than any other type of pizza I've encountered.

The first thing I noticed, and flipped for, was the snap of the crust and the slight smoky taste from the coals. Each bite is an explosive burst of flavor, distinct from every bite that follows. The pizzas are not cut into wedges, but instead served with a knife and fork and either cut into squares at the table or simply torn apart as they are eaten. One pie can serve four as an appetizer, but I think of them like a *Napoletana*, that is, one per person. They look large, but because the dough is so thin, it is easy for one person to consume a whole pie.

Al Forno is not a pizzeria. It is a destination restaurant. I always order other wonderful things from the menu, usually something baked in the *forno*, and I always save room for Johanne's desserts. But, sorry about this George, despite your dad's fears, you will always be the pizza guy to me.

CHICAGO

People from Chicago, or anyone who has fallen under the spell of its celebrated pizza style, are quite passionate about the local deep-dish pizza. Susan and I met a man in Rome just outside the Pantheon, standing in line at an ATM machine. He was a large, handsome guy who looked like he could have been a professional football player. When he heard us speaking English, he recognized us as fellow Americans and asked how we liked Rome and what had brought us there. We told him about the pizza research and asked him back the same two questions.

He answered, "I'm with the Secret Service and President Bush is coming to town tomorrow. I'm just part of the advance, not the regular, team." He explained that they needed some volunteers to handle logistics, and even though he worked out of the Los Angeles office, he thought, "Hey, it's Rome, why not?"

Before we could ask him more about what the Secret Service was like and what a cool job it must be, he said, "Pizza, I love pizza! But if it's pizza you're looking for, I have two words for you: Pizzeria Due."

"But that's in Chicago," I said, trying to show I really knew my pizza stuff.

"Exactly. I'm totally a Chicago deep-dish kind of guy, but it has to be from Due. Look, my wife's an airline attendant, so we can fly anywhere. Our idea of a great date is to hop on a plane to Chicago, grab some pizza at Due, and then fly home. That's how much we love it."

I was convinced, so I made Pizzeria Due my first stop when I got to Chicago a few weeks later. Even though it's owned by the same people who own Pizzeria Uno, and it's just a couple of blocks away from the original Uno, I had been told by many people that Due does the classic deep-dish better. It was, indeed, very good, though later that day my Chicago guide, cookbook writer Kathleen Kennedy, took me to her favorite place, Lou Malnatti's, or more correctly, to one of the many Lou Malnatti's in and around Chicago.

"This isn't the one I usually go to, which is closer to where I live, so I can't guarantee it will be just as good," she warned. But when the pizza arrived, after the usual thirty-minute wait I encountered at every deep-dish place (these pizzas definitely take longer and must be made to order, not in advance), Kathleen proudly said, "Actually, this pizza is pretty much identical to the Lou Malnatti's I get in my neighborhood."

I agreed with Kathleen that the crust was every bit as good as at Due, maybe even a touch crisper and thinner, which I loved, and the filling was even better. With deep-dish pizza, the differentiating factors are the style of the crust and the quality of the ingredients, and sausage is one of the definitive ingredients in Chicago pizza. It seemed as if all the pizzerias made a big deal about how their sausage is specially made for them, how proud they are of it, and how it sets them apart from their rivals. I had the sausage pizza at all three of the places I tried—Gino's East was the third— and it was excellent at all three, with probably Gino's full-sized patty, which covered the whole pie, getting the edge.

When it came to crust, I decided that Lou Malnatti's was my favorite, just edging out Due. Gino's crust was thicker and softer, more like corn bread. I had gone to Gino's with Rick Bayless, who, along with his wife, Deann, owns two hugely popular Chicago restaurants, the Frontera Grill and Topolobampo. He was more positive about the crust, insisting that he kind of liked "that corn bread quality" for a change. Those differences, I guess, are why each place has cultivated its own loyal, fanatical following.

The fact is, I am not like that guy at the Pantheon. Prior to my visit to Chicago I'd had excellent versions of the deep-dish style outside of Chicago, at Zachary's in Berkeley and Sicilia's in Providence (where they also do a pretty mean version of deep-dish's fraternal twin, the double-crusted stuffed pizza, for which another Chicago pizzeria, Giordano's, is the headliner). There's a lot to like about the concept: it's a big pie, either single or double crust, filled with lots of great stuff. How could it be bad? It can't and it isn't. But it just doesn't do it for me.

I was hoping I'd become a convert to the genre when I visited the fabled originators. On paper, I'm there. I love cornmeal-flavored doughs, spicy sausage, and oozy, gooey cheese of all sorts, but when I actually sit down to eat a deep-dish pie, I have the feeling of being assaulted—yes, in a good flavor sort of way, but relentlessly.

There's just so much going on; the sheer massiveness of it overwhelms me. It's like one of those couples-breakup scenarios where one person says to another, "It's not you it's me." That's the only way I can explain my lack of burning passion for deep-dish pizza: yes, you're beautiful and interesting, but you're just not my type. To take a stab at a qualitative reason, I think it's that the ratio of filling to crust is out of balance (remember the crust-to-topping scorecard of five to one in importance).

But that's just me. I am not one of the regulars who carved my initials into a table at Gino's, I didn't grow up on this style of pizza, and I don't have any past associations or food memories connecting me to the Chicago tradition. Yet I have dear friends who fell in love at Gino's thirty-five years ago and got married as a result, and others who no longer live in Chicago and can't stop lamenting how they miss their deep-dish pizza. Nearly everyone I know from Chicago has a marvelous, yet almost pathological sense of loyalty to it that I can't help but respect. And, to be fair, plenty of non-Chicagoans also love deep-dish and stuffed pizza.

The deep-dish pizza subculture has been around since at least 1943, when Ike Sewell and Ric Riccardo opened their first Pizzeria Uno at the corner of Wabash Avenue and Ohio Street, followed twelve years later by Pizzeria Due just a block away. Gino's East debuted in 1966, started by two cab drivers, Sam Levine and Fred Bartoli. Other deep-dish restaurants followed, contributing innovations like the two-crusted stuffed pizzas found at Giordano's and at Nancy's. (The latter is now a successful pizza chain built upon a layered pizza recipe developed by original founder Rocco Palese, modeled on an Easter pastry called *scarciedda*.) Edwardo's introduced a spinach soufflé pizza in 1979 on Howard Street, and the Chicago-style deep-dish wars were on.

Because I am a Philadelphia kid who grew up amid the cult of the cheese steak and its many denominations, I can relate. Chicagoans are entitled. Deep-dish is, like the grilled pizza of Providence, a legitimate category in the pizza lexicon. I know that I am not the only one who has not been swept away by the glories of the Chicago pizza paradigm. But I also admire the pluck of anyone who has decided that a perfect date consists of jumping on a plane in Los Angeles, flying to Chicago for dinner at Pizzeria Due, and then flying home.

While I was flying home from Chicago, I recalled a story I'd heard years ago about a woman in a museum who, while staring at a Picasso painting, began complaining to anyone within her vicinity, "I don't see what's so great about this painting. I don't see why everyone thinks Picasso is so great."

Most people distanced themselves from her, moving as far away as possible, everyone except for a single quiet fellow standing to her right. He kept looking at the painting. The woman complained again, "I just don't get it."

This time the quiet fellow said, "Yes, but lady, don't you wish that you could?"

When I arrived home, I felt an obligation to master making my own deep-dish versions, ones that did meet my (admittedly subjective) criterion of balance. I wanted my own climactic moment when I could say, "Oh yeah, now I get it." It took a few months and some burnt pies, but I acquired an appreciation for deep-dish pizza. I guess I just needed to spend some time with the thing itself to establish the connection that many Chicagoans have as their birthright.

PIZZERIA BIANCO

My Chicago experience—that is, my initial resistance to diving fully and passionately into the deep-dish genre—may have been preordained by an encounter I had a few days before I arrived in Chicago. My travels had, at long last, brought me back through Phoenix, Arizona, where I made arrangements to spend some time with Chris Bianco. It had been a few years since my last Pizzeria Bianco visit. Chris's stature within the chef community had continued to grow; he's the only *pizzaiolo* ever to be nominated by the James Beard Foundation for one of their "best chef" awards (after twice being nominated, he won the Best Chef: Southwest award in May 2003). I needed to find out, after all my pizza hunting, and having embraced the Steingarten challenge to taste and taste again, whether I had deluded myself before. In other words, was Chris the real deal, and if so, what made him so?

Chris and I sat in the new air-conditioned Pizzeria Bianco wine bar, a small, recently renovated brick building next door to the pizzeria. "I felt bad about everyone standing out there in the heat, so we finally got this place fixed up. We were using it for storage before. It kind of takes the pain out of waiting for a table. It's pleasant in here." He showed me some of the artwork on the walls. "Those are painted by my father. He's very good, actually quite well-known." Then we sat down with a couple of bottles of sparkling water and continued our conversation.

I asked him if he could explain what made his pizza so special, so much better than anyone else's. He took a deep breath, as if to signal that I had better hold on because he had a lot to say.

"Many people have asked me that and have even wanted to give me money to open branches of Pizzeria Bianco in Las Vegas and other cities. They want to take it national. They want me to teach other *pizzaioli* all my secrets. But they don't understand. They think I have all these secret tricks, and I do have some pretty good tricks, but that's not the point. That's not the secret to my pizza. The secret to my pizza is not the tomatoes, though I am picky about those and I'm extremely proud of the growers I purchase all my produce from. It's not the cheese, even though I make it myself fresh every day. It's not the wood-fired oven, though the pizza wouldn't be as good without it. People ask for my secrets, but I think it might be a disservice to give out so-called cooking secrets. They might think they are the keys, but they're not. Here's the secret and I hope this doesn't sound vain or conceited. The secret is . . . the secret is . . ."

He was having trouble saying it, and although I knew what he was going to say, I wanted to hear him say it.

"The secret is, well, it's me. I'm the secret. It's my passion, my energy, my commitment. I can't bottle that and give it to someone else. Maybe someone else has the talent and the passion and I could teach them, but, really, there aren't too many people who feel the way I do, who care as much as I care. I can remember nearly every pizza I've ever made, and what many of my customers had the last time they were here, and I try to make decisions to make it right for each of them. Has every pizza been perfect? No. I'm still working on getting it perfect. I don't know if I ever will, but sometimes I really nail one. It's like hitting the perfect golf shot. When people come into my restaurant, what I really want is for them to say, 'Why don't you pick out the pizza you think I should have.' I want them to trust me to choose the exact right one for them. I like it when people trust me to read them and match them up with the perfect choice. That makes me feel like I'm connecting with them. When I was a kid I connected with the pizza guy. He wore a white shirt and he was respected in our neighborhood. He was cool. You know what I mean? I want the respect of my peers, and I want people to like what I do."

He paused for a moment and I could see he was thinking about what he had just said, reflecting on that guy in the white jacket. So I asked Chris what experience he wants his customers to have when they eat one of his pizzas. What would he like them to get when they take a bite? He took a deep breath and started doodling on a pad as he spoke, as if drawing might help him put his feelings into words.

"Pizza is my metaphor, and I believe my mission in life is to make the best pizza in the world. I really do. In many places, maybe not here but in Italy, the pizzeria represents the soul of a village. Every pizza I make is an extension of my hand, even of my imperfection. When someone comes into my restaurant and eats my pizza I," and here he paused, "I want them to . . ." The room got very quiet, then slowly he finished, "I want . . . them to . . . experience . . . my soul."

We sat in silence for a few moments, letting the sobriety that hovered in the room settle. I asked him, "Do they?"

"Do they experience my soul? I don't know. Maybe sometimes. Pizza really is the metaphor of my life, but if you really want to get me, to experience who I am, there is one particular pizza that really defines me. It's called the Rosa. There's no sauce, only red onions, but special red onions that someone grows for me, similar to torpedo onions, with a little heat but not too much. And I use the best Parmigiano-Reggiano, the real thing, aged at least twenty-four to thirty-six months. It kind of bites you right here," he said, pointing to his cheeks and then under the back of his jaw. "And when I can get them I use pistachios from Tucson, you know, locally grown. That's important to me. If I can't get them, I use pignolias, pine nuts. Then just a small amount of fresh rosemary, not too much but enough to, you know, say 'I'm here.' It's an intense pizza, and not everyone likes it. But it's like the metaphor within the metaphor. If you get that pizza, you get me."

We talked for nearly three hours about food, art, mission, connecting with people, but then it was almost time for the restaurant to open. He said, "Let's go. I want to make you some pizza."

He set me up at the bar, just in front of the oven so I could watch him work. The doors were opened and customers streamed in. It was 112 degrees outside so being indoors was a relief; a feeling of general goodwill filled the air. Chris emerged from the back kitchen wearing an apron over his T-shirt and a baseball cap with the

The metaphor within the metaphor, the Rosa pizza from Pizzeria Bianco.

visor sloped backward over his neck. It was a garage band kind of entrance. Regulars came over to him as he took his position at the oven, chatting, glad-handing, high-fiving, and schmoozing. He asked me if I wanted to choose my pizzas or leave it up to him. After all we had talked about, I hardly needed to answer.

He smiled and nodded.

Before I knew it, a fresh cucumber, onion, and tomato salad dressed with a boldly flavored vinaigrette was in front of me. I devoured it and had half a mind to ask for another, but I knew what was still to come.

"I want you to try this. It's real basic but classic," Chris said from behind the counter as he assembled pizzas, including mine. His movements were economical. No great fanfare or showmanship. The most dramatic aspect of his performance was the subtle movement of pies from one position in the oven to another. Occasionally he checked the wood, maybe adding a small log or two. His team was clicking, with one guy making up and baking the *spiedini* appetizer (rolled prosciutto and fontina) and others keeping the bread and salads moving. The wait staff was lively and attentive to the customers, while Chris's business partner and fiancée, Susan Pool, was charmingly handling the front of the house. This was a small, vibrant restaurant community fully in the glow of its Camelot era, both staff and customers aware of a special bond they were sharing.

Chris continued, "I want to start you off with a *marinara*. Is that okay? I mean, it doesn't have cheese; can you handle that?"

"Like I said, I'm totally in your hands."

A few minutes later, a basic, classic *marinara* pizza arrived: sauce, oregano, and garlic, but no cheese. It was similar to, yet different from, the one I'd flipped for at Da Michele in Naples.

Two attractive women had seated themselves next to me at the bar and saw my pizza. One of them said, "That's my favorite, too, although I also really like the Wiseguy."

I looked quickly at the menu and saw that she was referring to a pizza topped with wood oven–roasted onions, house-smoked mozzarella, and fennel sausage. We spent the next ten minutes talking about what being a regular at Pizzeria Bianco was like, and how one of them was initiating the other, an out-of-towner, into the world of Bianco.

The *marinara* pizza was delicious, and for the second or third time in my life I came to believe that I did not have to be a cheese pizza kind of guy forever. The sauce was tangy and fresh tasting. It had the flavor burst of fresh herbs with each bite, and the crust was charred and ancient looking, as if excavated from the ruins of Pompeii. The *cornicione* was not as puffy as those made in Naples, but it still had that airy, *ciabatta*-like structure that seduces me every time. I remembered the pizzas that I'd had at Bianco nearly four years earlier, and it was as if time had compressed like the bellows of an accordion. I was back there again.

When their Wiseguy pizza arrived, the women gave me a slice. It was excellent. I was thoroughly enjoying the universe according to Bianco.

Then Chris brought me a Rosa, the definitive metaphor within the metaphor, the "this is me" pizza. I was pretty full by now and wondered how I could eat the whole thing. I didn't want to upset Chris or cause him to think I didn't get him. The pizza did have a kind of bite, just as he said it would, in the back of my mouth near my cheeks. It did get me on the inner sides of my jaw the way some wines do, again just as he had predicted. The fresh rosemary and red onion slices played off the pine nuts (he was out of Tucson pistachios until the next harvest). There was no red sauce to blunt the edginess of the Parmigiano-Reggiano. All of these factors collectively left an impression that I can still taste months later as I write these words. It was an impression of intensity. I got Chris on my first bite and it was, he was, intense. I couldn't finish the pizza; I was shot, my palate was shorted out, and my stomach was full. I offered it to my counter mates, hoping they would eat it all before Chris returned, but he came over before they could cover my tracks. He saw that I had bailed out about halfway through the pie, and he just chuckled and said, "Pretty intense, huh?"

Over the course of my pizza hunts, the name Pizzeria Bianco often came up in discussion. The word had gotten out about this place, and quite a number of people that I encountered had been there. Rick Bayless, who had joined me for a pizza at Gino's East in Chicago, was one of them. When we finished our analysis of the pizza at hand, we found ourselves discussing weightier, more personal matters. This is how we got there: He asked me if I had discovered any really great pizza on my hunts. Before I could answer, he asked, "Have you been to Pizzeria Bianco?"

"Well, actually, I was just about to say that."

"Yes, it's definitely my favorite," he responded.

"I had an interesting conversation with Chris," I told him. "Somehow, during our discussion, he said that he had discovered that his mission in life was to make the best pizza in the world and that pizza was the metaphor that defined him."

Rick's eyes got very wide. "He said that pizza was his metaphor?" He started to chuckle. "That's so great, pizza is his metaphor. So what did you say?"

"I told him I totally understood. Why are you chuckling?"

"Well, I've often said that I think of Mexican food as my metaphor, and Deann and I have talked about how our mission is to bring authentic Mexican cuisine and flavors to the world."

So I told him how Chris even had one pizza that was his metaphor of metaphors, his ur-metaphor, the one he called the Rosa, and how that pizza really defined his personality. I explained that Chris feels that if people can get what that pizza is about they can get who he is. Rick chuckled again.

"I can believe it. I have one friend who told me he had a life-changing experience because of a pizza he ate in Florence."

Before I could ask him if it happened to be a *pizza Vesuvio* with lots of black truffles, he continued, "I don't think that I have one particular dish that is the defining metaphor of who I am. They all add up to that, I suppose, but my favorites change pretty regularly, so maybe that means I'm still a work in progress. But I think it's great that Chris said pizza was his metaphor. I really like that."

We spent the next hour talking about things like mission in life, how food is both an end in itself and a means to an end, and how having a successful restaurant creates opportunities not only to support farmers and others in the food chain, but also to bring growers, cooks, and even customers together into a community with shared values.

Rick said, "Having a restaurant has its rewards, but it also carries responsibilities to the environment, to support sustainable agriculture, to bring together people who might not otherwise come together. At least that's what makes it rewarding to me. It really is a pretty deep metaphor."

We talked about everything that two hours and one deep-dish pizza would allow, another reminder that all this pizza hunting was more about people and conversations than it was about the pizza.

PHILADELPHIA AND MAMA'S

Eventually I made my way back to Philly. I had some unfinished business there at Mama's. I needed to get to the bottom of the crust issue. What had changed, me or the crust?

I stayed with my mother and we went on two pizza hunts together to prepare me for my visit to Mama's. The first was to Morimoto, the new sushi palace of Iron Chef Morimoto Masaharu. I had seen a documentary on the Food Network about the opening of Morimoto and noticed that one of the chef's signature dishes was sushi pizza. I had no illusions that this would be pizza in the traditional sense, but one of my definitions for pizza is "a crust with something on top." Nobody said it had to be topped with sauce and cheese. I like sushi almost as much as I like pizza, so in the spirit of the hunt, I was in a bring-it-on mood.

Maybe it was because I'd been eating too much pizza, or maybe I am just a sucker for bold flavors, but I could have eaten a lot of Morimoto's sushi pizza. He used a crisply grilled flour tortilla, topped it with an eel sauce, raw tuna, red onion and jalapeño slivers, fresh tomatoes, and cilantro, and then finished it with an anchovy aioli and some Tabasco sauce. I'm sure the sushi police are all over his case, but I don't care and I doubt that he does either. The sushi pizza was similar to the ahi tuna pizzetta I had eaten at Viognier in San Mateo, except that the California pie had a paper-thin rye crust that was baked in a wood-burning oven. Obviously, raw tuna seasoned with a zingy sauce is a wonderful flavor explosion. Put it on a crust and who is to say it is not a pizza.

A few hours after lunch at Morimoto, we went on a dinner hunt to Philadelphia's most famous pizzeria, Tacconelli's, in north Philly's Fish Town section. I never went to Tacconelli's when I was growing up in Philadelphia, which means if I want to beat myself up over my misspent youth, I now have a good reason. Tacconelli's has been around since the 1940s, but kids of my era didn't often leave the Main Line suburbs for Fish Town. Regrettably, I missed years of golden opportunities to indulge in a rare level of superb pizza. Fortunately, one of my boyhood friends, Jeff Frank, is a pizzaholic. When we were kids, he favored a place called Boston Style Pizza in a section of town called Manoa, while I was a die-hard Mama's boy. Sometimes I'd indulge him and go to Boston Style, and sometimes he'd relent and accept a Mama's slice or two. Boston Style was owned by a couple of Greeks, so we called it Greek-style pizza, and the crust was a little thicker than at Mama's. Jeff and I, along with our regular gang of food-crazy, poker-playing friends, alternated between pizza and cheese steaks as our nourishment of choice. As any good Philadelphian must, we had our favorite places for cheese steaks (either Larry's or Mama's—yes the same Mama's) and for all the other essentials of our everyday food-support system: pizza, hoagies, water ice (Overbrook), soft pretzels (any street corner in Center City), Chinese food (Happy Garden in Chinatown, but it was always called Pepsi Garden because of the Pepsi sign over the door), and corned beef sandwiches at Hymies, Kip's, or Murray's Deli—the debates raged for years over who made the best. It was a small but well-stocked universe.

Jeff never tired of pizza, and in his adulthood he discovered Tacconelli's. When we reconnected after many peripatetic years on my part, he took me there. It is the real deal and, in addition to the quality of the pizza, which is nearly the caliber and style of New Haven pies, here's what I like about it best: you cannot eat there unless you call ahead and reserve—not a table, but a dough ball. When you call, you tell them how many dough balls you want, and they make only as many as are ordered (well, probably a few extra for those on their forgiveness list). Under ordinary circumstances, if you have not ordered a dough ball, you do not get a pizza. Jeff knew the drill and he took care of ordering the dough balls earlier in the day. We put together a hunting party of seven people, including Jeff and his wife, Alyson; two of their friends, Norma and Sherman; my nephew Christopher, who was only fourteen at the time but a true *fresser* (Yiddish for "big eater"); and me and my mom. Despite the sushi pizza we'd had for lunch, I was hungry for real pizza by dinnertime and so was my mom. Earlier in the day, Jeff had ordered five dough balls for us, which meant that we could order five large pizzas of our choice. One of them I knew would be pepperoni because Jeff, for as long as I could remember, always got pepperoni on his pizza. Spacing the arrival of the pies at ten-minute intervals, we also ordered a white pizza, loaded with garlic; another with spinach, sweet peppers, and onions; next was a sausage pizza; and finally one with prosciutto and mushrooms. Five large pizzas sounded like more than we could possibly need, and the idea was that there might be some left to take home. I am embarrassed to report that we ate them all.

This was not my first visit to Tacconelli's. The previous year Jeff had initiated me into the dough-ball society when we went with some other friends of ours, again accompanied by my mom. She is the one who first discovered and introduced our family and all our neighbors to Mama's Pizzeria back in the late 1950s, so it was fitting that she be along for my discovery of Tacconelli's. One good turn deserves another, and it took me only forty or so years to complete that loop. Since we enjoyed the pizza at Tacconelli's so much the first time, we were actually very excited about going back again.

Tacconelli's is also famous for its oven. It really is a big, beautiful brick oven—not the original 400-square-foot oven built in 1920 by Giovanni Tacconelli and his friends, but a re-creation that was built to replace the original in 1992. New Haven and New York City have a long history of coal-fired brick pizza ovens, but Philadelphia does not, so a large brick oven is kind of special, even if it is gas fired. Two things set brick ovens apart: they get very hot and, well, they are made of bricks. Of course, this would all be for naught if a brick oven did not also bake beautiful pizzas. Are the pizzas from Tacconelli's gas-fired brick oven as good as the pizzas from New Haven's coal-fired beauties? Not quite, but they are very close. Outside of what I tried in New Haven and in a few places in New York City (Totonno's, for one), Tacconelli's pizzas were about as good as any I hunted down. They were big, gorgeous, thin-crusted, crisp, charred pies.

With our waitress Lucille's permission, I went into the kitchen and met Vince Tacconelli, the grandson of founder Giovanni. He was cranking out pizzas, sliding them into the oven on eight-foot-long peels, but he didn't seem to mind me hovering near him. A couple of times he had to warn me to watch out for the end of the peel, a long, unwieldy paddle that seemed to have a mind of its own. The pizza action was a well-rehearsed drama, with a minimum of movements. Most of the skill involved the ability to move the pizzas into, around, and then finally out of the huge brick oven. The oven was the width of the entire kitchen, about eight feet, and was about twelve feet deep, and it could handle up to fifteen or so pizzas at once. I asked Vince what he thought made their pizza so special. His answer was simple: "We've been making them for a long time."

Brick ovens do not, of themselves, guarantee a great pizza. I've been to places, such as my local Bertucci's, that simply break my heart. Their wood-fired brick oven is everything you want a pizza oven to be, yet the pizzas that emerge, while decent, are uninspired. So while Tacconelli's gets a lot of publicity because of its big brick oven, I know that the quality of the pizza is due to some other factors, including the quality of the ingredients and the skill of the *pizzaiolo*. The notable thing about a Tacconelli's pizza is that every aspect of it is of high quality. It is not dominated by the crust, the sauce, or the cheese and toppings, but is cohesive and unified, what my students are taught to call BUFF—balance, unity, focus, and flow. It is a balanced pie and both times I was there the quality was the same. If I had known about Tacconelli's when I was growing up, I would have overcome my fear of venturing into North Philadelphia and made it my hangout pizzeria.

Which brings me, at last, back to Mama's.

I drove to Bala Cynwyd by myself the day after our big Tacconelli's blowout. I wanted to meet with Paul Sr., but he is rarely there anymore. His son, Paul Jr., runs the show now, and even though I had not seen him for over thirty years, I instantly recognized him. When I last saw him, he was about fourteen, and I would notice him sometimes working the cash register or watching his mom make cheese steaks, sometimes stepping in himself to take over the grill.

"When you were coming in back then, most of our business was pizza with a little cheese steak and hoagie action on the side, but my passion was always with the cheese steaks," he told me. "I took it over from Mom, and that was always my station. Later, when I started running things, the cheese steak demand grew and now it's about 80 percent of our business."

I was not surprised. I always loved Mama's cheese steaks, even though they were totally different from everyone else's. First of all, they were loaded with cheese, pizza cheese, not American cheese or Cheese Whiz. My recollection was that they always seemed more loaded with steak than all the others, too. Just a few days before coming to Philly, I received my monthly issue of *The Rosengarten Report*, David Rosengarten's wildly entertaining food newsletter. It happened to feature Philly cheese steaks and guess what? He named Mama's the best cheese steak in the universe. I congratulated Paul and discovered that he had not yet heard about the recognition. "Well, I'm here most of the time, and a little out of touch with stuff like that."

Then I asked, "Listen, I have to know. Who makes the pizzas now and did you change the crust?"

"You noticed, eh? Well, my dad did change it a few years ago. When he was making them he had the feel. But when he stopped, we needed to make it so that anyone could make them, so he changed the formula a little, made it a little thicker, easier to work with. Of course, we haven't touched the sauce or the cheese. It's the same as it's always been—some mozzarella, a little Cheddar, some Parm. You know, our secret blend."

My pizza came out of the oven and I had a slice. It was good, the cheese and sauce really were the same as in my memory vault, but the crust was definitely thicker, not at all as I remembered it. I would have to call my brother Fred as soon as I got home to gloat.

While I was eating the pizza, Paul made me two cheese steaks, one to eat there and one to take back to Providence for Susan, who I knew would be disappointed— I mean *very* disappointed—if I came home empty-handed. I watched him work the grill. His movements were fluid; he was in rhythm, at one with his tools. He had to fill a large take-out order plus mine, and he was working the grill like a maestro. When I was a kid, the grill in Mama's was maybe two and a half feet long. Now it dominated the kitchen, probably eight or nine feet long, and the pizza oven looked puny in comparison. Paul Jr. covered the stacks of shaved steak with a big pile of the house-blend pizza cheese, and then, with a smooth, practiced motion honed over thirty years, he divided the piles into portions and rolled each portion over so that it became enrobed in the molten cheese. One at a time, he swung his metal spatula under the glistening cheese steaks and laid each one in a long Italian roll, not from Amoroso's Bakery as everyone assumes about Philly cheese steaks, but in rolls custom-made for Mama's by a bakery that he wouldn't name. They were quickly wrapped in butcher paper and bagged.

I looked down for a second to take another bite of pizza, and when I looked up, Paul was standing next to my table, handing me my two cheese steaks, one of them wrapped for the long train ride home.

"One of the things that makes these so good is that we use better meat than everyone else, real rib eye roast, and, of course, there's our cheese blend," he told me, as I sighed rapturously between bites. "I love making them. It gives me pleasure to work the grill, always has. It's like it's my mission."

I told him about my conversations with Chris Bianco and Rick Bayless, and about my pizza hunts and my search for the perfect pizza. He smiled and nodded, and then returned to the grill.

POSTSCRIPT

After many hunts, many adventures, many conversations, I have come to the conclusion that there are two kinds of perfect pizza: contextually perfect and paradigmatically perfect. They are both important. Mama's, I now realize, was contextually perfect, as was the Brothers Pizzeria in Raleigh where I brought the kids when they needed comfort. It's the pizzeria where we have a special history, a memory that is woven together with the flavors, textures, and atmosphere of the place. It is necessary, I think, that such a contextually perfect pizza—that is, perfect because of the circumstances of a time and situation—at least aspires, even if it fails, to be paradigmatically perfect as well. There must be someone, the *pizzaiolo*, who believes, rightly or wrongly, that this is the best way to make pizza, that no one does it better. It's like the pizza lady in the movie *Mystic Pizza* who was convinced that the special herbs and spices from the Azores, with a recipe passed down from her father and his father before him, made her pizza the best in the world. If the *pizzaiolo* brings this effort and attitude to the workbench, then the pizza hunters like me, and probably you, can declare whether it is as perfect in this world as it is in the mind of the *pizzaiolo*.

Once in awhile, and only rarely, these two perfections come together in one pie, in one perfect pizza moment, and then we know a different reality, a moment of grace, and we attain an indelible memory. When that happens, if we are conscious enough even to recognize it when it occurs, it is like a gift, and the best we can do is to be grateful.

In 1986, I went to a new ribs place in Sebastopol, California, with a friend of mine, a restaurateur who shared my passion for barbecue. Barbecue has its own dynamic, similar but distinct from the world of pizza, but the passions run equally deep. The three main veins that barbecue freaks explore are smoking techniques, rubs, and sauces. At that time my primary interest was sauce, though later I completed the circuit by going after smoking techniques and rubs. We brought along a bottle of my homemade sauce, Holy Smoke, a name coined by my mother, who recognized well before I did the sweet irony of a barbecue sauce created at a seminary, which is where I lived at the time. When the ribs arrived, slathered in the restaurant's house sauce, we took out the Holy Smoke and poured a little next to the ribs. The owner happened to be watching, probably hoping to see us going bonkers over his ribs, as any new rib-house guy would. He was deeply offended that we had our own sauce and rushed to the table.

"What the hell's going on here, boys? Did you bring your own sauce?"

Unfazed, I replied, "Yeah, I always do. I'm searching for the perfect barbecue and I use this sauce as my benchmark. Want to try some?"

"Nah, I like mine." It was the expected reply. "I'm just about to get into bottling that sucker."

It was said with such fatherly pride that I was touched. So I said, "Well I'm looking forward to it. Let's give it a test drive."

With great fanfare my friend and I attacked our ribs with the house sauce and then, instinctively, made simultaneous eye contact, communicating quickly, without the owner's catching it, the message: "No way!" Of course, our new friend was waiting for our review, so I did the politic thing and said, "Hey, this is, you know, pretty good stuff. Yeah, pretty darn good . . ."

"There's a gallon of pure Tennessee whiskey in that baby, and real butter, too." His eyes glazed over and a warm smile inched up his face. He was obviously experiencing a Kodak-like memory of some great barbecue moment, a reverie that we wouldn't dare disturb. When he snapped to, his eyes refocusing and narrowing on us, the smile slowly ebbing, he looked intently, checking us out to see if we were also properly transported. Our fakery couldn't extend that far, but when he looked away I dipped a rib in my own sauce, took a bite, and happily tapped into my own taste-memory moment. When he looked back and saw the glazed eyes and involuntary smile on my face, he figured it was from his sauce and said, "Well, yeah, that's what I'm talkin' about," and walked to the kitchen, his shoulders back, his head held high.

"This guy won't last two months," my table companion said. He was right. Six weeks later the place was gone, the doors padlocked. The owner had passion and conviction, and he had linkage to deeply felt memories. He just didn't have barbecue that was perceived by others as he saw it. But his passion at least got him into the game, and I'm sure he's still enjoying that Tennessee whiskey barbecue somewhere, wondering how the rest of the world could be so wrong.

I know now that in the world of pizza only a few pizzerias offer both contextual and paradigmatic perfection, and that there are many more places that would like to be part of that special club and many that don't care. On one pizza hunt with my childhood friend Michael Goldfarb (who is now an award-winning public radio journalist), we were enjoying a pizza at his favorite Boston pizzeria, the venerable Pizzeria Regina in the North End. He and his wife, Christen, have accumulated a lot of good pizza memories associated with Regina's, and they consider it their place for pizza whenever they're in Boston. I was explaining to Michael my theory of paradigmatic and contextual perfection. Trained reporter that he is, he turned the tables and began interviewing me. He asked if I found many people as passionate about pizza as me.

Before I knew it, he had me on a roll. I said, "The type of pizza that most people like today is usually the one they grew up with. In some communities there are still great independent pizzerias, but in most areas it's Pizza Hut, Papa John's, Papa Gino's, or some other franchise. It seems that the younger the taster, the more the taste gravitates toward the generic pizzas, the mainstream *pizza americana*. It has become the new reference point for this generation. These are not," I admitted, "bad pizzas, but neither are they of the caliber of the great neighborhood or by-the-slice pizzas that people of our generation grew up with. They are not made at the kind of pizzerias that people feel passionate about and say, 'Oh yeah, the Pizza Hut on Reservoir Avenue is the only good Pizza Hut—fuhgeddabout the one on Quaker Lane!'"

Michael just nodded, knowing he had me going.

"But to be fair, it's not just pizza. This trend toward a generic middle ground applies to every food that has been franchised, like hamburgers, fried or roasted chicken, and even Mexican and Chinese food. But when we grew up in the 1950s and early '60s, pizza was a find, it was special and, remember, we'd have fights over which pizzeria was the best."

Michael said, "Yeah, I liked Pagano's better than Mama's, but you were always a die-hard Mama's guy."

"But Mike, we're native Philadelphians; we grew up in the land of Philly cheese steaks and hoagies. Philadelphians are still, even now, chauvinistically passionate regarding their foodstuffs. But when pizza emerged from ethnic neighborhoods and became Americanized, something besides the pizza changed. Our standards and expectations became noticeably lowered. In New Haven, I can still get into very heated discussions about whether Sally's Apizza or Frank Pepe Pizzeria Napoletana makes the best pie on Wooster Street, but now, outside of New York or Chicago, I couldn't pick a fight over the matter."

We continued delving into the subject as we devoured our Regina's saucy, cheesy rustic-style pizza. Michael told me about Stromboli in the Lower East Side of Manhattan at St. Mark's Place and First Avenue, where he would go for solace when he was a struggling actor.

"I can't say it was the greatest pizza in the world, but it a had a flavor that was different, kind of sweet and sour, and I really liked it. I couldn't quite figure out the accents of the owners, so I thought maybe they were from an obscure part of Sicily where they had their own style of spicing. But when I asked the guys where they were from, they said Albania. Then it all clicked, the sweet and sour flavors were not Sicilian at all, but a whole different ethnic region. Yet the pizza was still really good pizza. I tried to find out what spices they put in it, but they'd just smile back and wouldn't ever tell me. But even more important, the pizza at Stromboli was all I could afford. For a couple of bucks, to be able to get a big slice of pizza with their sauce that I knew I'd never taste anywhere else, and to be so utterly satisfied—it really worked, it fed me. I still make it a point to go there when I'm in the city even though the original crew isn't there anymore. I'm not sure if it's as good as when I went there years ago, but it's good enough; it still works for me. What's really important to me is that it's still there."

"That's it," I jumped in, "That's the contextual perfection. Without a connection to a place's history or without a history with a place, it's hard to recognize it. Otherwise, all we have is anecdotal, apocryphal history, or we have to sense it subjectively in the air, on the walls, carved into the booths, or in the eyes of the regulars. New Haven," I continued, "is rife with such storied places. A newcomer can get sucked into the context almost on the first visit."

"Yes, that's context, but how can you tell if a pizza is paradigmatically perfect?" he asked. "Are there actual criteria?"

I tried to define such criteria—the snap and char of the crust, the balance of flavors, the quality of the cheeses, the type of tomatoes, and the dedication of the *pizzaiolo*. I spoke of how the criteria must be broad enough to include an appreciation for diversity, and a recognition that truly great styles of pizza exist apart from the idealized *Napoletana* form. I even explained how this pizza diversity is a controversial point, not unlike religious ecumenism.

We sat there in silence for a few moments, rubbing our *cornicione* scraps into the dribs of sauce and cheese still stuck on the pan. Finally, as we finished off our last pieces of crust, I said what we both knew all along, "You know, sometimes it just comes down to the old truism: I'll recognize it when I see it."

[PART 2]
THE
RECIPES

Attempting to replicate perfect pizza at home, especially without the high temperatures of a wood- or coal-burning oven, may seem like a daunting task. In fact, you may believe that the limitations of home ovens make it impossible to reproduce the pizzas of the truly great pizzerias. Though many home cooks are adventurous in other areas, most are content to satisfy their pizza craving with a stop at a favorite local pizzeria, home delivery, or a pie out of the freezer. (It is a tribute to pizza's flavor potency that even when it is prepared on a mass scale, people keep coming back for more.) This is totally understandable if you live near one of the great pizzerias and you don't believe you can match their pie at home. But what if you can? Pizza is, after all, a peasant food at heart and should be as easy to make at home as meat loaf or macaroni and cheese. My goal is to win you over to this view by teaching you some basic principles and methods that, when applied, yield wonderful home-baked pizzas in a variety of styles.

Pizza and its various cousins, including focaccia, calzone, *stromboli* (rolled pizza), and *schiacciata* (the Tuscan version of focaccia), have two components in countless variations: crust and topping or filling cooked in a very hot oven or over or near fire or coals. The best pizza has an extraordinary crust and an equally exceptional topping in flawless symbiosis and balance. It has been called a perfect food by many nutritionists because it is easily assembled with a healthful balance of protein, carbohydrate, and fat, yet many pizzerias have abandoned the rules of sound nutrition, supersizing their pies to appeal to Americans' love of fat and volume. With relatively little effort, however, pizza can be a platform both for balanced flavor and balanced nutrition.

In the next few pages, I present my take on the two key components of pizza, crust and toppings, and then conclude with an overview of the baking process. In these discussions, and in the recipes that follow, there is a guiding principle at work, something that I emphasize again and again with my culinary-school students: flavor rules. Yes, we teach presentation, knife skills, gastronomy, food history, kitchen and business management, and nutrition. All of these, however, are merely pillars that support the one indispensable experience that a cook must deliver to a customer. It is flavor that brings people back, and noble philosophy, captivating history, or brilliant presentation cannot replace it.

THE CRUST

I agree with Jeffrey Steingarten: crust is at least 80 percent of the pizza experience and is worth five times more than the topping when it comes to total satisfaction. The crust is the unifier of the pizza and the toppings play off of it, not unlike the role of bread in a sandwich. The most wonderful toppings in the world are wasted if not delivered on a great crust; and since it is no harder to make a great crust than it is to make a mediocre one, the crust is the prime area where a home cook can shine with modest effort.

The major cause of indifferent crusts is that many pizzerias, especially chains and manufacturers of frozen pizzas, need to have a system in place that guarantees what could be called no-brainer consistency. Unfortunately, there are few trained *pizzaioli* in this country, and many pizzerias are staffed not by pizza professionals but by kids, or by adults who are underpaid, undertrained, or underqualified, or who simply don't care. Cost-effectiveness requires them to produce a consistent product, not a great one. More than one pizzeria owner of a multigenerational family operation told me that only a handful of employees ever care as much about the quality as the family members do, but now even their own younger generation doesn't want to carry on the business. When that happens in the pizza world, the first thing to go is the crust.

If the enemy is mediocrity, then one solution is logging some well-spent hours learning how to make great pizza dough at home. As you will see in the dough chapter beginning on page 103, there are many variations on the basic ingredients of flour, water, salt, yeast, fat, and sugar. Each of the combinations creates a slightly different result, and everyone has his or her own style preference. While the true

Napoletana pizza is held to be the purest and highest expression, it is not the most popular style in the United States. The cognoscenti may support a great *Napoletana*-style pizzeria, as they do in Phoenix with Pizzeria Bianco, but mass-produced pizzas laden with cheese and other toppings remain ubiquitous because people buy them. However, I am convinced, having witnessed it in a few places, that even in the realm of standard commercial pies, there is a way to prepare them at the highest level.

The first thing you will notice about most of my dough recipes is that the instructions call for making them the day before you plan to use them. This is not a hard and fast rule. After all, Pizzeria Bianco and many other excellent pizzerias make the dough the same day they use it, but they make it early in the day so that it has a long time to ferment. An explanation of why this fermentation period is important begins on page 103.

THE TOPPINGS

For many pizza eaters, the crust, though visible only on the edges and the underside, is the medium through which the other ingredients are experienced. If instead you are primarily a sauce person or a cheese person—and I know many of you—the focus shifts and everything works in a different order. There were times, such as at DiFara's in Brooklyn, when the sauce was so good that my own focus was forced to shift and a quick adjustment was necessary. Once I did that, everything else fell nicely into place. Similarly, when I am at the Cheese Board in Berkeley, my initial focus is always on the topping because the cooks have access to such an amazing array of cheeses.

While some of the best pizzerias rely on only a few toppings and others employ many, they all share a commitment to using cheese, sauce, and other ingredients of the highest caliber. The toppings suggested in this book are not limited to the usual suspects, such as pepperoni, sausage, and ground beef, but I don't avoid them either. There is a reason why these ingredients are so popular, especially when used in harmony with other toppings.

When teaching my students about this sense of harmony, I refer to the BUFF system of evaluation, which was explained to me by chef Mial Parker when I was teaching at the California Culinary Academy in San Francisco. He and his teammates developed this rubric, which stands for balance, unity, focus, and flow, when they represented the United States in the Culinary Olympics in the 1980s. While these principles are usually applied to the visual aspect of a product, I find them even more useful when evaluating the relationship between presentation and flavor. Space itself is an ingredient and is often the most important one. Proper spacing keeps the topping flavors in equilibrium so that the full flavor of each ingredient, both individually and in concert with the other ingredients, comes through. Each bite should have a balance of clearly identifiable flavors, not a muddle. Simply put, when topping any pizza, use only enough ingredients to enhance the whole, and select ingredients that work in harmony.

The Sauce

Recipes for a handful of easy-to-make sauces and specialty toppings begin on page 141. One of the favorite hot-button pizza issues is the tomato sauce. Hard-core partisans of the *Napoletana* style insist on the sweet, elongated San Marzano tomatoes, grown in mineral-rich, volcanic soil near Naples and Salerno, in the Campania region of southern Italy. Chris Bianco imports cans of these tomatoes for his pizzeria and also contracts with American farmers to grow tomatoes of equal quality. Many pizzerias choose 6 in 1 brand tomatoes, while others make special deals with California or even Ohio farmers and canneries to produce to their specifications. Still others use generic tomato sauce and doctor it up with their own blend of spices and herbs. During tomato season, I peel and dice fresh tomatoes, usually what are called plum or Roma style, and marinate them in olive oil, basil, salt, and pepper. Fresh cherry and grape tomatoes, with their intense sweetness, are also fabulous additions to the top of a pizza. But most of the time I used canned plum tomatoes, typically but not exclusively from California; I find them reliable and consistent. The most important quality for pizza sauce is the brightness of the flavors, and most brands of canned tomatoes make fine pizza sauce. However, if you have a favorite brand and are convinced that it is better than other labels, stay with it.

The two types of pizza sauce I prefer are crushed tomatoes with a blend of seasonings (page 142) and a quickly made *marinara* using tomato purée, water, spices, and herbs (page 143). In neither case do I cook the sauce, as the tomatoes are already cooked when they are canned. Any further cooking of your pizza sauce will kill the bright flavor, especially since the sauce will cook again when the pizzas are baked. A little acid in the sauce, either from wine vinegar or fresh lemon juice, helps preserve and bring out the brightness. The sauce should be neither too thick nor too thin. Remember, too, it will thicken somewhat in the oven as the moisture evaporates in the intense heat. Only a small amount of sauce is needed to accomplish the job; too much sauce makes the crust soggy.

The Cheese

Not every pizza requires cheese, but molten cheese on a great crust, with or without other toppings, is what excites many pizza lovers. The most popular pizza cheeses are mozzarella in its various forms and a dry aged cheese such as Parmigiano-Reggiano or one of its cousins. However, aside from the rules that govern *la vera pizza Napoletana,* there are no restrictions on the types or combinations of cheese you can use. For example, the Cheese Board, with its daily long line of devoted fans, has pretty much blown the lid off of any attempt to limit the choice of cheese, and they are not alone.

Not all cheeses are created equal, however, and some do work better on pizza than others. For classic Italian or Italian American pizza, there is no better choice for the foundation cheese than mozzarella. Some classic pizzas call only for mozzarella, but most pizzerias use a blend of mozzarella with other, saltier cheeses.

Mozzarella is not a single cheese, but rather a family of cheeses, each of which is made by separating the curds and whey of either water buffalo's milk (for *mozzarella di bufala*) or cow's milk (for *fior di latte*); heating the curds until they become elastic; and then kneading the curds to form a flexible paste. The paste is then shaped into balls, which are stored in whey or water. This cheese is known as fresh mozzarella. Alternatively, the curds may be fully drained, pressed into firm bricks, aged briefly, and then processed and packaged. This low-moisture mozzarella can be made from either full-fat or reduced-fat milk. Most pizzas in the United States are topped with one of these two types of low-moisture mozzarella, each of which has completely different characteristics when it melts. Although the reduced-fat cheese melts fairly nicely and results in a less greasy pizza, I prefer the full-fat mozzarella, or "mutz" as it's called in New Haven. It has a wonderful stringy, oozy, buttery quality.

Fresh mozzarella, especially *mozzarella di bufala*, is spectacular in appropriate situations, but it can be watery and it cools quickly, becoming rubbery and chewy. This is not a problem if you make small pizzas and eat them while they're still hot. Because fresh mozzarella is much moister than its processed counterpart, it tends to puddle, causing the dough to soften. This is a question of personal preference, however. Many people are happy to trade the softer dough for the wonderful creaminess of the cheese. There are certainly times when I am.

For some people, a good melting cheese—that is, a semisoft cheese with some fat in it, whether mozzarella, Bel Paese, Swiss, Monterey Jack, or some type of Cheddar or Gouda—is enough by itself. But I like the added saltiness delivered by a dry aged cheese such as Parmigiano-Reggiano, *grana padano* (a less expensive, less aged Parmesan-style cheese), Asiago, pecorino Romano (made from sheep's milk), or dry Jack, so I blend a small amount of dry aged cheese with a melting cheese, or sprinkle a little on top of my pizza just before baking. Smoked cheeses, of which there are now many, are also a wonderful way to add complexity to your pizza, creating a wood-fired brick oven flavor even in a home oven.

In some instances, fresh or very creamy cheeses like mascarpone, ricotta, and even American cream cheese or an herbed variation like Boursin are appropriate. I especially like these rich types on grilled pizza and in some variations of deep-dish or stuffed pizza.

The pizza recipes that follow come with recommended cheeses, but no pizza police will knock on your door if you choose to substitute an unconventional cheese (that is, unless you plan on opening a traditional pizzeria in Naples). If you are attempting to replicate a classic pizza, such as one of the official *Napoletana* pies, I recommend starting with the traditional cheeses and ingredients. But do not be afraid to adapt; pizza is an everyday hearth food, a peasant food, which means that it is a great way to use whatever ingredients you have on hand. If you have a great crust, heat the oven properly, and choose your cheese and other toppings wisely, flavor is certain to rule.

For more on some great pizza cheeses, see page 160.

BAKING

The final element in making perfect pizza is oven technique. It's disheartening when you have invested hours making excellent dough and have assembled wonderful toppings, only to pull a so-so pizza from your oven. At most pizzerias, pizzas go into ovens heated to between 650 and 1,000 degrees, and occasionally up to 1,200 degrees in a coal-fired brick oven in which many pizzas have to be baked all at the same time.

The high heat is essential, but even more critical is the thermodynamic configuration of the oven. Brick ovens offer the ideal environment for baking pizza because of how the heat radiates and flows; the heat is first absorbed by the thick bricks and is then released back evenly into the baking cavity, ensuring that the top of the pizza bakes at the same rate as the crust. Perfect coordination of top and crust is rare in a home oven and is only partially improved by a pizza stone or unglazed quarry tiles, as neither addition solves the actual problem: lack of insulation. As soon you open the door to slide in the pizza, about one hundred degrees escape. Even when the door is closed, the heating chamber does not always bake evenly because there isn't sufficient thermal mass or insulation to absorb and radiate heat evenly.

However, adjustments can be made to improve any baking setup. You will probably be in one the following situations: standard home oven with no baking stone, standard home oven with a baking stone or tiles, standard home oven with a Hearth Kit oven insert, commercial oven (restaurant quality) with or without a stone, or one of the above with a convection option.

BAKING SITUATION I:
Standard Home Oven with No Baking Stone

This is the most difficult situation in which to try to make great pizza. The oven will work okay for focaccia and other pan dough, but there is not enough thermal mass to hold in the highest heat the oven can produce, which is probably 500 or 550 degrees. There are basically three options for solving this problem.

The first option is to use a sheet pan and brush it lightly with olive oil. After shaping the dough, place it on the pan, finish topping it, and bake it on the lowest shelf, closest to the heat source. As the oil gets hot it will, in essence, fry the bottom of the crust, crisping it more than usual while the cheese and toppings finish off. You may need to experiment with the position of the shelf to achieve the simultaneous baking of crust and toppings.

A second option is to create a thermal mass either by preheating an inverted sheet pan (the thicker the better) or an inverted large, flat-bottomed cast-iron frying pan. Place it on the middle shelf the first time you make a pizza. Raise or lower it for the second pizza according to whether the top or bottom baked first on the initial pie (be sure to use a heavy-duty pot holder to move the hot pan). Do not oil these makeshift metal hearths in advance, or they will smoke in your oven. Instead, just before you slide the pizza onto the preheated inverted pan, mist the pan with a quick shot of nonstick cooking spray, or wipe it with a paper towel dipped in a very small amount of olive oil.

Finally, if the bottom is baking faster than the top, try this trick I learned from Chris Bianco, who not only makes what is arguably the best pizza in America, but also teaches classes for home *pizzaioli*. Before you put the pizza in the oven, turn the dial to broil for a few minutes to heat the oven to the maximum. Then, as soon as you slide the pizza onto the makeshift hearth, switch to the regular bake setting of 500 or 550 degrees, depending on which is the highest setting on your oven. The residual broiler heat will give the top a head start and should even out the baking.

Regardless of which of the three options you choose, you should preheat the oven for 45 minutes, rather than the usual 15 minutes needed for most baking.

BAKING SITUATION II:
Standard Oven with a Baking Stone or Tiles

Baking stones, which provide thermal mass to absorb heat, can make a big difference in the effectiveness of a home oven. The trick, however, is to find the best shelf for the thermal mass. Some ovens perform better with the stone closer to the bottom, while others do better with it on a higher shelf. You may need to experiment a few times before you nail what's best for your oven. I used to think that the ideal location was the oven floor, and this may work in some gas ovens, but it is the least likely location for good thermodynamics in many other home ovens. One friend of mine has success only when he bakes on tiles set on the oven floor, while the middle shelf works best in my oven.

As a general rule, the thicker the mass, the better the radiant heat. Allow at least one hour for your oven and stone to absorb the heat. From time to time during the preheat cycle, switch to the broiler, as described above; this will speed up the process and heat the stone to the maximum capability of the oven.

Another option is to use two pizza stones to create a top and bottom effect. This may improve the evenness of the bake, although the preheating step will take longer and there is no benefit in using the broiler option described above. I have not found that using two stones improves the performance of my oven, but some people have told me that it works wonderfully for them. Again, it depends on the oven.

BAKING SITUATION III:
Standard Home Oven with a Hearth Kit Oven Insert

I use the Hearth Kit insert so much that I volunteered myself as a product spokesperson (mentioned in the interest of full disclosure). It does seem to me to be the best solution, though it is also the costliest one at about two hundred dollars (well, not as costly as buying or building a brick oven). Its success is due to its thermodynamic design that includes two slightly curved sidewalls. The hearth is placed in the upper half of the oven so that the ceiling of the oven serves as a fourth wall. It is as close to brick-oven baking as a home oven is likely to get. Because it is big and heavy, once you install the insert, you will want to leave it in your oven and use it for all your baking and roasting. Allow at least a full hour for it to preheat to your oven's maximum temperature. I use the broiler setting for about five minutes midway through to speed the preheating process. The insert's most important benefit is that once it reaches full temperature, the mass is so thick that barely any heat is lost when you open the oven door to introduce the pizza. Also, in most ovens, the insert helps to even out the heat flow, eliminating the need to rotate the pizza for even baking.

BAKING SITUATION IV:
Commercial Oven with or without a Stone

Most commercial ovens are larger than any home oven, which means that you can use a full-sized sheet pan for the makeshift hearth described in Situation I. It is more difficult to find a baking stone large enough to cover a commercial-oven shelf, however. But these ovens also tend to be better insulated than home ovens, and, as a result, lose less heat when you open the door. While a regular-sized baking stone can improve the oven's performance, it is better to place two stones side by side to cover the entire shelf, or to use unglazed quarry tiles to line a shelf or the oven floor. Every oven brand will have its own idiosyncrasies, so the same performance suggestions described in Situations I through III apply.

BAKING SITUATION V:
One of the Above with a Convection Option

Convection, or moving air, improves almost any oven, making the heat more efficient and, seemingly, hotter. For example, an oven with a Hearth Kit with the convection turned on will bake with the efficiency of a 650- to 700-degree brick oven. For this reason, any pizza will bake about 25 percent faster in a convection oven, with or without a stone, so you will need to keep your eye on it. Even though convection ovens typically bake more evenly than conventional ovens, the pizzas may still need to be turned. If possible, turn off the fan before opening the door so the hot air doesn't blow out (and into your face!).

When using a convection oven without a stone or insert, the top of the pizza may bake faster than the crust. To prevent this, use the cast-iron frying pan technique described in Situation I to create as much thermal mass as possible. If the top is still cooking too fast, turn off the fan (or turn off the oven) and let the residual heat from the frying pan radiate into the crust.

Mise en Place

The following list is a *mise en place* of tools and ingredients to keep on hand for pizza occasions. All of the sauces and specialty toppings beginning on page 141 can also be prepared in advance to speed up the pizza-making process.

TOOLS

Peels, wooden and metal

Baking stone, quarry tiles, or Hearth Kit insert

Mixing bowls

Blender

Food processor

Electric stand mixer (optional)

Wooden and metal mixing spoons

Plastic bowl scraper

Metal pastry blade (also called a bencher)

Rubber and metal spatulas

Good knives, including a chef's knife or *mezzaluna* (knife with a curved blade and two handles)

Pizza cutter (roller style)

Cutting boards

Measuring spoons and scoops

Ingredient scale (optional)

Cheese grater

Zester, preferably Microplane

Two 9- or 10-inch cake pans

One or more 14-inch round baking or cake pans (or other sizes)

Two 12 by 17-inch sheet pans

Saucepans and frying pans

Baking parchment or nonstick silicone baking pan liners (Silpat)

Plastic wrap

Charcoal grill and other grilling accoutrements (see page 219)

BASIC INGREDIENTS

Unbleached high-gluten flour

Unbleached bread flour

Unbleached all-purpose flour

Whole-wheat flour

Rye flour (optional)

Semolina flour and/or cornmeal (optional)

Instant or active dry yeast

Table-grind salt and coarse salt such as kosher or sea salt

Black peppercorns or coarsely ground black pepper

Chile flakes

Fresh and/or dried herbs such as basil, thyme, oregano, and parsley

Sugar

Honey

Olive oil and other vegetable oil

Nonstick cooking spray, olive oil flavored and vegetable oil flavored

Canned plum or San Marzano tomatoes

Canned crushed tomatoes

Canned tomato purée

Yellow, sweet, red, and torpedo onions

Fresh garlic and granulated garlic powder

Canned baby or cocktail clams

Capers

Olives

Balsamic vinegar

High-quality cheeses, both fresh and aged, including mozzarella, Parmigiano-Reggiano or other dry aged cheese, Cheddar, smoked cheese (mozzarella or Gouda), *stracchino* or other fresh, creamy cheeses such as mascarpone

The Family of Doughs

There are an infinite number of pizza dough recipes. Most are simply variations of basic bread dough, sometimes differing only in their percentage of water, oil, or sugar. Another variable is the percentage of yeast or salt. The final, and often most significant determinant, is the fermentation time. While the dough is not fermented overnight at every pizzeria, most of the great pizzas are made with dough that has had a long fermentation—longer than for most bread recipes. Here's why.

Flour, the main ingredient in dough, is composed primarily of starch with a smaller amount of protein. Starch is a complex carbohydrate, which means it is a complex version of simple carbohydrates, that is, sugar. In other words, flour is a complex version of, well, confectioner's sugar, with a little protein thrown in. Great bread makers intuitively understand that the key to making world-class bread from flour, water, salt, and yeast is to draw out the natural sweetness trapped in the complex carbohydrates. This takes time.

In all fermentation processes, from beer making to bread baking, the flavors emerge slowly from the ingredients, coaxed out by the brewmaster or winemaker through an understanding of the relationship between time, temperature, biological processes, and ingredients. The key biological process is the effect of enzymes on the proteins and, more important, on the starches. Enzymes, in effect, break apart the molecules by acting like little wedges, freeing up the simple sugars trapped in the complex carbohydrates. This takes at least five to seven hours to properly accomplish, making it possible to make and bake the dough on the same day, but only under a watchful eye and patient hand.

If you are a home cook, the best way to take advantage of the role that enzymes play in fermentation is to use the refrigerator as a primary tool. The fundamental fermentation activity of yeast is to convert the simple sugars liberated by the enzymes into alcohol and carbon dioxide. The carbon dioxide is what raises, or leavens, the dough, and the alcohol is baked off in the oven, leaving a residual, but not primary, flavor in the finished product. The goal for bakers is to let enzyme activity draw out the maximum natural sugar trapped in the starchy carbohydrates while controlling the amount of sugar converted by the yeast. By putting the dough in the refrigerator soon after it is mixed and letting it ferment overnight, the goal is achieved since the cool temperature slows yeast activity while the enzymes continue to break down the starches. Thus, less sugar is converted to carbon dioxide and alcohol, leaving more of it available to our palates as flavor.

I learned this delayed-fermentation technique from Parisian baker Philippe Gosselin, and I have found that it evokes the maximum flavor potential inherent in the flour. The color of the crust also benefits from this technique because, like the flavor, it is related to the amount of sugar released by the flour while it ferments. It is the caramelizing of these sugars that creates the rich golden color we admire visually. Although flavor is always paramount, we eat first with our eyes, and a golden crusts looks and tastes better. The final plus of using the refrigerator for fermentation is that it allows you more flexibility in your schedule: you can take up to three days to bake off your pizzas. I am not kidding when I say that the one trick of chilling your pizza dough will improve any recipe that you are currently using.

In every recipe, regardless of the type of dough, the guiding principle is to use a method that will deliver the best flavor and the best appearance. To that end, oil, sugar, honey, or milk is sometimes added to doughs for texture or to balance out some of the hardness of the gluten proteins. Fats and sugars create softness because they are hydroscopic, that is, they hold in moisture. The added sugars also foster caramelizing and flavor, but they are not the primary source of flavor; to use them in place of long fermentation is like trying to make wine by adding sugar to premium grape juice—it works, but not at the highest level. This is why the most classic dough is the true Neapolitan *(Napoletana)*, which calls for no oil or sugar. Like true French or Italian bread, it tests the skill of the *pizzaiolo* to extract the full flavor potential from the flour alone.

Little things can make a big difference in pizza dough. In many instances, simply applying a longer, slower fermentation cycle to your already favorite dough recipe produces a dramatic increase in flavor and performance. In other instances, the addition of even 1 or 2 percent more water to an existing recipe will result in a major improvement. The kind of flour you use is also a factor and is one of the defining elements of the type of pizza dough you intend to bake. For instance, the chewier crust and higher tolerance for handling characteristic of *Americana* dough demand a stronger flour than what is used for *Napoletana* dough.

The following recipes encompass a full range of pizza dough styles. Topping and baking are described in subsequent chapters.

Ten Tips for Making Pizza Dough

1. Unbleached flour is always preferable to bleached because it still has beta-carotene pigments, which give the dough better flavor and aroma. If you have only bleached flour, you can still make the recipes as written, but I suggest switching to unbleached in the future and seeing if you notice the difference.

2. If you are using an electric mixer, use the dough hook and mix on low speed as directed. For a very wet dough, you can start the mixing with the paddle attachment to gather the ingredients into a ball and then switch to the hook. You will minimize the stress on your mixer and reduce oxidation in your dough by letting the dough rest as directed after it first comes together in the bowl. (In general, mixing causes oxidation, which bleaches out the flavor benefits of the beta-carotene pigments; less oxidation translates into better flavor.) The rest period also allows the ingredients to hydrate fully. After the rest, you can resume mixing for an additional few minutes.

3. Sticky dough will not stick to wet hands or tools. If you are mixing by hand, repeatedly dip one of your hands or the spoon into room-temperature water (or cold water, if specified) and use it much like a dough hook, working the dough vigorously into a smooth mass as you rotate the bowl with your other hand. It usually takes about 6 minutes for the dough to firm up and for the gluten to develop. If you have measured your flour by cups rather than by weight, it is more probable that you will have to make water or flour adjustments, as everyone scoops flour differently. If the dough does not feel the way it is described (that is, the dough is either too tight or too slack and sticky), do not be afraid to make the appropriate adjustments. In the end, it is the dough that dictates the amount of water or flour, not the exact measurements specified in the recipe.

4. Use the *windowpane test* to determine when your dough has been sufficiently mixed. This is done by snipping off a piece of dough from the larger ball and gently tugging and turning it, stretching it out until it forms a paper-thin, translucent membrane somewhere near the center. If the dough does not form this membrane, or windowpane, it probably needs another minute or two of mixing. Remember to rotate the piece of dough as you tug. Even

properly developed dough will rip if you stretch it in only one direction. This windowpane is a signal that the gluten protein has properly bonded in the dough. (Gluten is a combination of two smaller flour proteins, gliaden and glutenin, linked together as a result of hydration and mixing. Developing the gluten is one of the critical reasons we mix dough; the other reasons are to distribute the ingredients evenly and to activate the yeast in order to initiate fermentation.)

5. Wetter dough is more difficult to handle but usually produces a superior crust, with a better, puffier *cornicione*, or edge.

6. Oil or another fat is added to American-style pizza dough made with high-protein flour to tenderize it. It is usually not needed in dough made with all-purpose flour, such as *Napoletana* dough.

7. Less yeast and longer fermentation are preferable to more yeast and fast fermentation. Artisanal bakers are taught to use only the minimum amount of yeast needed to leaven the dough. More yeast will speed up the fermentation, but the yeast consumes all the available sugar in the dough, converting it into alcohol, and thus diminishes flavor. (Please note that while the recipes in this book call for instant yeast, you can also use active dry yeast. If using active dry yeast, increase the amount by 25 percent; that is, for 1 teaspoon of instant yeast substitute $1^{1}/4$ teaspoon of active dry yeast. Also, active dry yeast must be dissolved first in a few tablespoons of the water that you will be using in the dough.)

8. Overnight fermentation almost always improves your dough, although you can also mix it early in the day for evening pizzas.

9. Many pizza dough recipes can be used interchangeably. *Napoletana* and other soft, sticky doughs are best for smaller, individual-sized pizzas, as they are difficult to stretch into larger sizes. If you want to make family-sized pizzas, use the stronger neo-Neapolitan, New York, or *Americana* variations. Otherwise, feel free to mix and match.

10. The best crust is the one that enhances the pizza without drawing too much attention to itself. When a crust does attract attention, it's frequently negative, prompting such comments as "this crust is too soft" or "this crust is too dry." You often recognize the perfect crust only afterward, in retrospect, when you recall the sigh of pleasure created by the snap, the natural sweetness, and the creamy melt-in-your-mouth quality of each bite.

Note on mixing with a food processor: In this book, the dough recipes always include instructions for mixing by hand and by stand mixer. Although mixing in a food processor, which is an increasingly popular option, is not covered, all of the doughs can be made in this way as well. One major adjustment is necessary, however: most of the dough recipes are too large for a standard home food processor, so you must cut all of the ingredient amounts in half.

The trick for mixing dough in a food processor is to use only the pulse switch in the beginning and mix only until the ingredients are hydrated and form a ball. Then let the dough rest for at least 5 minutes or for up to 20 minutes before mixing again. The resting phase allows the flour to absorb the water fully. Otherwise, the machine mixes the dough before the developing gluten can handle the agitation, tearing the strands and damaging the dough. When you resume mixing, use the on switch and mix for an additional 45 to 60 seconds. The short rest period followed by the short final mixing cycle is all that you need to complete the job.

NAPOLETANA PIZZA DOUGH

If you want the DOC designation for your pizza, the dough must be made according to the rules of the Associazione della Vera Pizza Napoletana, which means it cannot contain oil or sugar. This works fine when you have the right kind of flour (Italian "00" or unbleached all-purpose American flour), but you'll end up with a tough, chewy crust if you use bread flour or high-gluten flour. In such instances, a little oil tenderizes the dough to achieve the desired texture (see *Napoletana* Pizza Dough Variations). The DOC-approved pizzerias I visited in Naples each used their own blend of "00" flour mixed with a small amount of American bread flour. American all-purpose flour, which is actually a little stronger and more elastic than "00" flour, performs closest to this blend, but even then you may need to adjust the water amount depending on the brand. As you become more comfortable with wetter dough, feel free to increase the amount of water, in small increments, to make the dough sticky rather than tacky.

If possible, make this dough either the day before you plan to make the pizzas, or make it well in advance and keep the dough balls in the freezer. When I shape the pizzas, I always keep a couple of extra dough balls ready in case of mishaps, such as dropping or tearing. If you don't use the extra dough balls, they can still be chilled for later use, preferably within 24 hours.

Makes six 6-ounce dough balls

5 cups (22 1/2 ounces) unbleached all-purpose flour

1 3/4 teaspoons table salt or 3 1/4 teaspoons kosher salt

1 teaspoon instant yeast

1 3/4 cups plus 2 tablespoons cool water (65°F)

1. With a large metal spoon, stir together all the ingredients in a 4-quart bowl or the bowl of an electric stand mixer until combined. *If mixing with an electric mixer,* fit it with the dough hook and mix on low speed for about 4 minutes, or until all the flour gathers to form a coarse ball. Let the dough rest for 5 minutes, then mix again on medium-low speed for an additional 2 minutes, or until the dough clears the sides of the bowl and sticks just a little to the bottom. If the dough is too soft and sticky to hold its shape, mix in more flour

by the tablespoonful; if it is too stiff or dry, mix in more water by the table-spoonful. The dough should pass the windowpane test (see page 105). *If mixing by hand,* repeatedly dip one of your hands or the spoon into room-temperature water and use it much like a dough hook, working the dough vigorously into a coarse ball as you rotate the bowl with your other hand. As all the flour is incorporated into the ball, about 4 minutes, the dough will begin to strengthen; when this occurs, let the dough rest for 5 minutes and then resume mixing for an additional 2 to 3 minutes, or until the dough is slightly sticky, soft, and supple. If the dough is too soft and sticky to hold its shape, mix in more flour by the tablespoonful; if it is too stiff or dry, mix in more water by the table-spoonful. The dough should pass the windowpane test (see page 105).

2. Transfer the dough to a floured counter, dust the top of the dough with flour to absorb the surface moisture, and then, working from the 4 corners, fold the dough into a ball. Place the ball in a bowl that has been brushed with olive oil, turn the dough to coat it with the oil, and cover the bowl with plastic wrap. Let the dough sit at room temperature for 30 minutes, then put the bowl in the refrigerator overnight. (Or, if you are making the pizzas on the same day, let the dough sit at room temperature for 1 1/2 hours, punch it down, reshape it into a ball, return the ball to the bowl, and then cover and refrigerate for at least 2 hours.)

3. The next day (or later the same day if refrigerated for only 2 hours), remove the bowl of dough from the refrigerator 2 hours before you plan to make the pizzas. The dough will have expanded somewhat and the gluten will be very relaxed. Using a plastic bowl scraper dipped in water, or using wet hands, gently transfer the dough to a floured counter, trying to degas the dough as little as possible. Using a pastry blade that has been dipped in water, divide it into 6 equal pieces. Gently round each piece into a ball and brush or rub each ball with olive oil. Line a sheet pan with baking parchment or a nonstick silicone baking liner and brush with olive oil. Place each dough ball on the pan and loosely cover the pan with either plastic wrap or a food-grade plastic bag. (If you do not plan to use all the pieces, place the extra ones in individual zippered freezer bags and refrigerate or freeze. Use the refrigerated balls within 2 days and the frozen balls within 3 months.) Allow the dough balls to sit at room temperature for 2 hours before making the pizzas.

Napoletana **Pizza Dough Variations**

Unless you are seeking DOC status, you will probably not be worried about the rules of *la vera pizza napoletana*. Therefore, you should feel free to vary some of the ingredients or proportions. For instance, if you choose to use bread or high-gluten flour instead of all-purpose flour, add 1 teaspoon olive or vegetable oil for every cup of flour. You may also substitute a small amount, up to 1 tablespoon per cup of flour, of whole-wheat or rye flour for the all-purpose flour. The addition of a small amount of whole-grain flour gives the dough a pleasant country-style quality; many people actually prefer it.

ROMAN PIZZA DOUGH

I used to think the world of pizza preference was divided between two types of people, but now I know there are three: those who prefer a thick crust, those who prefer a thin crust, and those who prefer a Roman ultrathin crust. The latter is the style of crust that is served at Da Baffetto and at many other pizzerias in Rome. Everything about the pizza is essentially the same as for the *Napoletana*, except that the dough is stretched much thinner, to form an almost crackerlike crust. I add some semolina flour to the *Napoletana* dough recipe to make it stiffer, and thus easier to stretch thinly, and to give it some extra crispness in the oven.

Makes six 6-ounce dough balls
5 cups (22 1/2 ounces) unbleached all-purpose flour
1/4 cup (1 ounce) semolina flour
1 3/4 teaspoons table salt or 3 1/4 teaspoons kosher salt
1 teaspoon instant yeast
1 3/4 cups plus 2 tablespoons cool water (65°F)

1. With a large metal spoon, stir together all the ingredients in a 4-quart bowl or the bowl of an electric stand mixer until combined. *If mixing with an electric mixer,* fit it with the dough hook and mix on low speed for about 4 minutes, or until all the flour gathers to form a coarse ball. Let the dough rest for 5 minutes, then mix again on medium-low speed for an additional 2 minutes, or until the dough clears the sides of the bowl and sticks just a little to the bottom. If the dough is too soft and sticky to hold its shape, mix in more flour by the tablespoonful; if it is too stiff or dry, mix in more water by the tablespoonful. The dough should pass the windowpane test (see page 105). *If mixing by hand,* repeatedly dip one of your hands or the spoon into room-temperature water and use it much like a dough hook, working the dough vigorously into a coarse ball as you rotate the bowl with your other hand. As all the flour is incorporated into the ball, about 4 minutes, the dough will begin to strengthen; when this occurs, let the dough rest for 5 minutes and then resume mixing for an additional 2 to 3 minutes, or until the dough is tacky, soft, and supple. If the dough is too soft and sticky to hold its shape,

mix in more flour by the tablespoonful; if it is too stiff or dry, mix in more water by the tablespoonful. The dough should pass the windowpane test (see page 105).

2. Transfer the dough to a floured counter, dust the top of the dough with flour to absorb the surface moisture, and then, working from the 4 corners, fold the dough into a ball. Place the ball in a bowl that has been brushed with olive oil, turn the dough to coat it with the oil, and cover the bowl with plastic wrap. Let the dough sit at room temperature for 30 minutes, then put the bowl in the refrigerator overnight. (Or, if you are making the pizzas on the same day, let the dough sit at room temperature for $1^1/2$ hours, punch it down, reshape it into a ball, return the ball to the bowl, and then cover and refrigerate for at least 2 hours.)

3. The next day (or later the same day if refrigerated for only 2 hours), remove the bowl of dough from the refrigerator 2 hours before you plan to make the pizzas. The dough will have expanded somewhat and the gluten will be very relaxed. Using a plastic bowl scraper dipped in water, or using wet hands, gently transfer the dough to a floured counter, trying to degas the dough as little as possible. Using a pastry blade that has been dipped in water, divide it into 6 equal pieces. Gently round each piece into a ball and brush or rub each ball with olive oil. Line a sheet pan with baking parchment or a nonstick silicone baking liner and brush with olive oil. Place each dough ball on the pan and loosely cover the pan with either plastic wrap or a food-grade plastic bag. (If you do not plan to use all the pieces, place the extra ones in individual zippered freezer bags and refrigerate or freeze. Use the refrigerated balls within 2 days and the frozen balls within 3 months.) Allow the dough balls to sit at room temperature for 2 hours before making the pizzas.

NEO-NEAPOLITAN PIZZA DOUGH

This is the dough for making New Haven–style pizzas and pizzas in the style of Lombardi's, Totonno's, John's, Grimaldi's, and Tacconelli's. It makes a thin, crisp crust with airy pockets in the crown. It's a little sticky and a touch tricky to handle, but the payoff is in the snap when you take that first bite. This dough stays crisp better than *Napoletana* dough, which softens under the toppings. Neo-Neapolitan dough requires high-gluten flour (about 14 percent protein), or strong bread flour if you cannot get high-gluten, rather than the all-purpose flour used in *Napoletana*. If you do not have a retail resource for high-gluten flour, ask a local pizzeria that makes its own dough or a local bakery if you can buy a few pounds.

Makes four 10-ounce dough balls

5 cups (22 1/2 ounces) unbleached high-gluten or bread flour

1 tablespoon sugar or honey

2 teaspoons table salt or 3 1/2 teaspoons kosher salt

1 teaspoon instant yeast

2 tablespoons olive or vegetable oil or solid vegetable shortening

1 3/4 cups plus 1 tablespoon room-temperature water (70°F)

1. With a large metal spoon, stir together all the ingredients in a 4-quart bowl or the bowl of an electric stand mixer until combined. *If mixing with an electric mixer,* fit it with the dough hook and mix on low speed for about 4 minutes, or until all the flour gathers to form a coarse ball. Let the dough rest for 5 minutes, then mix again on medium-low speed for an additional 2 minutes, or until the dough clears the sides of the bowl and sticks just a little to the bottom. If the dough is too soft and sticky to hold its shape, mix in more flour by the tablespoonful; if it is too stiff or dry, mix in more water by the tablespoonful. The dough should pass the windowpane test (see page 105). *If mixing by hand,* repeatedly dip one of your hands or the spoon into room-temperature water and use it much like a dough hook, working the dough vigorously into a coarse ball as you rotate the bowl with your other hand. As all the flour is incorporated into the ball, about 4 minutes, the dough will begin to strengthen;

when this occurs, let the dough rest for 5 minutes and then resume mixing for an additional 2 to 3 minutes, or until the dough is slightly sticky, soft, and supple. If the dough is too soft and sticky to hold its shape, mix in more flour by the tablespoonful; if it is too stiff or dry, mix in more water by the table-spoonful. The dough should pass the windowpane test (see page 105).

2. Immediately divide the dough into 4 equal pieces. Round each piece into a ball and brush or rub each ball with olive or vegetable oil. Place each ball inside its own zippered freezer bag. Let the balls sit at room temperature for 15 min-utes, then put them in the refrigerator overnight or freeze any pieces you will not be using the next day. (Or, if you are making the pizzas on the same day, let the dough balls sit in the bags at room temperature for 1 hour, remove them from the bags, punch them down, reshape them into balls, return them to the bags, and refrigerate for at least 2 hours.)

3. The next day (or later the same day if refrigerated for only 2 hours), remove the balls from the refrigerator 2 hours before you plan to roll them out to take off the chill and to relax the gluten. At this point, you can hold any balls you don't want to use right away in the refrigerator for another day, or you can freeze them for up to 3 months.

NEW YORK–STYLE PIZZA DOUGH

Here is the dough for the pizza with a medium-thick crust that you find in New York City, any college town, or anywhere else that pizza is sold by the slice. It can be spun in the air and stretched into big disks, calls for high-protein (high-gluten) flour, and requires some fat or oil to lubricate and tenderize it. New York–style dough is designed to handle heavy toppings, so it must be rolled out about 1/4 inch thick. A defining characteristic of the pizza is that when it comes out of the oven and is cut, the nose of each slice droops and must be flipped back into the center of the wedge. You can reheat the slices in a hot oven to bring a true snap and crackle to the crust.

Makes three 12-ounce dough balls

5 cups (22 1/2 ounces) unbleached high-gluten or bread flour

1 1/2 tablespoons sugar or honey

2 teaspoons table salt or 3 1/2 teaspoons kosher salt

1 1/2 teaspoons instant yeast

3 tablespoons olive or vegetable oil or solid vegetable
   shortening

1 3/4 cups room-temperature water (70°F)

1. With a large metal spoon, stir together all the ingredients in a 4-quart bowl or the bowl of an electric stand mixer until combined. *If mixing with an electric mixer,* fit it with the dough hook and mix on low speed for about 4 minutes, or until all the flour gathers to form a coarse ball. Let the dough rest for 5 minutes, then mix again on medium-low speed for an additional 2 minutes, or until the dough clears the sides of the bowl and sticks just a little to the bottom. If the dough is too soft and sticky to hold its shape, mix in more flour by the tablespoonful; if it is too stiff or dry, mix in more water by the tablespoonful. The dough should pass the windowpane test (see page 105). *If mixing by hand,* repeatedly dip one of your hands or the spoon into room-temperature water and use it much like a dough hook, working the dough vigorously into a coarse ball as you rotate the bowl with your other hand. As all the flour is incorporated into the ball, about 4 minutes, the dough will begin to strengthen; when this occurs, let the dough rest for 5 minutes and then resume mixing for

an additional 2 to 3 minutes, or until the dough is slightly sticky, soft, and supple. If the dough is too soft and sticky to hold its shape, mix in more flour by the tablespoonful; if it is too stiff or dry, mix in more water by the tablespoonful. The dough should pass the windowpane test (see page 105).

2. Immediately divide the dough into 3 equal pieces. Round each piece into a ball and brush or rub each ball with olive or vegetable oil. Place each ball inside its own zippered freezer bag. Let the balls sit at room temperature for 15 minutes, then put them in the refrigerator overnight or freeze any pieces you will not be using the next day. (Or, if you are making the pizzas on the same day, let the dough balls sit at room temperature in the bags for 1 hour, remove them from the bags, punch them down, reshape them into balls, return them to the bags, and refrigerate for at least 2 hours.)

3. The next day (or later the same day if refrigerated for only 2 hours), remove the balls from the refrigerator 2 hours before you plan to roll them out to take off the chill and to relax the gluten. At this point, you can hold any balls you don't want to use right away in the refrigerator for another day, or you can freeze them for up to 3 months.

PIZZA AMERICANA DOUGH

Say what you will about generic pizza franchises, but they represent the single largest category of fresh pizza sales. In other words, they work for a lot of people. I've given this style the name *pizza americana* simply because pizza of this type is now the definitive American food, catching up even to hamburgers in total consumption. What makes this dough so useful is its strength and ability to stand up to heavy toppings. It produces a breadlike crust that is both filling and tasty in its own right. This dough also works well as a take-and-bake crust, meaning that you can dress up your pizza, chill it, take it to a party, and bake it later—anytime within twenty-four hours. While every pizzeria has its proprietary formula, the following version produces a crust equal to, or even better than, what you can eat at your favorite chain.

Makes four 10-ounce dough balls

5 cups (22 1/2 ounces) unbleached high-gluten or bread flour

3 tablespoons sugar or honey

2 teaspoons table salt or 3 1/2 teaspoons kosher salt

2 teaspoons instant yeast

1/4 cup olive or vegetable oil or solid vegetable shortening

1 cup whole or low-fat milk

3/4 cup room-temperature water (70°F)

1. With a large metal spoon, stir together all the ingredients in a 4-quart bowl or the bowl of an electric stand mixer until combined. *If mixing with an electric mixer,* fit it with the dough hook and mix on low speed for about 4 minutes, or until all the flour gathers to form a coarse ball. Let the dough rest for 5 minutes, then mix again on medium-low speed for an additional 2 minutes, or until the dough clears the sides of the bowl and sticks just a little to the bottom. If the dough is too soft and sticky to hold its shape, mix in more flour by the tablespoonful; if it is too stiff or dry, mix in more water by the tablespoonful. The dough should pass the windowpane test (see page 105). *If mixing by hand,* repeatedly dip one of your hands or the spoon into room-temperature water and use it much like a dough hook, working the dough vigorously into a coarse ball as you rotate the bowl with your other hand. As all the flour is

incorporated into the ball, about 4 minutes, the dough will begin to strengthen; when this occurs, let the dough rest for 5 minutes and then resume mixing for an additional 2 to 3 minutes, or until the dough is slightly sticky, soft, and supple. If the dough is too soft and sticky to hold its shape, mix in more flour by the tablespoonful; if it is too stiff or dry, mix in more water by the table-spoonful. The dough should pass the windowpane test (see page 105).

2. Immediately divide the dough into 4 equal pieces. Round each piece into a ball and brush or rub each ball with olive or vegetable oil. Place each ball inside its own zippered freezer bag. Let the balls sit at room temperature for 15 minutes, then put them in the refrigerator overnight or freeze any pieces you will not be using the next day. (Or, if you are making the pizzas on the same day, let the dough balls sit at room temperature in the bags for 1 hour, remove them from the bags, punch them down, reshape them into balls, return them to the bags, and refrigerate for at least 2 hours.)

3. The next day (or later the same day if refrigerated for only 2 hours), remove the balls from the refrigerator 2 hours before you plan to roll them out to take off the chill and to relax the gluten. At this point, you can hold any balls you don't want to use right away in the refrigerator for another day, or you can freeze them for up to 3 months.

PREBAKED PIZZA FREEZER DOUGH

This is the way to go if you want to throw a great pizza together on a moment's notice. I always have a few prebaked pizza crusts in the freezer, and they perform amazingly well. The key to a twice-baked dough is to make it with lots of water so that it doesn't turn into something reminiscent of cardboard after the second baking. Most commercial frozen pizzas emphasize the toppings because the manufacturers know the crusts are going to be inferior to pizzeria crusts. When Freschetta, DiGiorno, and even the California Pizza Kitchen came up with their new oven-rising crusts, they found a way to eliminate the factory bake that stabilizes the dough. Instead, they flash-freeze the still-active unbaked dough so that it will have some rise in it during the final bake. These products are good and sales show that the public clearly loves them. In early 2003, these three companies alone were producing more than two hundred thousand oven-rising pizzas every day. Yet even with this new technology, a frozen oven-rising crust is still not as good as a pizzeria crust. Nor do I believe it is as good as the following prebaked crust, which, in addition to the extra water, benefits from a long fermentation period. Try this crust side by side with the leading freezer brands and I think you'll agree.

Review the shaping and baking techniques beginning on page 167 before you make this dough. Also, this recipe assumes that you are using a baking stone in a conventional home oven. Refer to page 97 if your oven arrangement is different.

Makes four 10-inch prebaked crusts

4 1/2 cups (20 1/4 ounces) unbleached high-gluten or
   bread flour

1/2 cup (2 1/4 ounces) whole-wheat flour

2 teaspoons table salt or 3 1/2 teaspoons kosher salt

1 1/4 teaspoons instant yeast

3 tablespoons honey

2 cups plus 2 tablespoons ice-cold water (40°F)

1/4 cup olive oil

Unbleached high-gluten or bread flour, cornmeal, or
   semolina flour for dusting peel

1. With a large metal spoon, stir together all the ingredients except the olive oil in a 4-quart bowl or the bowl of an electric stand mixer until combined. *If mixing with an electric mixer,* fit it with the paddle attachment and mix on low speed for about 2 minutes, or until all the ingredients are hydrated and begin to form a wet ball of dough. Let the dough rest for 5 minutes. Switch to the dough hook, add the olive oil, and resume mixing on medium-low speed for 3 to 4 minutes, or until the all of the oil is incorporated and the dough is sticky, supple, and smooth; it should clear the sides of the bowl and stick just a little to the bottom. If the dough seems like a batter and does not have sufficient structure to hold itself together, mix in more flour by the tablespoonful. Even though it is sticky, the dough should pass the windowpane test (see page 105). *If mixing by hand,* repeatedly dip one of your hands or the spoon into cold water and use it much like a dough hook, working the dough vigorously as you rotate the bowl with your other hand. As all the flour is incorporated and the dough becomes a wet ball, about 3 minutes, stop mixing and let the dough rest for 5 minutes. Then add the olive oil, dip your hand or spoon again in water, and continue to work the dough for another 3 to 4 minutes. The dough should be very sticky, but it should also have some texture and structure. If the dough seems like a batter and does not have sufficient structure to hold itself together, mix in more flour by the tablespoonful. Even though it is sticky, the dough should pass the windowpane test (see page 105).

2. Form the dough into a ball and place it in a bowl brushed with olive oil. Turn the dough to coat it with the oil, and cover the bowl with plastic wrap. Let the dough sit at room temperature for 30 minutes, then put the bowl in the refrigerator overnight.

3. The next day, remove the bowl of dough from the refrigerator 3 hours before you plan to bake the crusts. The dough should have nearly doubled in size. Using a plastic bowl scraper dipped in water, or using wet hands, gently transfer the dough to a floured counter, trying to degas the dough as little as possible. Using a pastry blade that has been dipped in water, divide it into 4 equal pieces. Gently round each piece into a ball and brush or rub each ball with olive oil. Line a sheet pan with baking parchment or a nonstick silicone baking liner and brush with olive oil. Place each dough ball on the pan and loosely cover the pan with either plastic wrap or a food-grade plastic bag. Allow the dough balls to sit at room temperature for 2 hours to relax the gluten and to take off the chill.

4. Place a baking stone on the middle shelf of the oven (unless you know your oven well enough to place it on a different shelf) and preheat on the highest setting for at least 1 hour. While the oven is heating, uncover the balls of dough on the pan, dip your hand in some room-temperature water, and flatten each piece of dough into a thick, round disk. Separate the disks so they are not touching each other; if necessary, transfer some of the pieces to another sheet pan prepared in the same manner. Cover the disks with the plastic and let them relax at room temperature for 15 to 20 minutes.

5. One at a time, begin to work the disks of dough into rounds 10 inches in diameter, using the method for shaping on the counter described on page 168. (The wet, sticky nature of this dough makes it difficult to toss and spin it, as you would for other high-gluten doughs.) As each piece begins to get springy and refuses to extend any farther, move on to another. Return to each disk after it has rested for about 5 minutes, which allows time for the gluten to relax. Eventually all the disks will achieve the desired size.

6. Transfer the first dough round to a peel or an inverted sheet pan that has been dusted with flour, sliding it around to make sure it is not sticking. If it sticks, lift the dough and sprinkle the peel with more flour. Brush the top of the dough with olive oil and prick the entire surface with a fork to minimize bubbling in the oven. Check again to be sure the dough is not sticking to the peel, then slide the dough round onto the baking stone. (If your baking surface is large enough to hold 2 dough rounds at the same time, go ahead and bake 2 rounds at once.) Bake for 10 to 12 minutes, or until the dough is set and is just beginning to show signs of browning. If the dough puffs up like a pita bread, poke it with a fork to deflate.

7. Remove the baked crust from the oven and place it on a cooling rack. Repeat the process with the remaining dough rounds. Let the crusts cool completely, then double wrap them individually in plastic wrap and freeze for up to 3 months. You can top and bake the crusts while they are still frozen, or you can thaw them before topping. In either case, they will crisp up nicely during the rebake. If the crusts are thawed, the rebaking time will be about the same as a pizza made from scratch. If the crusts are frozen, add 2 additional minutes to the bake.

SOURDOUGH PIZZA DOUGH

I have written extensively about sourdough or, more properly, wild yeast dough, in two previous books, but it is important to review the unique dynamics of wild yeast fermentation here, especially for those who have not worked with sourdough before. What follows is a crash course in sourdough.

Yeast fermentation is what makes bread dough rise, and most pizza dough is made with commercial yeast, or *Saccharamyces cerevisiae*, a reliable and predictable strain of the yeast family. Many yeast strains exist, most of which will ferment sugar and convert it into alcohol and carbon dioxide, but this strain has been chosen for commercial yeast because it works the best and is the easiest to grow and package. In addition to creating alcohol (ethyl alcohol, to be more precise) and carbon dioxide, it also generates a small amount of acid, which *S. cerevisiae* does not really like. As dough becomes more acidic, the yeast activity slows and the yeast cells begin to die. So, in a sense, it paves the way for its own demise.

This short-circuiting of yeast activity is exacerbated by another kind of fermentation that occurs more slowly in bread dough. This is bacterial fermentation, especially of lactobacillus and acetobacillus organisms. The primary byproduct that occurs when these bacteria eat the sugar and enzyme nutrients in bread dough is acid, either lactic acid or vinegar. If a bread dough is allowed to acidify, it will eventually kill the *S. cerevisiae* yeast, and the dough will lose the ability to rise. Yet *S. exiguus*, a different strain of yeast, can tolerate an acidic environment. It lives in the wild (thus *exiguus*, or "wild"), often on the skins of fruit and seeds, and is the strain that is cultivated in a sourdough starter. As the wild yeast grows in the starter, bacteria also grow, and after a few days, a culture medium made primarily of flour and water will become the home to thousands, perhaps millions, of living wild yeast and bacteria cells. The result of all of this biological activity is a dough that has a distinctly acidic flavor due to the particular strains of bacteria predominant in the starter. The bacteria will vary from region to region, but all regions are home to all sorts of good and bad bacteria, and so sourdough or wild yeast bread can be made anywhere and have its own distinctive regional tang. This is how bread was made for thousands of years before people like the Fleischmann brothers figured out how to grow and package commercial yeast.

Armed with this rudimentary knowledge and the instructions that follow, you can make your own sourdough starters and use them for baking many types of breads, including sourdough pizza. There are many ways to make sourdough starters, so if you already have a starter or a method for making one that you like, by all means use it. Any established starter, regardless of how it was made, will make great dough if you also follow proper fermentation procedures. For example, milk is a good medium for the growth of microorganisms, so some methods call for it. Grapes and raisins, onions, plums, potatoes, and other fruits and vegetables are all hosts to wild yeast and bacteria, so some methods extol their use. All of these examples work, but they are not necessary for the method I describe here.

The following system, which is based on a French method, is a variation of the version I used in *The Bread Baker's Apprentice.* I have altered it here because sometimes the starters were hindered by the presence of a strain of bacteria that interfered with yeast fermentation. I learned from a group of dedicated home bakers (all contributors to the King Arthur Flour Baker's Circle website) that the bacteria are defeated by the presence of a small amount of acid during the early stages. The best solution, with nearly 100 percent success, was to use pineapple juice on the first day only. By following this revised sourdough system, you will end up with a starter that you can keep using for as long as you like to make bread or pizza in the style of places like the Cheese Board Collective in Berkeley, California.

The system has three distinct phases. The first is to make a seed culture that will inoculate the actual permanent starter. The permanent starter, which is called either the "mother," "sponge," or "barm," is then used to make the final dough. I usually advocate building your mother starter into a second starter, what the French call the *levain,* for more complex flavor development. For pizza dough, however, I find that the mother starter is all you need to make perfect dough. What follows are instructions for completing the three distinct stages. Once you have established a healthy mother starter, you will not have to return to the seed stage again unless you kill your mother starter and have to start over. I've done just that, but it takes only a few days to get back to the same point. You can use the starter right away, although it will reach peak flavor development in about two weeks. Once it reaches its optimal flavor, it will remain at that level, so there is no advantage to having a two-year-old starter over a two-week-old starter, other than bragging rights.

STAGE ONE: *Making the Seed Culture*

This is a four-day process, although in warmer climates it may take only three days.

Day One: Combine 1 cup (4 1/2 ounces) whole-wheat or rye flour and just enough pineapple juice (about 3 ounces) to form the mixture into a fairly firm mass. Continue to mix and knead until all the flour is hydrated and the dough forms a firm ball. It should be about the size of a small tennis ball, weigh about about 7 1/2 ounces, and be only slightly tacky to the touch. Press the ball into a 2-cup clear glass or plastic container, place a piece of tape on the outside of the container that marks the height of the dough, cover with a lid or plastic wrap, and leave the container at room temperature for 24 hours. (You do not have to capture yeast or bacteria from the air. They are already in the flour.)

Day Two: There will probably be little or no growth of the dough. Discard half of the ball from Day One (or give it to a friend to carry on). Crumble the remaining dough into a bowl and add 1/2 cup (2 1/4 ounces) unbleached bread flour or high-gluten flour and about 3 tablespoons water, or as much water as needed to form the mixture into a ball of dough. Mix and knead until you have a ball about the same size as you had on the previous day. Repeat the procedure of pressing it into the container, checking the mark to see that it comes to the same place. Cover the container and leave at room temperature for 24 hours.

Day Three: If the dough has more than doubled in size, you can go on to Stage Two. If not, and most likely not, repeat the procedure described for Day Two, discarding half the dough and rebuilding it with 1/2 cup unbleached bread flour or high-gluten flour and enough water to form a firm ball. Press it into the container, cover, and leave at room temperature for 24 hours.

Day Four: The dough should have at least doubled in size and you can go on to Stage Two. If it has not at least doubled in size, repeat the procedure described for Day Three. In rare instances, you will have to continue this seed building for a few more days.

STAGE TWO: *Making the Mother Starter*

Once your seed culture has demonstrated sufficient fermentation for it to double in size, you can use it to inoculate a larger mass of dough. To do this, break the seed culture into about 6 equal pieces and place them in a 4-quart bowl. Add 3 1/2 cups (1 pound) unbleached bread flour or high-gluten flour and 2 cups room-temperature (70°F) water, and stir together to form a thick sponge. When all the flour is hydrated and the seed pieces are evenly distributed, cover the bowl with plastic wrap and leave it at room temperature for 3 to 4 hours, or until it begins to bubble and ferment visibly. The time it takes to ferment will vary according to the ambient conditions (the rate of yeast fermentation doubles for every 17°F between 40°F and 140°F). Once it begins to bubble, place the bowl in the refrigerator overnight (or transfer the sponge to a permanent container, either glass, plastic, or stainless steel, before refrigerating). The sponge, or mother starter, will be ready to use the following day and for up to 3 days.

After the third day, the acid in the sponge will eat much of the gluten, weakening the structure. Thus, you will need to refresh, or feed, the mother starter after the third day to keep it strong and active. When feeding it, you must always at least double it in size, although you should never more than quadruple it. To feed the sponge, first estimate the amount remaining in the container. For instance, if there is 1 cup of sponge left, double it by adding 1 cup (4 1/2 ounces) of bread flour or high gluten flour and 1/2 cup plus 1 tablespoon water (equal parts flour and water by weight). If you want to triple or quadruple the sponge, simply increase the flour and water at the same rate. Mix the sponge, flour, and water together thoroughly, cover the container, and let the sponge ferment at room temperature until it begins to bubble, usually about 3 hours. Once it begins to bubble, refrigerate it overnight and it will be ready to use the next day and for up to 3 days.

If you are not using the mother starter, you may leave it in the refrigerator for up to 3 months without refreshing it until you approach the day you need it. A day or two before you plan to make pizza (or bread), discard all but 1 1/2 cups of the starter (including any liquid that floats to the surface, which is sometimes called "hootch") and refresh it with 4 cups (18 ounces) unbleached bread flour or high-gluten flour and 2 1/4 cups water. Mix together thoroughly, cover the container, and let the sponge ferment at room temperature until it begins to bubble, about 3 hours, then refrigerate it overnight. The next day you will have a strong, fresh starter. You may also freeze the starter for up to 6 months. Remember to defrost it in the refrigerator a day or two before you plan to refresh it, and then refresh as described above.

　　　Once you have a fresh mother starter, you are ready to proceed to Stage Three.

STAGE THREE: *Making the Dough*

Making sourdough or wild yeast pizza dough is much like making any other pizza dough except that the sourdough starter is used in place of commercial yeast. Because the starter is wetter than regular dough, the amount of water in the final dough will be less than in dough made without starter. The total hydration of the final dough will conform with standard ratios, however, coming in somewhere between 60 percent and 75 percent of the flour weight, depending on the type of dough. As with other doughs, the wetter the dough, the more it will bubble and spring in the oven, so it is possible to make a sourdough pizza in the style of *Napoletana* dough, though this is rare. The following dough is more like the strong, elastic dough used at the Cheese Board, which must stand up to large amounts of cheese and other toppings. If you can find it, use high-gluten flour, although bread flour will produce a good dough as well. You can also replace up to 1 cup of the flour with an equal amount of whole-wheat or rye flour. Also, the amount of water is approximate because how much you need will depend on how wet you keep your mother starter and the type of flour you use. You can adjust the flour or water as needed while mixing to achieve the proper consistency. The Cheese Board–style pizza on page 199 is just a starting point for topping ideas; you can top this dough with any of the ingredients that go on the neo-Neapolitan, New York, or *Americana* dough.

Makes four 10-ounce dough balls
1 cup sourdough mother starter
4 cups (18 ounces) unbleached high-gluten or bread flour
2 teaspoons table salt or 3 1/2 teaspoons kosher salt
2 tablespoons honey or 3 tablespoons sugar
1/4 cup olive oil
1 to 1 1/4 cups lukewarm water or milk (90° to 95°F)

1. Remove the sourdough starter from the refrigerator about 2 hours before you begin mixing the dough to take off the chill. With a large metal spoon, stir together the starter, flour, salt, honey, olive oil, and 1 cup of the water in a 4-quart bowl or the bowl of an electric stand mixer until combined. *If mixing with an electric mixer,* fit it with the dough hook and mix on low speed for about 4 minutes, or until the dough forms a coarse ball and clears the sides and the bottom of the bowl. Add more flour or water by the tablespoonful as needed. Let the dough rest for 15 minutes, then mix again on low speed for an additional 2 to 3 minutes, or until the dough is smooth, supple, and tacky but not sticky. The dough should pass the windowpane test (see page 105). *If mixing by hand,* repeatedly dip one of your hands or the spoon into room-temperature water and use it much like a dough hook, working the dough vigorously as you rotate the bowl with your other hand. Continue mixing for about 4 minutes, or until the dough forms a coarse ball, adding more flour or water by the tablespoonful as needed. Let the dough rest for 15 minutes, then transfer it to a lightly floured counter. Dust the top with flour to absorb the surface moisture, then knead the dough by hand for 2 to 3 minutes, or until it is soft, supple, and tacky but not sticky. The dough should pass the windowpane test (see page 105).

2. Form the dough into a ball and place it in a bowl brushed with olive oil. Roll the dough in the oil to coat the entire surface and cover the bowl with plastic wrap. Let the dough sit at room temperature for 3 to 4 hours, or until it swells by at least 50 percent and up to 100 percent.

3. Divide the dough into 4 equal pieces. Gently round each piece into a ball and brush or rub each ball with olive oil. Place each ball inside its own zippered freezer bag. Let the balls sit at room temperature for about 1 hour, and then refrigerate the balls overnight.

4. The next day, remove the dough balls from the refrigerator 2 hours before you plan to make the pizzas to take off the chill and to relax the gluten. At this point, you can hold any balls you don't want to use right away in the refrigerator for another day, or you can freeze them for up to 3 months.

GRILLED PIZZA DOUGH

This dough needs to be very extensible and supple because it is pressed out
quite thin, almost as thin as a flour tortilla. The dough is easy to make, but the
technique for properly grilling a pizza, as perfected by George Germon of
Al Forno in Providence, requires practice, a good grasp of *mise en place*, and a
refusal to be intimidated. You can substitute up to 5 tablespoons whole-wheat
flour, rye flour, or cornmeal for an equal amount of the all-purpose flour for
a nice earthy flavor and texture, although you may also have to increase the
amount of water slightly. You can keep these dough balls in the freezer; that
way you will be ready to spring into action anytime the craving for grilled
pizza strikes—and it will!

Makes six 6 1/2-ounce dough balls
5 cups (22 1/2 ounces) unbleached all-purpose flour
1 tablespoon sugar
2 teaspoons table salt or 3 1/2 teaspoons kosher salt
1 teaspoon instant yeast
3 1/2 tablespoons olive oil
1 3/4 cups room-temperature water (70°F)

1. With a large metal spoon, stir together the flour, sugar, salt, yeast, 1 1/2 tablespoons of the olive oil, and the water in a 4-quart bowl or the bowl of an
   electric stand mixer until combined. *If mixing with an electric mixer,* fit it with
   the dough hook and mix on low speed for about 4 minutes, or until the
   dough forms a coarse ball and clears the sides and the bottom of the bowl.
   Add more flour or water by the tablespoonful as needed. Let the dough rest
   for 15 minutes, then mix again on medium-low speed for an additional 2 to
   4 minutes, or until the dough is smooth, supple, and tacky but not sticky. The
   dough should pass the windowpane test (see page 105). *If mixing by hand,*
   repeatedly dip one of your hands or the spoon into room-temperature water
   and use it much like a dough hook, working the dough vigorously as you
   rotate the bowl with your other hand. Continue mixing for about 4 minutes,
   or until the dough forms a coarse ball, adding more flour or water by the

tablespoonful as needed. Let the dough rest for 15 minutes, then transfer it to a lightly floured counter. Dust the top with flour to absorb the surface moisture, then knead the dough by hand for 2 to 4 minutes, or until it is smooth, supply, and tacky but not sticky. The dough should pass the windowpane test (see page 105).

2. Immediately divide the dough into 6 equal pieces. Gently round each piece into a ball and brush or rub each ball with olive oil. Place each ball inside its own zippered freezer bag. Using the remaining 2 tablespoons olive oil, drizzle 1 teaspoon olive oil over the ball in each bag and seal the bags closed. Let the balls sit at room temperature for about 30 minutes, then refrigerate the balls for at least 3 hours or preferably overnight.

3. Remove the dough balls from the refrigerator 2 hours before you plan to roll them out to take off the chill and to relax the gluten. At this point, you can hold any balls you don't want to use right away in the refrigerator for up to 3 days, or you can freeze them for up to 3 months.

CHICAGO DEEP-DISH PIZZA DOUGH

Chicago deep-dish pizza has come to national attention through the expansion of the Pizzeria Uno chain and a number of independent Chicago-style pizzerias in many cities, such as Zachary's in Berkeley and Sicilia's, my local verison in Providence. Most Americans associate the crust with a cornmeal flavor and texture. While this is often accurate, it is not always the case; there is also a version that calls for no cornmeal, but is instead a soft, white dough made with a small amount of milk. But a cornmeal crust is the most definitive style, and even within that category differences exist. Gino's East, for example, makes a thick, airy cornmeal crust, while Lou Malnatti's and the original Pizzeria Uno (and Pizzeria Due, its even better sister restaurant) make a thinner, crispier crust. I much prefer the latter, and this dough recipe is my version of it, although the same dough can be used for the thicker style as well. Unlike most pizza dough, this one does not improve from an overnight rise.

Makes two 18-ounce dough balls
4 cups (18 ounces) unbleached bread flour
2/3 cup fine-grind yellow cornmeal
2 tablespoons sugar
1 1/4 teaspoons table salt or 2 1/2 teaspoons kosher salt
2 1/4 teaspoons instant yeast
5 tablespoons corn oil
1 1/2 cups lukewarm water (90° to 95°F)

1. With a large metal spoon, stir together all the ingredients in a 4-quart bowl or the bowl of an electric stand mixer until combined. *If mixing with an electric mixer,* fit it with the dough hook and mix on low speed for about 4 minutes, or until the dough forms a coarse ball and clears the sides and the bottom of the bowl. Add more flour or water by the tablespoonful as needed. Let the dough rest for 15 minutes, then mix again on low speed for an additional 2 to 3 minutes, or until the dough is smooth, stretchy, and tacky but not sticky. The dough should pass the windowpane test (see page 105). *If mixing by hand,* repeatedly dip one of your hands or the spoon into room-temperature water and use it much like a dough hook, working the dough vigorously as you

rotate the bowl with your other hand. Continue mixing for about 4 minutes, or until the dough forms a coarse ball, adding more flour or water by the tablespoonful as needed. Let the dough rest for 15 minutes, then transfer it to a lightly floured counter. Dust the top with flour to absorb the surface moisture, then knead the dough by hand for 2 to 3 minutes, or until it is smooth, stretchy, and tacky but not sticky. The dough should pass the windowpane test (see page 105).

2. Form the dough into a ball and place it in a bowl brushed with olive oil. Roll the dough in the oil to coat the entire surface, and cover the bowl with plastic wrap. Let the dough sit at room temperature for about 2 hours, or until doubled in size.

3. Divide the dough into 2 equal pieces and round them into balls. Rub the surface of the dough balls with olive oil, place them on the countertop, and cover them with plastic wrap. Let the dough sit at room temperature for 15 to 20 minutes before making the pizzas.

SARDINIAN *CARTA DI MUSICA* DOUGH

This dough makes the crispiest, thinnest pizza crusts you'll ever eat. It calls for a two-step process, but it does not take a long time to accomplish, and the crusts can double as soft or crisp flatbreads. Once crisped, the crusts will keep in an airtight container at room temperature for up to 2 weeks. This recipe is written for the cook using a baking stone in a conventional home oven. If this is not your situation, review the information on other baking arrangements beginning on page 97.

Makes 8 soft or crisp 10 by 7-inch crusts

5 cups (22^1/2 ounces) unbleached bread flour

1 tablespoon sugar or honey

2 teaspoons table salt or 3^1/2 teaspoons kosher salt

1^3/4 teaspoons instant yeast

^{1}/4 cup olive or vegetable oil or solid vegetable shortening

1^2/3 cups room-temperature water (70°F)

Unbleached bread flour, cornmeal, or semolina flour for
   dusting peel

1. With a large metal spoon, stir together all the ingredients in a 4-quart bowl or the bowl of an electric stand mixer until combined. *If mixing with an electric mixer,* fit it with the dough hook and mix on low speed for about 4 minutes, or until the dough forms a coarse ball and clears the sides and the bottom of the bowl. Add more flour or water by the tablespoonful as needed. Let the dough rest for 15 minutes, then mix again on low speed for an additional 2 to 4 minutes, or until the dough is smooth, stretchy, and tacky but not sticky. The dough should pass the windowpane test (see page 105). *If mixing by hand,* repeatedly dip one of your hands or the spoon into room-temperature water and use it much like a dough hook, working the dough vigorously as you rotate the bowl with your other hand. Continue mixing for about 4 minutes, or until the dough forms a coarse ball, adding more flour or water by the tablespoonful as needed. Let the dough rest for 15 minutes, then transfer it to a lightly floured counter. Dust the top with flour to absorb the surface moisture, then knead the dough by hand for 2 to 4 minutes, or until

it is smooth, stretchy, and tacky but not sticky. The dough should pass the windowpane test (see page 105).

2. Form the dough into a ball and place it in a bowl brushed with olive oil. Roll the dough in the oil to coat the entire surface and cover the bowl with plastic wrap. Let the dough sit at room temperature for 1 to 1^1/$_2$ hours, or until doubled in size.

3. Place a baking stone on the middle shelf of the oven (unless you know your oven well enough to place it on a different shelf) and preheat on the highest setting for at least 1 hour.

4. While the oven is heating, sprinkle some flour on the counter and transfer the dough from the bowl to the floured counter. Divide the dough into 4 equal pieces. Round each piece into a ball, flatten each ball with the palm of your hand into a disk, and lay the disks on a clean counter lightly dusted again with flour. Lightly dust the tops of the disks with more flour, cover them loosely with plastic wrap, and let rest for 15 to 20 minutes.

5. With a rolling pin, evenly roll out each disk into a rectangle or oblong about 10 by 7 inches. If the dough resists extending to the full size, cover it with a kitchen towel and let it rest for at least 5 minutes. Move on to another dough disk and then return to the first piece. When it is fully rolled, it should be a scant ^{1}/$_4$ inch thick. If it is slightly longer or shorter than 10 inches or is not a perfect rectangle, yet appears to be the proper thickness, stop rolling. Let the rolled-out dough rest uncovered on the counter for about 3 minutes, then gently lift one (you may need to use a metal or plastic scraper) onto a wooden or metal peel that has been lightly dusted with flour.

6. Slide the dough from the peel onto the stone, close the oven door, and wait for 2 minutes before opening the door. The dough should begin separating horizontally into 2 thin halves, puffing up into a large pitalike bread. When this occurs, count to 20 and then remove the bread, placing it on a wire rack to cool; do not wait for it to brown or crisp. While the first piece is baking, prepare the next piece and continue in this manner until all 4 pieces are baked. If any do not begin to puff and separate within 4 minutes, remove them from the oven and use them as soft flatbreads.

7. When the puffed breads have cooled, they will release their air and flatten. Separate the halves with a sharp, serrated knife into 2 very thin disks (one side may be thinner than the other, but unless it is too thin to hold together, it will be okay). These halved breads may be used in this soft form for pizza crusts, or they can be crisped in the same preheated oven and used either as ultracrisp pizza crusts or cracker bread *(carta di musica)*.

8. To make crisp crusts, place as many halved pieces as will fit on the baking stone or inverted sheet pan in the still-hot oven and bake for about 5 minutes, or until the disks begin to brown and curl. Remove them from the oven to a wire rack to cool.

FOCACCIA DOUGH

Focaccia has been growing in popularity as its overall quality has improved. It is no longer regarded as the big, starchy, underfermented "pizza bread" usually found in supermarkets. Now, there are as many ways to make great focaccia dough as there are to make pizza dough. Some recipes call for milk or wine in addition to water. Most have olive oil, either in the dough or on top. Not all focaccia is crowned with herbs, cheese, potatoes, or other savories. There are some versions that incorporate raisins, whole wine grapes, and other sweet fruits.

This recipe makes the best-tasting all-purpose focaccia dough that I've ever had and is also the easiest to make. Like many of the dough recipes in this book, it utilizes a delayed-fermentation technique, a method so perfectly suited to focaccia that I now use this recipe in place of most of the previous focaccia recipes that I've learned or developed.

You can vary this basic recipe by substituting an equal amount of either milk or wine for up to half of the water. Both are traditional ingredients in various regional Ligurian and Tuscan *(schiacciata)* recipes. It is also definitely within the rules to play around with whole-grain flour substitutions to create different textures and flavors. See *Napoletana* Pizza Dough Variations on page 109 for tips on using whole-wheat and rye flours.

Makes one 12 by 17-inch sheet
5 3/4 cups (26 ounces) unbleached bread flour
2 teaspoons table salt or 3 1/2 teaspoons kosher salt
2 1/4 teaspoons instant yeast
2 1/2 cups ice-cold water (40° F)
1/4 cup olive oil

1. With a large metal spoon, stir together the flour, salt, yeast, and water in a 4-quart bowl or the bowl of an electric mixer until combined. *If mixing with an electric mixer,* fit it with the paddle attachment and mix on low speed for about 2 minutes, or until all the ingredients are hydrated and begin to form a wet ball of dough. Let the dough rest for 5 minutes. Switch to the dough hook, add the olive oil, and resume mixing on medium-low speed for 3 to

4 minutes, or until all of the oil is incorporated and the dough is sticky, supple, and smooth; it should clear the sides of the bowl and stick just a little to the bottom. If the dough seems like a batter and does not have sufficient structure to hold itself together, mix in more flour by the tablespoonful. Even though it is sticky, the dough should still pass the windowpane test (see page 105). *If mixing by hand,* repeatedly dip one of your hands or the spoon into cold water and use it much like a dough hook, working the dough vigorously as you rotate the bowl with your other hand. As all the flour is incorporated and the dough becomes a wet ball, about 3 minutes, stop mixing and let the dough rest for 5 minutes. Then add the olive oil, dip your hand or spoon again in water, and continue to work the dough for another 3 to 4 minutes. The dough should be very sticky, but it should also have some texture and structure. If the dough seems like a batter and does not have sufficient structure to hold itself together, mix in more flour by the tablespoonful. Even though it is sticky, the dough should still pass the windowpane test (see page 105).

2. Form the dough into a ball and place it in a bowl brushed with olive oil. Turn the dough to coat it with the oil, cover the bowl with plastic wrap, and immediately refrigerate it overnight. The next day the dough should have nearly doubled in size. Allow it to sit at room temperature for about 2 hours before making the focaccia.

Pizza al Taglio Dough

For more information on this unique style of pizza, see page 26. The only difference between this and the Focaccia Dough is that it requires slightly less water; substitute 2 1/4 cups for the amount called for above. The recipe makes about 3 pounds of dough, or enough for 3 "planks."

FOCACCIA COL FORMAGGIO AND GREEK PITA DOUGH

This is the simplest of all doughs, yet it makes an extraordinary type of focaccia. The dough is unleavened and, when rolled out paper-thin, is not that different from Greek phyllo or German strudel dough. It is used not only in the Ligurian *focaccia col formaggio di Recco,* but also in countless Greek and Macedonian pastries of the pita tradition (see page 245). While the authentic *focaccia col formaggio* is baked in large copper pans or directly on the hearth, this version uses a 10-inch cake pan. (You can also use a 12-inch pizza pan.) As you become more experienced making these crusts, you will be able to bake them directly on a baking stone and make them as large as your stone allows. It's hard to eat just one of these; they are not nearly as filling as they look because the dough is so thin.

Makes twenty 1 1/2-ounce dough balls, enough for 10 *focaccie col formaggio* or one 14-inch pita

4 1/2 cups (20 ounces) unbleached all-purpose flour

3/4 teaspoon table salt or 1 1/2 teaspoons kosher salt

1 1/2 cups room-temperature water (70°F)

1. With a large metal spoon, stir together all the ingredients in a 4-quart bowl or the bowl of an electric stand mixer until combined. *If mixing with an electric mixer,* fit it with the dough hook and mix on low speed for about 4 minutes, or until the dough forms a coarse ball and clears the sides and the bottom of the bowl. Add more flour or water by the tablespoonful as needed. Let the dough rest for 5 minutes, then mix again on low speed for an additional 2 minutes, or until the dough is smooth, supple, and satiny. *If mixing by hand,* repeatedly dip one of your hands or the spoon into room-temperature water and use it much like a dough hook, working the dough vigorously into as you rotate the bowl with your other hand. Continue mixing for about 4 minutes, or until the dough forms a coarse ball, adding more flour or water by the tablespoonful as needed. Let the dough rest for 5 minutes, then transfer it to a lightly floured counter. Dust the top with flour to absorb the surface moisture, then knead the dough by hand for about 2 minutes, or until it is smooth, supple, and satiny.

2. Divide the dough into 20 equal pieces. Gently round each piece into a ball and brush or rub each ball with olive oil. Line a sheet pan with baking parchment or a nonstick silicone baking liner and brush with olive oil. Place each dough ball on the pan and loosely cover the pan with either plastic wrap or a food-grade plastic bag. (If you do not plan to use all the pieces, place the extra ones in individual zippered freezer bags and refrigerate or freeze. Use the refrigerated balls within 2 days and the frozen balls within 3 months.) Allow the dough balls to rest for about 15 minutes before rolling them out.

Sauces and Specialty Toppings

When a great crust meets a delicious topping, the key elements for memorable, even legendary, pizza are in place. The following sauces and toppings are easy to make and are guaranteed to deliver great flavor; add them to your repertoire of recipes you already love. These recipes are merely a starting point—feel free to tweak them to suit your own palate preferences and those of your friends and family. And, above all, have fun with them.

TOMATO SAUCES

The key word for tomato sauces is *bright*. Flavor in a sauce, especially a tomato sauce, should evoke a sense of brightness, or vibrancy. Two simple tricks contribute to a bright sauce. One of them is acidity. Lemon juice or red wine vinegar can brighten up a flat sauce. The other trick is to not overcook the tomatoes. Crushed tomatoes and tomato purée come out of a can already cooked. They may not be sufficiently cooked for a pasta sauce, in which the herb and vegetable flavors need some time to blend over heat, but they are fine for pizza sauce because they cook a second time in the oven, at which point the necessary blending can take place.

I use one of the two following pizza sauces for any pizza calling for tomato sauce. (Sometimes I use fresh tomatoes as well, of course, either sliced or diced.) Both sauces can be made quickly and then kept in the refrigerator until needed. If you do not plan to use all the sauce within a week, freeze the excess in an airtight container; it will keep for several months.

CRUSHED TOMATO SAUCE

Some canned tomato brands are more heavily salted than others, so you will need to adjust the amount of salt in this recipe to your taste. You can purchase canned crushed tomatoes, or you can buy canned whole tomatoes and crush them with your fingers or in a food processor, mixing all the juice back into the tomato pulp. The basil and oregano are optional. I use both, but when Neapolitan cooks make a *pizza alla marinara*, they use only oregano in the sauce. The flavors of the herbs and garlic will intensify while the pizza is baking, so resist the urge to increase the amount.

Makes 4 cups

1 can (28 ounces) crushed tomatoes

1/4 teaspoon freshly ground black pepper

1 teaspoon dried basil or 2 tablespoons minced fresh basil
   (optional)

1 teaspoon dried oregano or 1 tablespoon minced fresh basil
   (optional)

1 tablespoon granulated garlic powder, or 5 cloves fresh
   garlic, minced or pressed

2 tablespoons red wine vinegar or freshly squeezed lemon
   juice, or a combination

1 teaspoon salt, or to taste

In a bowl, stir together all the ingredients, starting with 1/2 teaspoon salt and adding more to taste. Store in a tightly covered container in the refrigerator for up to 1 week.

ALL-PURPOSE *MARINARA* PIZZA SAUCE

The flavors are fresher and brighter in this sauce than they are in any commercially bottled or canned pizza sauce. Dried herbs are preferable to fresh herbs here, but if you want to use fresh herbs, sprinkle them on the pizzas either just before you put them in the oven or as soon as they come out. Also, if you do not have thyme or marjoram, you can substitute additional oregano or basil to taste.

Makes about 6 cups

1 can (28 ounces) tomato purée

1 3/4 cups water

1 tablespoon dried parsley

2 teaspoons dried basil

1 teaspoon dried oregano

1/2 teaspoon dried thyme

1/2 teaspoon dried marjoram (optional)

1/4 teaspoon freshly ground black pepper

1/4 cup olive oil

2 tablespoons granulated garlic powder, or 10 cloves fresh
garlic, minced or pressed, and lightly sautéed in the
olive oil, above

1/4 cup red wine vinegar or freshly squeezed lemon juice,
or a combination

1 1/2 teaspoons salt, or to taste

In a bowl, stir together all the ingredients, starting with 1/2 teaspoon salt and adding more to taste. Store in a tightly covered container in the refrigerator for up to 1 week.

PESTO

When I first discovered pesto in the mid-1970s, I thought the heavens had opened and revealed a special secret. It was new to Americans then, but now has become so familiar that it is almost a culinary cliché. Yet throughout my travels in Liguria, where pesto has been a staple for centuries, nobody seems to have tired of it, and my passion for it was reborn.

The problem with much of the pesto in this country is the same as it is for many tomato sauces: a lack of brightness. Pesto is too often dull green, thick, and pasty, with the flavors trapped in the cheese. This could be caused by anything from a mediocre olive oil or too little oil to poor-quality cheese to a lack of freshness (it should be made just before you use it).

The best pesto I ever ate in America was at San Francisco's legendary Caffè Sport during its glory years in the 1970s. It was the pesto of then-chef/owner Tony Latona, and it was bright green with a basil flavor that exploded in my mouth—a flavor transported by freshly grated cheese (I assume it was Parmigiano-Reggiano, but I never asked), bold Sicilian olive oil, and rich pine nuts. It had been a long time since pesto sent me into such ecstasy, but when I ate it over *trofie* at Da Vittorio in Recco, the flavors carried me back to Caffè Sport. With those flavors in mind, I set out to recapture my favorite pesto memories in the following recipes.

PESTO ALLA GENOVESE

This recipe makes a smooth, creamy pesto. It can be baked on top of focaccia or pizza, or drizzled over it after it comes out of the oven. It will keep for about a week in the refrigerator, but will be at its best during the first 24 hours. It begins to lose some of its bright color and flavor the longer it sits. You can substitute toasted walnuts for the pine nuts, or add them in equal parts.

Makes about 2 cups
2 cups fresh basil leaves
8 cloves garlic, minced
1 cup extra virgin olive oil

1 tablespoon freshly squeezed lemon juice

1 cup pine nuts, lightly toasted

3/4 cup freshly grated Parmigiano-Reggiano or pecorino
Romano cheese

1/4 teaspoon freshly ground black pepper

Salt

1. In a blender or food processor, combine the basil, garlic, olive oil, and lemon juice and purée until smooth. Add half the pine nuts and blend for a few seconds to grind them coarsely.

2. Transfer the purée to a bowl and fold in the cheese, the remaining pine nuts, the pepper, and salt to taste. Place in an airtight container and keep refrigerated until needed.

Pesto Variations

PARSLEY PESTO: Substitute an equal amount of flat-leaf parsley for the basil, or use parsley and basil in any combination equaling 2 cups.

SPINACH PESTO: Increase the olive oil to 1 1/4 cups and add 1 cup thawed, frozen chopped spinach, well drained, and 1/2 teaspoon salt to the blender or processor with the other ingredients. Proceed as directed. This makes a beautiful bright green pesto.

ROASTED PEPPER PESTO: Substitute an equal amount of roasted red peppers for the basil, or use basil and roasted peppers in any combination equaling 2 cups. The peppers provide a rich, earthy flavor.

SUN-DRIED TOMATO PESTO: Add 5 olive oil–packed sun-dried tomatoes, drained and chopped, to the blender or processor with the other ingredients. Proceed as directed. The sun-dried tomatoes give the pesto a greater complexity. I prefer to use sun-dried tomatoes in tandem with other ingredients or in small doses, as they have a particularly intense flavor. For a milder option, use oven-roasted tomatoes. You can purchase them at gourmet delicatessens, or you can roast them at home by brushing tomato slices with Herb Oil (page 147) and then roasting them in a 400°F oven for about 20 minutes, or until they begin to bubble and lightly char on top.

SPECIALTY TOPPINGS

The following are specialty preparations that are worth keeping on hand. They are the fine touches that can make a big difference in the final flavor of a pizza. Some of the toppings can be kept in the refrigerator for an extended period, others need to be kept frozen, and still others are best made just before using them.

Additional Toppings (before Baking) or Garnishes (after Baking)

Roasted or grilled peppers (topping or garnish)

Eggplant, sliced and broiled or sautéed in olive oil (topping or garnish)

Broccoli rabe, blanched (topping)

Capers (brined, topping; or salt cured, garnish)

Marinated or fresh artichoke hearts or stems (topping or garnish)

Any seafood (topping or garnish, depending on type)

Sliced cured meats (*salumi*) such as mortadella and prosciutto, and salami of any type (topping or garnish)

BALSAMIC SYRUP

This syrup is useful for many things, not just pizza. It is wonderful on salads, drizzled over vegetables, and even splashed over fruit and ice cream. But it really enlivens a pizza. Because the vinegar is reduced to a syrup, it concentrates the flavors and brings out the sweetness of the grapes. For this reason, you do not need to start with an expensive balsamic, but you do need to be sure that you are using true balsamic and not a flavored wine vinegar masquerading as balsamic.

Makes about 1 cup

2 cups balsamic vinegar

In a saucepan, bring the vinegar to a boil over high heat, reduce the heat to low, and simmer until the vinegar is reduced to about 1 cup. It should be thick and syrupy. Remove from the heat and let cool completely. Store the syrup in a squirt bottle for ease of use. It will keep indefinitely at room temperature.

HERB OIL

I use this oil more than any other specialty ingredient. Its primary use is on focaccia, but it also is excellent drizzled over many types of pizza and can be used to marinate or coat various toppings, especially fresh tomatoes. There are a number of ways to make an herb-flavored oil. For example, this recipe calls for dried herbs (except for the rosemary), but fresh herbs will work as well. If you substitute fresh herbs for dried, triple the amounts called for below and stir the fresh herbs into the olive oil immediately to prevent oxidation. You can also change the amounts to your taste, or substitute an herb blend, such as herbes de Provence. You should consider this recipe only a starting point for creating your own herb combination.

Use only whole-leaf dried herbs, not ground ones; the latter will muddy the oil and settle to the bottom. Oil made with dried herbs will keep for several months in the refrigerator, while oil made with fresh herbs will keep for only a week. Store the oil in a tightly capped container.

Makes about 2 cups

2 cups olive oil

2 tablespoon dried basil

2 tablespoons dried parsley

1 tablespoon dried oregano

1 tablespoon fresh rosemary leaves

1 teaspoon dried thyme

2 tablespoons granulated garlic powder, or 10 cloves
fresh garlic, pressed and lightly sautéed in $1/2$ cup of
the olive oil, above

1 tablespoon kosher salt or coarse sea salt

$1/4$ teaspoon freshly ground black pepper

1 teaspoon chile flakes (optional)

1 teaspoon sweet or hot paprika (optional)

In a bowl, whisk together all the ingredients. Let sit at room temperature for 2 hours before using.

SPICY OIL

My wife and I fell in love with the spicy oil at Al Forno in Providence the first time we tasted it. This is a variation of that distinctive oil, adapted from a recipe in *Cucina Simpatica*, authored by the restaurant's owners. One change is that I add salt because I find that it intensifies the flavor of the oil, but it is not in the original, so you may omit it if you like. The oil is excellent for small drizzles over almost any kind of pizza.

Makes 1 cup

1 cup olive oil

4 teaspoons sweet or hot paprika

4 teaspoons chile flakes

1 large clove garlic, peeled

1/4 teaspoon salt (optional)

In a saucepan, combine the olive oil, paprika, chile flakes, and garlic and bring to a boil over medium heat. Reduce the heat to low and simmer gently for 10 minutes. Remove from the heat and let cool for 30 minutes. Strain the oil into a jar, add the salt, and let cool completely. Cover and store in the refrigerator for up to 2 weeks.

CARAMELIZED GARLIC PURÉE OR WHOLE CLOVES AND GARLIC OIL

There are so many uses for caramelized garlic, both whole and puréed, as well as for garlic oil, that I always make this in large batches and keep it on hand in the freezer or refrigerator. You can buy a large jar of peeled garlic cloves, or you can peel your own. There are a number of ways to caramelize garlic, but this is my favorite method.

Makes about 2 cups purée or 150 whole cloves and 1 cup oil
10 heads garlic, cloves separated and peeled
About 1 1/2 cups olive oil

1. Arrange the garlic cloves in a frying pan large enough to accommodate them in a single layer. Pour in the olive oil to cover the cloves (about 1 inch of oil), place over medium heat, and cook, stirring from time to time, for 10 to 15 minutes, or until the garlic softens and turns a beautiful golden brown. Remove from the heat and, using a slotted spoon, scoop the garlic cloves from the oil and place them in a bowl. Let the cloves and the oil cool, returning any oil that collects in the bottom of the bowl to the frying pan.

2. Once the garlic and oil have cooled, you can either purée some of the garlic into a paste, or package the whole cloves in zippered snack-sized freezer bags. Don't overfill the bags, packing perhaps 20 to 25 cloves in each one. Freeze any bags that won't be used within the next 3 days. Transfer the garlic oil to a glass or plastic container, cover, and refrigerate. It will keep for several months.

SMOKED EGGPLANT PURÉE

Making this purée has become an annual rite for both of us, but especially for Susan, who buys a bushel of eggplants from a local farm, sets up the kettle grill, and systematically fire roasts them until they are all reduced to a smoky-flavored pulp. Then we season it, divvy it up into small freezer bags, and freeze it. Whenever we have a craving for any number of things that we make from this purée, including the best baba ghanouj I've ever had, we just pull out a bag from the freezer, let it defrost, and the purée is ready to use. Use small dollops of this purée on top of a pizza, especially a grilled pizza, for a memorable treat.

Makes about 4 cups

4 eggplants

1/2 cup freshly squeezed lemon juice

1/4 cup olive oil

Salt

1. Fire up a charcoal grill with natural hardwood charcoal and set the grate so that it is about 4 inches from the coals. When the coals are white hot, lay the whole eggplants on the grate as it comfortably holds and let them cook for about 5 minutes, then give each eggplant a quarter turn. If the hot side is not charred, give them a few minutes longer before turning. Continue until all the sides of the eggplants have been exposed to the heat. It may be necessary to turn them for two complete rotations before they begin to turn soft. (The average cooking time is 20 to 25 minutes, depending on the level of heat.) When they are very charred and very soft, remove the eggplants from the grill with a large spoon (they may be too soft for tongs), and put them in a large bowl to cool.

2. When the eggplants are cool enough to handle, scoop out the pulp into a bowl, discarding the charred skins. Add the lemon juice, olive oil, and salt to taste to the pulp and stir until well combined and the mixture is very soft. Alternatively, process the mixture in a food processor.

3. Package the eggplant pulp in zippered snack-sized freezer bags and freeze for up to 12 months. One bag is usually enough topping for 2 or 3 small pizzas.

SWEET-AND-SOUR ONION MARMALADE

There are so many ways to use this marmalade, you can never have too much of it on hand. However, my favorite use is on the top of focaccia or grilled pizza. It takes about a half hour to make, so you will need to plan ahead. You can store it in the refrigerator for up to 2 weeks.

Makes about 2 cups

1/4 cup olive or vegetable oil

4 large yellow or white onions, cut into thin strips

3/4 cup sugar

1/4 cup balsamic vinegar

1/4 teaspoon salt

1/8 teaspoon freshly ground black pepper

1. In a large frying pan, heat the oil over medium heat. Add the onions and sauté for 20 to 25 minutes, or until they begin to turn a light golden brown. (Do not cook over high heat, as the outside of the onions will char too quickly before the insides have softened and sweetened.) Add the sugar and continue cooking and stirring for about 3 minutes, or until the sugar melts and begins to bubble.

2. As the onions turn a richer brown, clear a space in the center of the pan, pour the vinegar directly onto the hot pan, and then stir the vinegar into the onions. When the vinegar has reduced, leaving a syrupy coating on the onions, remove from the heat, stir in the salt and pepper, and let cool completely before using or storing.

SAUTÉED MUSHROOMS

Mushrooms, especially porcini and other wild mushrooms, are wonderful on a *pizza bianca* (pizza with white sauce). They are actually pretty wonderful on almost any kind of pizza, especially in conjunction with savory herbs and vegetables like arugula, glazed onions, and spinach.

Makes about $1/2$ cup, enough for 1 pizza

2 tablespoons olive oil

5 porcini or other mushrooms (about 4 ounces), cut into
   $1/4$-inch-thick slices

1 clove garlic, minced (optional)

Salt and freshly ground black pepper

1 tablespoon chopped fresh flat-leaf parsley or arugula
   (optional)

1. In a frying pan, heat the olive oil over medium heat. Add the mushrooms and garlic and sauté for 2 to 3 minutes, or just until the mushrooms begin to sweat. Season to taste with salt and pepper and remove from the heat.

2. Let the mushrooms cool completely. Spread the mushroom mixture over the top of the pizza, either before or after baking. Garnish the pizza with the parsley when it comes out of the oven.

BUTTERNUT SQUASH PURÉE

Make this purée during the late fall and winter, when winter squashes and root vegetables are abundant and are appreciated on the dinner table. You can use the same method to make similar purées with turnips, parsnips, carrots, acorn squashes, or pumpkins, but I think butternut squash is the king of this category. The yield will depend on the size of the squash; for example, a 3-pound squash will yield about 5 cups purée.

1 butternut squash, any size, cut into 8 sections and seeds discarded
1 cup water
Salt and freshly ground black pepper

1. In a large saucepan, combine the squash and water, cover, and bring to a boil over high heat. (If you have an expandable steamer insert, you can use it if you like, although it is not necessary.) Lower the heat to low and simmer for about 20 minutes, or until the squash is fork-tender. Remove from the heat and drain off the water, reserving it.

2. When the squash pieces are cool enough to handle, scoop out the flesh into a bowl and discard the skin. Working in batches, process the squash flesh in a food processor until smooth and creamy, adding the reserved cooking water if necessary to achieve a good consistency. Package the purée in zippered snack-sized freezer bags and refrigerate for up to 2 weeks or freeze for up to 6 months.

WHITE SAUCE

This sauce is especially good on white pizzas, particularly mushroom pizzas. It makes them deliciously creamy and rich.

Makes about $1/2$ cup, enough for 1 or 2 pizzas, depending on size

2 tablespoons olive oil

1 small yellow onion, diced

1 clove garlic, minced or pressed

$1/4$ cup heavy cream

$1/2$ teaspoon minced fresh thyme or marjoram

Salt and freshly ground black pepper

1. In a heavy saucepan or frying pan, heat the olive oil over medium heat. Add the onion and sauté for 5 or 6 minutes, or until translucent. Add the garlic and stir for 1 minute longer. Add the cream, lower the heat to medium–low, and cook for about 3 minutes, or until the cream thickens and reduces slightly.

2. Remove from the heat, stir in the thyme, and season to taste with salt and pepper. Let cool completely before using. It will keep tightly covered in the refrigerator for up to 5 days.

CRAB AND CREAM CHEESE TOPPING

Although this topping has the consistency of cream cheese, it melts into a creamy sauce when you bake it on pizza. It can also be served straight from the refrigerator as a dip for crackers. If you do not have an organic lemon, blanch a regular lemon in boiling water for 15 seconds to remove any pesticide residue before zesting. When zesting, use either a rasp-style zester, such as a Microplane, or the finest rasps on a box grater. Also, do not remove any of the white of the peel with the colored portion, as it will impart a bitter flavor.

Makes about 2 cups

1 can (6 ounces) crabmeat, drained and picked over for shell
  fragments, or an equal amount of fresh cooked crab

1/2 pound full-fat cream cheese, at room temperature

1/4 cup finely minced Vidalia, Walla Walla, Maui, or other
  sweet onion

Finely grated zest and juice of 1 lemon, preferably organic

1/2 teaspoon Tabasco or other hot-pepper sauce

1/8 teaspoon freshly ground black pepper, or to taste

In a bowl, combine the crabmeat, cream cheese, onion, half of the lemon zest, all of the lemon juice, and the hot-pepper sauce. Using a sturdy spoon, beat until well blended. (Alternatively, combine the ingredients in an electric stand mixer fitted with the paddle attachment and beat on low speed until blended.) Mix in 1/8 teaspoon pepper and adjust the seasoning, adding more lemon zest to taste. Cover and refrigerate for up to 1 week.

DILL AND CHIVE SAUCE

Here is a wonderful low-fat sauce for smoked salmon or other seafood pizzas, drizzled under the toppings or over them. It can also be used as a dip for vegetables and crackers. You can make it thicker and richer by substituting sour cream for the yogurt.

Makes about 1 cup

1 cup low-fat plain yogurt

2 tablespoons minced fresh chives or 1 tablespoon dried chives

2 tablespoons finely chopped fresh dill

1 tablespoon capers

1/4 teaspoon salt

1/4 teaspoon freshly ground black pepper

In a small bowl, combine all the ingredients, mix well, and then taste and adjust the seasoning. Cover and refrigerate for at least 1 hour before using to meld the flavors. It will keep refrigerated for up to 1 week.

TAPENADE

Wonderful tangy tapenades, or relishes made from savory ingredients like olives and capers, are now widely available and are showing up in all sorts of creative, nontraditional variations. They make excellent pizza toppings, and my wife, Susan, has come up with her own version, which is now a refrigerator mainstay for topping pizzas and for eating with crackers. It is not only easy to prepare, but also, packed into small jars, makes a wonderful gift at holiday time. We use it primarily on grilled pizzas, but it will deliver a flavor burst on any kind of oven pizza as well. If you cannot locate dry-packed sun-dried tomatoes (buy the reddest ones you can find), you can use marinated ones. Drain off and discard the oil and seasonings unless the olive oil is of high quality. If you do not have an organic lemon, blanch a regular lemon in boiling water for 15 seconds to remove pesticide residue before zesting.

Makes about 1 cup

1/2 pound dry-packed sun-dried tomatoes, coarsely chopped

20 Kalamata olives, pitted

1/2 cup extra virgin olive oil

1 teaspoon red wine vinegar

3 large cloves garlic

1/4 teaspoon dried oregano

Finely grated zest and juice of 1 lemon, preferably organic

Salt

In a food processor, combine the sun-dried tomatoes, olives, olive oil, vinegar, garlic, oregano, and lemon zest and juice and process until a smooth paste forms, stopping to scrape down the sides of the bowl as necessary. Taste and season with salt, though it may not need any. Store in a tightly covered container in the refrigerator for up to several months.

ROASTED EGGPLANT, TOMATO, AND LEMON TOPPING

You will need to set aside a little time to make this rustic, full-flavored topping, but it is time well spent, as it can be used in many ways. We often serve it over hot or cold pasta or over rice, or sometimes we just eat it on crackers. But a pizza is its best medium. Use it in small dollops—the flavor is too intense to use over the entire surface—on oven or grilled pizzas. You can make a large batch and keep it in the refrigerator for about 2 weeks, or freeze it in zippered plastic bags for up to 6 months. If you can find only nonorganic lemons, blanch them for 15 seconds in boiling water to remove any pesticide residue before zesting.

Makes about 4 cups

1 large eggplant, cut crosswise into 1/3-inch-thick slices

1 large yellow or white onion, cut into thin strips

4 large tomatoes, cut into 1/2-inch-thick slices

1 pound Kalamata olives, pitted

1 tablespoon coarse sea salt or kosher salt

Finely grated zest and juice of 3 lemons, preferably organic

3/4 cup olive oil

1/4 teaspoon freshly ground black pepper

1. Preheat the oven to 500°F. In a large bowl, combine all of the ingredients except the pepper and mix thoroughly. Spread the mixture in an even layer on a sheet pan.

2. Place the pan in the oven and roast the mixture, stirring it every 15 minutes for even cooking, for about 50 minutes, or until the eggplant is easily pierced with a fork. Turn the oven dial to the broiler setting and cook on the middle shelf under the broiler for about 8 minutes, or until the ingredients char slightly, crisp, and caramelize. Remove from the oven, stir in the pepper, and then taste and adjust the seasoning. Let the mixture cool before using or storing.

Pizza–Cheese Primer

Many cheeses taste good on pizza, so you should feel unrestrained in trying a variety of types and combinations. Italian cheeses are a pizza maker's first thought, of course, but cheeses from elsewhere will work beautifully, too. For instance, low-moisture mozzarella and Monterey Jack cheese are often interchangeable, or Sonoma dry Jack is a wonderful option to replace Parmesan or pecorino Romano cheese.

The following list briefly describes some of the Italian cheeses that appear in the recipes that follow, or in other pizza recipes you may have seen. If you know of other cheeses, domestic or international, with similar characteristics, you should be able to make substitutions freely.

Asiago: Named for a plateau in northeastern Italy, Asiago is a DOC cow's milk cheese produced in areas around Padua and Treviso and in the provinces of Trento and Vincenza. It is sold at a variety of ages, from very young, aged about three weeks, to more than a year old, the latter called *Asiago stravecchio*. The longer-aged versions are excellent for grating and can be used in place of Parmesan-type cheeses

Bel Paese: Literally "beautiful country," this soft, slightly tangy cow's milk cheese is growing in popularity. A very buttery cheese—made from milk with a butterfat content that can be as high as 50 percent—it originated in Lombardy, although an American-made version is also widely sold. Bel Paese can be substituted for full-fat low-moisture mozzarella.

Caciocavallo: This southern Italian cheese has a long history; as the story goes, it was originally made from mare's milk, thus the name, "cheese on horseback." Another tale attributes the name to how the cheeses are traditionally ripened,

hung from poles in pairs, as if carried on horseback. In any case, today *caciocavallo* is a cow's milk cheese and is in the same family of cheeses as provolone and mozzarella, meaning that it is stretched and shaped by hand. It is available plain or smoked, and may be young and smooth or aged and granular.

Crescenza: Sometimes called *crescenza stracchino*, this is a fresh cow's milk cheese from northern Italy with a rich, delicate flavor and a creamy texture similar to American cream cheese. Italian *crescenza* is difficult to find in this country because it is highly perishable. Bellwether Farms, an artisanal cheese maker in northern California, produces an excellent American version.

Fontina: This cheese originates in the Aosta Valley, in the northern corner of Italy, near Switzerland. It is a medium-ripened cow's milk cheese that has a buttery texture, a delicate flavor, and melts nicely.

Gorgonzola: A soft, blue-veined cheese native to Lombardy, Gorgonzola is made from cow's milk with a high butterfat content and has a pleasantly piquant flavor.

Grana: This is the name of a cheese group, of which the most famous members are Parmigiano-Reggiano, *grana padano*, and pecorino Romano. The word *grana* means "grain" or "of granular quality," which aptly describes the texture of these aged cheeses. *Grana padano* is generally aged for a shorter period than Parmigiano-Reggiano.

Mascarpone: A fresh, very rich cheese that has a texture similar to that of sour cream. It is made from cow's milk and was originally produced only in Lombardy, but now is made throughout Italy. Traditionally, it was commonly used in desserts, but it has become popular in savory dishes as well.

Mozzarella: The most well-known pizza cheese, mozzarella is made by the process known as *pasta* *filata,* in which the milk curds are dipped into hot water and then kneaded, stretched, and squeezed into shape. This process gives the cheese its unique texture. Originally mozzarella was made only from the milk of water buffalo, but now it is primarily made from cow's milk. It is usually, but not always, produced from whole milk and may be sold as a fresh cheese, called *fior di latte* if made from cow's milk and *mozzarella di bufala* if made from water buffalo's milk. It can also be made into a low-moisture cheese. Fresh mozzarella is typically sold in balls packed in water (called the governing liquid). Small mozzarella balls *(bocconcini)* are also sold marinated in olive oil or smoked *(affumicata)*. Even though the fresh and low-moisture versions have very different melting and flavor properties, they are often used interchangeably or in concert.

My friend Paula Lambert, who owns the Mozzarella Company in Dallas, Texas, explained to me that in the world of fresh mozzarellas, there are two distinct production methods. One is the traditional method and the other is the deli (or direct-acidification) method. The traditional method uses cultures and enzyme-rich rennet to set the curds, while the deli method uses acids like vinegar or lemon juice. The difference is that the traditional method requires careful monitoring of the pH levels and allows the cheese to develop natural lactic acids through biological fermentation. The deli method is more foolproof, is faster, and yields a cheese with a more milky taste because the lactose in the curds is not transformed into lactic acid. Though the deli mozzarella is quite tasty, it does not melt as well as traditional mozzarella, nor does it have the complexity of flavor. This may be one reason why pizzas in Naples almost always seem to be a little better than Naples-style pizzas in America, where most of the fresh mozzarella is made by the deli method.

Parmigiano-Reggiano: This member of the grana family comes from Emilia-Romagna, specifically the provinces of Parma, Bologna, Modena, Mantua, and Reggio Emilia. It has been made the same way for at least seven centuries from nonpasteurized cow's milk and is aged for at least nine months, but usually longer.

Pecorino Romano: Pecorino is a cheese made from sheep's milk. There are many types of pecorino cheeses, ranging from soft to hard, lean to rich, but pecorino Romano, from the region of Lazio, is a dry aged cheese with properties similar to the cheeses of the Parmesan family, yet with a sharper flavor.

Provolone: Not unlike an aged mozzarella, since it is made by the same method, provolone is a cow's milk cheese from southern Italy. The intensity of flavor is determined by how long it has been aged, and in what size and shape it has been molded.

Ricotta: The word *ricotta* means "recooked," and true ricotta is not a cheese, but rather a cheese by-product. It is made by cooking the whey that is expelled from Parmesan and other cheeses, salvaging all the remaining tiny curds and milk solids that escaped the primary cheese. American ricotta is more like cottage cheese because it is a first-generation collection of curds from fresh milk, combined with whey. Ricotta has many applications, few of them on pizza, although it is being used more and more as a topping for white pizzas.

Robiola: A family of cheeses from northern Italy, each of which has a creamy texture and a delicate flavor. One fine example is *robiola di Roccaverano,* made from a combination of cow's and goat's milk in the Piedmont region.

Stracchino: A generic term for a family of fresh, creamy cheeses of northern Italy, usually made from milk with a 50 percent butterfat content. Among them are *crescenza* and Taleggio. *Stracchino* cheeses tend to be more acidic than American cream cheese and do not travel or age well. Any of the *stracchino* cheeses can be used for *focaccia col formaggio di Recco,* depending on the time of year and availability.

Taleggio: Another in the *stracchino* family of cheeses, Taleggio is named for a small town in Lombardy, near Bergamo. This cow's milk cheese is mild, very soft—sometimes almost runny—and high in butterfat.

The Pizzas

True *Napoletana* pizza is experiencing a renaissance. Of course, it never went out of fashion in Naples, where it has been made much the same way for over 125 years. But when Neapolitan pizza took hold in the United States at the turn of the twentieth century, it took on a new style, what is called neo-Neapolitan, a long-used term that did not originate with me. Many pizzerias still describe their pizzas as Neapolitan, even though they bear no resemblance to those made in Naples. I think it is their way of saying, "We make a thin-crusted pizza." Ironically, I found the crust in the pizzerias in Naples not to be particularly thin, at least by American standards of the term, but instead somewhat breadlike, especially around the *cornicione*, where it puffs up and has big air holes. This quality is extremely appealing and is what sets true *Napoletana* pizza apart from American neo-Neapolitan, which may have a puffy edge, but rarely one with large, irregular holes and the cool, creamy texture of the original.

But most Americans have not eaten pizza in Naples, and if they have had a true *Napoletana* pizza here, they are often less than enthusiastic about it. A few notable exceptions to this general apathy exist, such as what is typically said after a visit to Pizzeria Bianco and a growing number of newer *Napoletana*-style pizzerias like Pizzetta 211. But such reactions are rare indeed.

The reason why a *Napoletana* pizza frequently elicits such cool responses is because the neo-Neapolitan is the definitive American pizza. People tend to like what they know. Even neo-Neapolitan has its subcategories, however. It is turned out in both independent and chain pizzerias. Domino's, Pizza Hut, Papa Gino's, Papa John's, and even frozen supermarket brands are all variations of the original

Neapolitan pizza as it was reinterpreted in the United States. Even the so-called gourmet or California-style pizzas with their fancy toppings are just logical extensions of the American interpretation of Neapolitan pizza.

I have divided the neo-Neapolitan category into three subcategories, each of which has emerged as a distinctive style. The first generation neo-Neapolitan—variations on the sauce and mutz (mozzarella) style—leads the pack. Everybody I know has a favorite sauce and mutz pizzeria in their past. I grew up on the East Coast where many of the pizzerias were connected to first-generation immigrants. Tomato pie, as it was often known, with or without cheese, did not have to compete with chains and standardized concepts, so there were many local versions from which to choose. All of them, for better or for worse, made indelible impressions on the palate memories of anyone who patronized them.

The second generation neo-Neapolitan includes the pizzas from most of the pizza chains, independents (including those that use sourdough crusts), frozen pizzas, and even New York–style pizza, or pizza by the slice. Most of the pizza made and sold across the country is a distinctive American hybrid with a wide range of manifestations. For this reason, I think of this subcategory under the umbrella term *pizza americana*, and have provided a recipe for an all-purpose dough under that name, as well as one for New York–style dough, which is similar. A rough working of the numbers would probably reveal this *Americana* subcategory to be well over 90 percent of all pizza consumed in the United States. DiGiorno alone sells more than 350 million dollars worth of pizza a year, or over 65 million pies. Much as we love to rhapsodize about the legendary pizzas of our youth, or even of our present, this is the category that most people consume. Within this category, by the way, are some pretty impressive pizzas and pizzerias, not just middle-of-the-road chains.

The third generation neo-Neapolitan encompasses the increasingly popular gourmet-style pizza that was pioneered at Spago, California Pizza Kitchen, and many upscale restaurants. This style can be made on any type of dough, sometimes even on an original dough with an unusual flour combination. The focus, however, is usually more on the creativity of the topping than on the crust, and as a result the toppings are typically more time-consuming to prepare than they are for the other neo-Neapolitan pies. This subcategory is often called California-style pizza, even though it exists everywhere.

Some pizza genres don't fit into any of the neo-Neapolitan styles, such as Chicago deep-dish and stuffed pizzas; grilled pizza; focaccia, *pizza al taglio* (otherwise known as "pizza by the meter"), and other thicker-crusted pizza types; the Sardinian *carta di musica* cracker-style crusts; and the traditional Greek pita variations, which may very well be the progenitor of *Napoletana* pizza. I provide recipes for all of these styles in the second half of the pizza chapter.

Choosing a Dough

The dough recipes beginning on page 107 are master recipes that will make excellent pizzas of any style. The main difference among them is the type and amount of flour and hydration. For example, some call for stronger (higher-protein) flour and less water, making them easier to handle and to stretch without tearing. Another difference is the addition of an enrichment such as olive oil, sugar, honey, or milk, all of which contribute flavor and texture. By applying the long-fermentation principles explained on pages 103 to 104, all of the dough recipes will produce crusts comparable to those found at quality pizzerias. In the recipes, I have indicated which dough to use with a specific topping, but you can mix and match them as you like, letting your flavor preferences and your comfort level with making a specific dough determine the final decision.

As you work with the doughs, you will find yourself drawn to certain ones, a preference that may change over time. Many people like to start with an easier-to-handle firmer, stronger dough, rather than a softer, stickier one like the classic *Napoletana*. Each dough has its charms and challenges, and you should feel confident making any of the recipes within a short time.

Topping a Pizza

Topping choices are as numerous and as creative as you wish, but I recommend first making a simple pizza of sauce and cheese to become comfortable with the process at its most prosaic. Then, feel free to top your pies as you like. Keep in mind that sometimes toppings are put on before baking, which is common for a *Napoletana* pie, for example, and other times the toppings are added after the pizza is pulled from the oven, which protects the toppings from burning and makes a particularly beautiful presentation.

When topping any style of pizza, a harmony of flavors is the goal. Here are a few guidelines and suggestions to help you achieve that ideal marriage of flavors.

Consider the rule of three, which states that more than three toppings creates confusion, muddling the flavors. How you count to three is up to you. That is, you can count the sauce and cheese and then add three other toppings, or you can be a topping minimalist and count the sauce and cheese as two toppings and then limit yourself to one additional topping. Remember that more is not always better, however.

Always reach for good-quality vegetables, meats, and cheeses and don't disguise them. Sometimes just seasoning some simply roasted or sautéed garden-fresh vegetables with salt, pepper, and garlic will take them to the next level. Vegetables like mushrooms, peppers, and onions can be applied raw, but they will deliver better flavor and stay more tender if lightly sautéed or roasted first, a step that opens their cell walls, releasing excess moisture.

The better the cheese, the better the pizza, is an obvious principle. But not as obvious is the fact that more cheese does not always mean a better pizza. Nor does a blend of more cheeses always mean a better pizza. Some cheeses are perfect as they are, or maybe need just a small amount of another supporting cheese, such as full-fat mozzarella blended with a little a dry aged cheese. Dry aged cheeses do not melt like full-fat moist cheeses, such as mozzarella, Cheddar, or Jack. They are also saltier and more intense; plus, if too much is applied, they may burn before the pizza finishes baking. Smoked cheeses, which are growing in popularity, add a wonderful wood-fired flavor and are excellent on certain types of pizza.

While pepperoni is the most popular pizza topping (I recommend sautéing or even boiling it in advance to release some of the fat), there are some even better cured meats available. Generically known in Italy as *salumi*, cured meats include the many varieties that we call Italian salami, of which pepperoni is but one. A few of my favorites are *coppa* and Genoa salami, as well as *soppressata*, a Calabrese-style *salumi* that, along with other paprika and chile–infused cured meats from the south of Italy, were the forerunners of pepperoni (which was actually developed here in the

United States). In addition to the Italian family of *salumi*, there are many other excellent spicy cured meats of Creole, Spanish, and Portuguese lineage, such as *chaurice*, chorizo, linguiça, and andouille, not to mention the array of new sausage creations available at gourmet markets.

Even though ground beef is an everyday topping, it can be a great one, too. I like to cook it until it begins to brown and crisp, then I drain it well and season it with salt and pepper. I protect it on the pizza by placing it under the cheese, rather than on top. Using the cheese as a protective layer is a good trick with many toppings, including meats like smoked turkey and chicken, anchovies, and uncooked vegetables like onions, mushrooms, and bell peppers. I prefer to cook most vegetables lightly first (see above), but you if want to add them raw, top them with cheese for the best result.

And finally, don't use too much sauce, but don't use too little either. Also, make sure it is a good sauce—neither too thick nor too thin.

Shaping and Baking a Pizza

Before you start using the pizza recipes, read through the shaping and baking techniques that follow. Most of the pizzas are made essentially the same way, so it is good to familiarize yourself fully with these general instructions before you set to work.

How a kitchen is equipped will vary among readers, so rather than explain every oven situation in each recipe, I have written the recipes for baking the pizza on a baking stone in a conventional home oven. If your kitchen setup is different, read the discussion of various oven situations beginning on page 97 and make the necessary adjustments in the recipes.

1. There are many ways to shape pizza dough, some of them dictated by the wetness or strength of the dough. Dough made with high-gluten flour can be tossed and spun, while softer dough, made with all-purpose flour, is better shaped on a floured counter or gently over the knuckles.

2. Whether you are shaping the dough by the spin-and-toss method or on a counter, remove the dough from the refrigerator 2 hours before you plan to shape the crusts; this gives the yeast time to wake up and gives the dough greater extensibility.

3. **To shape the dough by the toss-and-spin method,** first place a bowl of flour near at hand. Dip your hands in the flour, being careful to the coat the back as well as the palm completely, and lay the dough on

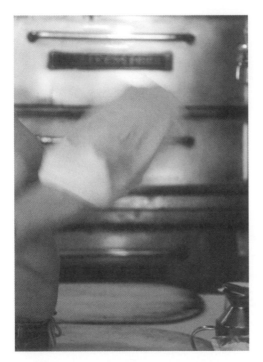

top of your knuckles, with the back of your hands serving as a platform of support. Gently pull and stretch, using only your knuckles and working only from the outer edge (the inside or center of the dough will follow on its own). Then toss the dough an inch or two off your hands, spinning it just slightly. When it lands back on your knuckles, gently stretch it out a bit more and repeat the toss, dusting your knuckles with more flour as needed to prevent sticking, until the dough achieves the desired diameter and thickness. Resist the urge to toss the dough high or to spin it wildly, at least until you have developed confidence in your feeling for its properties. Short tosses and spins may take longer, but they are less risky. The center of the dough will follow the gentle pull from the edges, becoming thinner and thinner. If you try to pull from the center instead of the edge, the dough will rip. The shaped dough should be slightly thicker around the edge than it is toward the center. It does not have to form a perfect circle.

4. **To shape the dough on a counter,** have a bowl of flour near at hand and liberally dust the counter with flour. Lay the dough ball on the counter and roll it over so that the entire ball is coated with flour. Dip your hands in the bowl of flour to coat them thoroughly, and firmly but gently press down on the dough to flatten it into a disk about 1 inch thick. Using your fingertips, press into and around the edge of the dough, turning it as you do, and continue in a spiral fashion, turning and pressing as you work your way to the center of the disk. Stop occasionally to dust your hands and the counter with more flour as needed to prevent sticking. Hang

the dough over the edge of the dusted counter so that half of it is suspended. Working with the portion of the dough still on the counter, use your fingertips to press around the inner lip of the dough, about 1/4 inch from the edge, and continue rotating the disk; gravity will stretch it as you press and rotate. You may also lift the entire piece, drape it over your flour-dusted knuckles, and gently pull from the edges as you carefully rotate it. Continue until the dough has reached the desired diameter and thickness. The edge should be slightly thicker than the center. It does not have to form a perfect circle.

5. If during shaping the dough tears, you may be able to patch it by overlapping the torn edges. Be sure that there are no holes when you lay it down on the peel to apply the toppings. If the dough will not patch or if

it becomes stuck while you are shaping it, just start over by re-forming it into a ball, rubbing it with oil, covering it with plastic wrap, and setting it aside for at least 30 minutes. While waiting, begin shaping another piece of dough.

6. If the shaped dough is going to be transferred from a peel to a baking stone, evenly dust the peel with flour, cornmeal, or semolina, or a combination of any two or all three, before laying the dough on it. When the dough is in place, jiggle the peel to be make sure the dough is not sticking to it. Wooden peels are better than metal peels for loading dough because the dough slides better on wood, but if all you have is metal, then by all means use it, making sure that it is well dusted. (Metal peels are better for removing pizzas from the oven because they are thinner and slip more easily

between the crust and the oven deck.) If you do not have a peel, use an inverted sheet pan, dusting it well with flour. To transfer the dough to the baking stone, use short vibratory pulses, rather than one long jerking stroke. The pulsing method gives you more control if the dough should stick to the peel; a longer thrust may flip the dough over or send it beyond the baking stone.

7. Apply the sauce and toppings only after the dough is on the peel. Periodically jiggle the peel slightly to be sure the dough still slides. If it sticks, use a pastry blade or plastic scraper to release the stuck part and sprinkle more flour under it.

8. If there is any doubt in your mind about your ability to slide the dough off the peel or sheet pan, cover the surface with baking parchment, mist the parchment with nonstick cooking spray, and set up the pizza on the parchment. It will then slide very easily off the peel onto the stone. After about 5 minutes in the oven, slip a metal spatula between the paper and the dough, pulling out the paper as you do.

9. To prepare the oven for baking, review the five oven situations discussed on pages 97 to 100, and set yours up accordingly. Preheat the oven to its highest setting for at least 1 hour, occasionally turning on the broiler to heat the baking stone or other surface from above. The best placement for baking stones or pans will depend on your oven, so you may need to experiment a few times before you settle on the position. Until you figure it out, always have on hand a few extra dough balls and topping ingredients in case you need to redo a pizza.

10. Baking times will vary from oven to oven and also from pizza to pizza. Wetter, thicker, or heavily topped dough takes longer than drier, thinner dough. Make note of the range of baking times for pizza in your oven for future reference. If your oven does not bake evenly, as is common, be prepared to rotate the pizza halfway though baking. If your topping is finished baking before the crust is sufficiently browned, you can buy a couple of extra minutes in the oven by loosely covering the top of the pizza with a sheet of aluminum foil, nonstick if possible, to protect the cheese or other topping.

11. Remove the pizza from the oven with a peel (preferably metal) if you have one, or with two long metal spatulas. If the pizza is a 9-inch *Napoletana*-style pizza, you can serve it whole (usually 1 pizza per person); otherwise, let the pizza cool for a few minutes before slicing and serving.

12. Using an oven brush or a wadded paper towel, sweep off any flour, semolina, or cornmeal from the baking surface onto a baking pan or other receptacle. Allow a few minutes for the oven to recover its heat before loading another pizza.

NAPOLETANA-STYLE PIZZAS

The following recipes are based on the authentic DOC pizzas of Naples and the variations they have inspired, both in Italy and abroad.

PIZZA MARGHERITA

Plain and simple, this is the standard by which every serious *pizzaiolo* is judged. My favorite version of this pizza was easily the one made at the fabled Da Michele in Naples, where the dough was stretched out a couple of inches wider than at the other pizzerias we visited. The result is a thinner, slightly crisper crust, with the puffy *cornicione* I've come to love. If it was easy to do everyone would be doing it, so start with a classic 9-inch version, and as your skill develops, try stretching the dough out to 10 to 12 inches.

Makes two 9-inch pizzas

2 *Napoletana* Pizza Dough balls, 6 ounces each (page 107)

Unbleached all-purpose flour, cornmeal, or semolina flour,
   or a combination, for dusting peel

1/2 cup Crushed Tomato Sauce (page 142)

16 fresh basil leaves

1/4 pound fresh mozzarella cheese, preferably *mozzarella di
   bufala*, sliced into rounds, coarsely shredded, or cut into
   small chunks

2 tablespoons freshly grated Parmigiano-Reggiano, pecorino
   Romano, Asiago, or other dry aged cheese (optional)

1. Place a baking stone on the middle shelf of the oven (unless you know your oven well enough to place it on a different shelf) and preheat on the highest setting for at least 1 hour. Make 1 pizza at a time unless your peel and oven can accommodate both pizzas. Shape the dough ball on a counter as described on page 168, and transfer it to a peel or an inverted sheet pan that has been dusted with flour.

2. Spread $1/4$ cup of the tomato sauce over the surface of the dough, leaving a
   $1/4$-inch border uncovered. Place 4 basil leaves on top of the sauce, one in
   each quadrant. Arrange half of the mozzarella over the top of the sauce and
   basil, and sprinkle with 1 tablespoon of the grated aged cheese.

3. Carefully slide the pizza from the peel onto the baking stone. It should take
   7 to 9 minutes to bake. When it is done, the crust should be puffy and slightly
   charred on the edge and thinner in the center, and the cheese should be fully
   melted and just beginning to brown in spots. The underside of the crust
   should be brown and crisp, not white and soft. If the underside is not ready
   when the top is finished, lower the shelf for the next pizza.

4. Remove the finished pizza from the oven and immediately lay 4 additional
   basil leaves on top, placing one in each quadrant but not directly on top of the
   previous basil leaves. Serve the pizza whole (usually 1 pizza per person), or let
   it cool for about 2 minutes before slicing and serving. Repeat with the
   remaining ingredients to make the second pizza.

PIZZA ALLA MARINARA

The predominant herb in this pizza should be oregano, and the distinguishing characteristic is the absence of cheese, at least of mozzarella cheese. I have had versions that include a sprinkle of a Parmesan-style or other hard grating cheese just prior to baking, which adds a nice flavor. Pizza without cheese is gaining in popularity, but I think it only works if the sauce is vibrant and the crust is superb. If you have All-Purpose *Marinara* Pizza Sauce (page 141) on hand, you can use it here, although I prefer the Crushed Tomato Sauce with this pie.

Makes two 9-inch pizzas

2 *Napoletana* Pizza Dough balls, 6 ounces each (page 107)

Unbleached all-purpose flour, cornmeal, or semolina flour for dusting peel

1 cup Crushed Tomato Sauce (page 142)

4 cloves garlic, slivered or thinly sliced

1/4 cup freshly grated Parmigiano-Reggiano, pecorino Romano, Asiago, or other dry aged cheese (optional)

2 tablespoons extra virgin olive oil

1 teaspoon dried oregano or 2 teaspoons chopped fresh oregano leaves

1. Place a baking stone on the middle shelf of the oven (unless you know your oven well enough to place it on a different shelf) and preheat on the highest setting for at least 1 hour. Make 1 pizza at a time unless your peel and oven can accommodate both pizzas. Shape the dough ball on a counter as described on page 168, and transfer it to a peel or an inverted sheet pan that has been dusted with flour.

2. Spread 1/2 cup of the tomato sauce over the surface of the dough, leaving a 1/4-inch border uncovered. Spread half of the garlic over the sauce, then top with 2 tablespoons of the grated cheese. Drizzle 1 tablespoon of the olive oil over the surface, spiraling it out from the center. Sprinkle half of the oregano evenly over the top.

3. Carefully slide the pizza from the peel onto the baking stone. It should take 7 to 9 minutes to bake. When it is done, the crust should be puffy and slightly charred on the edge and thinner in the center. The underside of the crust should be brown and crisp, not white and soft. If the underside is not ready when the top is finished, lower the shelf for the next pizza.

4. Remove the finished pizza from the oven and serve it whole (usually 1 pizza per person), or let it cool for about 2 minutes before slicing and serving. Repeat with the remaining ingredients to make the second pizza.

Pizza alla Puttanesca **Variation**

It is easy to give a classic *marinara* pizza a *puttanesca* twist. *Puttanesca*—in other words, "prostitute style"—is the name given to a southern Italian spicy tomato sauce for pasta that usually includes capers, olives, chile flakes, and sometimes anchovies. Any combination of these, added either to the sauce or distributed over the top of the pizza before it goes into the oven, will give your pie a memorable zing.

PIZZA QUATTRO STAGIONI

The idea behind the classic "four seasons" pizza is to evoke all of the seasons on a single pie—a form of tribute and thanks for the fruits of the earth enjoyed throughout the year. It makes a striking presentation. There are no rules as to what ingredients should represent each season, or limitations in terms of meats, fish, or vegetables. The following offers options from which you can choose, or you can substitute a favorite topping of your own.

Makes two 9-inch pizzas

3 *Napoletana* Pizza Dough balls, 6 ounces each (page 107)

Unbleached all-purpose flour, cornmeal, or semolina flour for dusting peel

1/2 cup All-Purpose *Marinara* Pizza Sauce (page 143)

3 ounces fresh mozzarella cheese *(fior di latte)*, cut into strips, or full-fat low-moisture mozzarella cheese, shredded

1/4 cup freshly grated Parmigiano-Reggiano, pecorino Romano, Asiago, or other dry aged cheese

SPRING: 8 asparagus tips, or 1/2 cup sliced fresh or marinated artichoke hearts (if fresh, blanch the slices and sauté lightly in olive oil with garlic)

SUMMER: 1 small zucchini or yellow summer squash, cut into 1/4-inch-thick slices and blanched for 1 minute, or 1/2 cup roasted red or yellow bell pepper or pimiento strips

FALL: 10 salt-brined Greek or Italian black olives or 1/2 cup mushrooms, any kind, thinly sliced and lightly sautéed in olive oil

WINTER: 1 potato, peeled, cut into 1/4-inch-thick slices, and blanched for 1 minute; 4 slices salami, each 1/4 inch thick; or 2 thin slices prosciutto or other cured ham

ANY SEASON: 4 anchovy fillets, or 4 peeled shrimp lightly sautéed in olive oil

2 tablespoons extra virgin olive oil

1. Place a baking stone on the middle shelf of the oven (unless you know your oven well enough to place it on a different shelf) and preheat on the highest setting for at least 1 hour. Make 1 pizza at a time unless your peel and oven can accommodate both pizzas. Shape the dough ball on a counter as described on page 168, and transfer it to a peel or an inverted sheet pan that has been dusted with flour. Two of the dough balls are used for making the crusts. Divide the third ball into 4 equal pieces. Lightly flour the counter and your hands. Using your palms and working with 1 dough piece at a time, roll the piece back and forth on the floured surface until it forms a strand about 10 inches long. If it springs back, let it relax for 3 minutes and roll again. Set the 4 strands aside.

2. Spread 1/4 cup of the tomato sauce over the surface of the dough, leaving a 1/4-inch border uncovered. Using 2 dough strands, form a cross on top of the dough, dividing it into equal quadrants; the ends should extend just to the edge, but do not need to be crimped onto it. Distribute half of the mozzarella cheese equally among the quadrants, and then sprinkle 2 tablespoons of the grated aged cheese evenly over the mozzarella. Select 1 topping choice from each season, and place half of it in a quadrant. If using prosciutto for the winter quadrant, ripple the slice rather than laying it flat, and place it under the cheese, rather than on top. If using anchovies, you can place 1/2 anchovy fillet in each quadrant, or 2 fillets in their own quadrant. Drizzle 1 tablespoon of the olive oil over the surface, spiraling it out from the center.

3. Carefully slide the pizza from the peel onto the baking stone. It should take 7 to 9 minutes to bake. When it is done, the crust should be puffy and slightly charred on the edge and thinner in the center. The underside of the crust should be brown and crisp, not white and soft. If the underside is not ready when the top is finished, lower the shelf for the next pizza.

4. Remove the finished pizza from the oven and serve it whole (usually 1 pizza per person), or let it cool for about 2 minutes before slicing and serving. Repeat with the remaining ingredients to make the second pizza.

PIZZA ALLA PUGLIESE

Apulia, which lies across the boot from Naples, has a glorious food tradition that includes pizzas built on the *Napoletana* foundation. The following version gets its distinctive flavor from smoked cheese, such as smoked mozzarella, smoked provolone, or *caciocavallo affumicato*, a hard, smooth cow's milk cheese from southern Italy.

Makes two 9-inch pizzas

1/4 cup extra virgin olive oil

1/2 cup sliced onion, any kind

1/4 teaspoon salt

2 *Napoletana* Pizza Dough balls, 6 ounces each (page 107)

Unbleached all-purpose flour, cornmeal, or semolina flour
   for dusting peel

6 ounces smoked cheese (see recipe introduction), grated
   or shredded

Freshly ground black pepper

1. Place a baking stone on the middle shelf of the oven (unless you know your oven well enough to place it on a different shelf) and preheat on the highest setting for at least 1 hour.

2. While the oven is heating, in a frying pan, heat 2 tablespoons of the olive oil over medium-high heat. Add the onion and sauté for 4 to 5 minutes, or until translucent. Season with the salt, remove from the heat, and let cool.

3. Make 1 pizza at a time unless your peel and oven can accommodate both pizzas. Shape the dough ball on a counter as described on page 168, and transfer it to a peel or an inverted sheet pan that has been dusted with flour.

4. Sprinkle half of the cheese evenly over the surface of the dough. Spread half of the sautéed onion on top. Drizzle 1 tablespoon of the olive oil over the surface, spiraling it out from the center. Sprinkle the top with pepper to taste.

5. Carefully slide the pizza from the peel onto the baking stone. It should take 7 to 9 minutes to bake. When it is done, the crust should be puffy and slightly charred on the edge and thinner in the center. The underside of the crust should be brown and crisp, not white and soft. If the underside is not ready when the top is finished, lower the shelf for the next pizza.

6. Remove the finished pizza from the oven and serve it whole (usually 1 pizza per person), or let it cool for about 2 minutes before slicing and serving. Repeat with the remaining ingredients to make the second pizza.

PIZZA CON ACCIUGHE (WITH ANCHOVIES)

Most *pizzaioli* put the anchovies on top of this classic pizza just before it goes into the oven. Others lay them on top of the finished pizza. However, I am in love with the technique I learned at Santarpio's in Boston, where they turn out a mean neo-Neapolitan anchovy pizza. The *pizzaioli* at Santarpio's put the anchovies under the cheese, where they soften and practically melt into the pie. I prefer low-moisture mozzarella cheese on this pizza, but you can substitute fresh mozzarella *(fior di latte)*.

Makes two 9-inch pizzas

2 *Napoletana* Pizza Dough balls, 6 ounces each (page 107)

Unbleached all-purpose flour, cornmeal, or semolina flour for dusting peel

1/2 cup Crushed Tomato Sauce (page 142)

4 to 6 anchovy fillets

6 ounces full-fat low-moisture mozzarella cheese, coarsely grated

2 cloves garlic, slivered or thinly sliced

2 tablespoons extra virgin olive oil

1/2 teaspoon dried oregano or 1 teaspoon chopped fresh oregano leaves

1. Place a baking stone on the middle shelf of the oven (unless you know your oven well enough to place it on a different shelf) and preheat on the highest setting for at least 1 hour. Make 1 pizza at a time unless your peel and oven can accommodate both pizzas. Shape the dough ball on a counter as described on page 168, and transfer it to a peel or an inverted sheet pan that has been dusted with flour.

2. Spread 1/4 cup of the tomato sauce over the surface of the dough, leaving a 1/4-inch border uncovered. Cut 2 or 3 anchovy fillets into a total of 6 or 9 lengthwise strips. Lay them on the surface of the dough like spokes on a wheel. Cover the surface with half of the cheese, then sprinkle half of the garlic evenly over the top. Drizzle 1 tablespoon of the olive oil over the surface, spiraling it out from the center. Sprinkle half of the oregano over the top.

3. Carefully slide the pizza from the peel onto the baking stone. It should take 7 to 9 minutes to bake. When it is done, the crust should be puffy and slightly charred on the edge and thinner in the center. The underside of the crust should be brown and crisp, not white and soft. If the underside is not ready when the top is finished, lower the shelf for the next pizza.

4. Remove the finished pizza from the oven and serve it whole (usually 1 pizza per person), or let it cool for about 2 minutes before slicing and serving. Repeat with the remaining ingredients to make the second pizza.

PIZZA QUATTRO FORMAGGI

Adding more types of cheese to a pizza does not always improve it. Sometimes the flavors cancel out one another or get muddled. American pizzerias often successfully blend mozzarella and Cheddar-style cheeses to make a tasty and distinctive pizza, but *pizza quattro formaggi* is designed to showcase four cheeses of different characteristics, usually without tomato (though slices of fresh tomato are not out of the question). The classic types are fresh *(fior di latte)* or processed mozzarella; blue-veined cheese, often Gorgonzola; a dry aged cheese like Parmigiano-Reggiano or pecorino Romano; and a fresh, creamy cheese such as *robiola, stracchino, crescenza,* or even mascarpone.

Makes two 9-inch pizzas

2 *Napoletana* Pizza Dough balls, 6 ounces each (page 107)

Unbleached all-purpose flour, cornmeal, or semolina flour for dusting peel

5 ounces fresh or full-fat low-moisture mozzarella cheese, shredded or coarsely grated

3 ounces blue cheese (see recipe introduction)

3 ounces fresh, creamy cheese (see recipe introduction)

2 tablespoons freshly grated dry aged cheese (see recipe introduction)

1. Place a baking stone on the middle shelf of the oven (unless you know your oven well enough to place it on a different shelf) and preheat on the highest setting for at least 1 hour. Make 1 pizza at a time unless your peel and oven can accommodate both pizzas. Shape the dough ball on a counter as described on page 168, and transfer it to a peel or an inverted sheet pan that has been dusted with flour.

2. Sprinkle half of the mozzarella evenly over the surface of the dough. Dot the top evenly with half of the blue cheese and then repeat with half of the creamy cheese.

3. Carefully slide the pizza from the peel onto the baking stone. It should take 7 to 9 minutes to bake. When it is done, the crust should be puffy and slightly charred on the edge and thinner in the center, and the cheese should be bubbling and golden. The underside of the crust should be brown and crisp, not white and soft. If the underside is not ready when the top is finished, lower the shelf for the next pizza.

4. Remove the finished pizza from the oven and sprinkle 1 tablespoon of the grated aged cheese over the top. Serve the pizza whole (usually 1 pizza per person), or let it cool for about 2 minutes before slicing and serving. Repeat with the remaining ingredients to make the second pizza.

PIZZA VESUVIO

This is my version of the wonderful pizza I ate at Antica Pizzeria dell'Arte in Florence. It is expensive to make because of the truffle paste, but it is a great conversation piece when you are throwing a fancy pizza party. Of course, it is a tribute to Vesuvius, the still-active volcano that dominates the Naples horizon but has never actually harmed the city because of favorable Mediterranean winds (nearby Pompeii was not so fortunate). You can buy the truffle paste, either black or white, at a gourmet-products store. It doesn't pack the wallop of freshly grated truffle (which you are free to use if you can afford it), but it still delivers the indescribably complex earthiness of the prized fungus. The best cheese to use for this pizza is true *mozzarella di bufala*. However, fresh cow's milk mozzarella is easier to find and less expensive, and if it is all you have, it will work fine. You can also use full-fat low-moisture mozzarella, but you will need to grate it and spread it in a 4 1/2-inch circle in the center of the dough. The flavor and texture will be markedly different, yet still wonderful, with this type of cheese.

Makes one 9-inch pizza

2 *Napoletana* Pizza Dough balls, 6 ounces each (page 107)

Unbleached all-purpose flour, cornmeal, or semolina flour
  for dusting peel

1/4 cup chopped, peeled tomatoes or quartered cherry
  tomatoes

3 ounces *mozzarella di bufala*

1 heaping tablespoon white or black truffle paste

2 tablespoons extra virgin olive oil

Freshly ground black pepper

1. Place a baking stone on the middle shelf of the oven (unless you know your oven well enough to place it on a different shelf) and preheat on the highest setting for at least 1 hour. Shape 1 dough ball on a counter as described on page 168, and transfer it to a peel or an inverted sheet pan that has been dusted with flour. Divide the second dough ball into 5 equal pieces. Lightly flour the counter and your hands. Using your palms and working with 1

dough piece at a time, roll the piece back and forth on the floured surface until it forms a strand about 9 inches long. If it springs back, let it relax for 3 minutes and roll again. Set the 5 strands aside.

2. Sprinkle the tomato pieces over the surface of the dough. Form the mozzarella into a soft ball, and then flatten it into a thick disk. Place it in the center of the dough. Spread or dollop the truffle paste over the top of the cheese. Drizzle 1 tablespoon of the olive oil over the truffle-topped cheese ball, and then sprinkle the pepper evenly over the pizza.

3. Lay the dough strands on top of the pizza, crossing them so that they divide the pizza into pielike wedges. The ends of the strands should extend just to the edge, but they do not need to be crimped onto it. Brush the remaining 1 tablespoon olive oil over the dough strands.

4. Carefully slide the pizza from the peel onto the baking stone. It should take 12 to 15 minutes to bake. When it is done, the top crust should have just begun turning a light gold and the bottom crust should be crisp and lightly charred.

5. Remove the finished pizza from the oven and let it cool for about 3 minutes before serving. Eat with a knife and fork.

PIZZA CON RUCOLA

One of my favorite pizza garnishes is arugula, known as rocket in England, as *roquette* in France, and as both *rucola* and *arugula* in Italy. Everywhere Susan and I went in Italy we saw beautiful pizzas covered with bright green, shredded leaves of arugula. Sometimes it wilted on the pizza surface and other times it stayed fresh and crisp. As much as I love arugula, I often thought it was added with too heavy a hand. But the flavor of the peppery leaves does grow on you, and by the time we left Italy, I was a full convert. However, I still think it is best when used as a garnish, rather than as a primary topping, and it is especially good sprinkled on top of prosciutto or other cured-meat-topped pizzas fresh out of the oven. The slightly bitter, radishlike flavor of arugula complements the sweet and spicy flavors in other ingredients. In addition to the variations provided below, arugula is also a great complement to toppings like Sautéed Mushrooms (page 152) and White Sauce (page 155).

Makes two 9-inch pizzas

2 *Napoletana* Pizza Dough balls, 6 ounces each (page 107)

Unbleached all-purpose flour, cornmeal, or semolina flour for dusting peel

3 ounces full-fat low-moisture or smoked mozzarella cheese, shredded or coarsely grated

2 tomatoes, cut into 1/4-inch-thick slices, or 12 cherry tomatoes, quartered (optional)

1/4 cup freshly grated Parmigiano-Reggiano, pecorino Romano, Asiago, or other dry aged cheese

5 large arugula leaves, or to taste

1. Place a baking stone on the middle shelf of the oven (unless you know your oven well enough to place it on a different shelf) and preheat on the highest setting for at least 1 hour. Make 1 pizza at a time unless your peel and oven can accommodate both pizzas. Shape the dough ball on a counter as described on page 168, and transfer it to a peel or an inverted sheet pan that has been dusted with flour.

2. Spread half of the mozzarella over the surface of the dough. Distribute half of the tomatoes over the cheese. Sprinkle half of the grated aged cheese over the top.

3. Carefully slide the pizza from the peel onto the baking stone. It should take 7 to 9 minutes to bake. When it is done, the crust should be puffy and slightly charred on the edge and thinner in the center, and the cheese should be golden. The underside of the crust should be brown and crisp, not white and soft. If the underside is not ready when the top is finished, lower the shelf for the next pizza.

4. While the pizza is baking, stack the arugula leaves, roll them up lengthwise, and cut thinly crosswise to create shreds (known as a chiffonade cut). Remove the finished pizza from the oven and immediately sprinkle half of the arugula over the top. Let the pizza cool for about 3 minutes so that the arugula can begin to wilt, then serve it whole (usually 1 pizza per person) or in slices. Repeat with the remaining ingredients to make the second pizza.

Prosciutto Variation

Lay a thin slice of prosciutto on the pizza before it goes in the oven, in which case it will become very crisp, or lay the slice on top of the arugula after the pizza is baked.

Mussel Variation

Just before assembling the pizza, place 8 mussels, well scrubbed, and 1/4 cup water in a saucepan, cover, place over medium heat, and cook for about 3 minutes, or until the mussels open. Remove from the heat and remove the mussels from the pan. When the mussels are cool enough to handle, remove them from their shells, discarding any that failed to open. Reserve half of the shells for serving. In a small frying pan, heat 2 tablespoons olive oil over low heat. Add 1 clove garlic, minced, and then stir in the mussels (the oil should be warm, not hot) until well coated with the oil and garlic. Season with a dusting of freshly ground black pepper and a touch of coarse sea salt or kosher salt. When the finished pizza is removed from the oven, garnish it lightly with shredded arugula (or basil, if you prefer). Place the 8 reserved shells on the pizza, and put 1 mussel in each shell. If any oil remains in the frying pan, pour it over the pizza. Clams or a combination of mussels and clams can be prepared the same way.

PIZZA ROSA AL BIANCO

This is my take on the pizza that Chris Bianco said is the metaphor within the metaphor, the pizza that defines him more than any other. Though this is technically a white pizza, Chris named it Rosa for the red torpedo onions on top, with a nod to the fresh rosemary. It is not unlike the *Pizza alla Pugliese* on page 177, with its use of cheese and onions, but Chris takes it in a slightly different direction. The strength of the Parmigiano-Reggiano and the other intensely flavored ingredients speak directly to the intensity of Chris's personality and commitment to his craft.

If you do not have pistachio nuts, you can substitute 1/4 cup pine nuts. You can also use another type of grated aged cheese, such as pecorino Romano, Asiago, or even dry Jack. Should you do that, I know what Chris would say, "You could do that, and it still would taste good, but then it would no longer be the metaphor of me." Perhaps it will be the metaphor of you!

Makes two 9-inch pizzas

2 *Napoletana* Pizza Dough balls, 6 ounces each (page 107)

Unbleached all-purpose flour, cornmeal, or semolina flour for dusting peel

1 red torpedo onion, thinly sliced

1 1/2 cups freshly grated Parmigiano-Reggiano cheese

24 pistachio nuts, very coarsely chopped

2 teaspoons fresh rosemary leaves

2 tablespoons extra virgin olive oil

1. Place a baking stone on the middle shelf of the oven (unless you know your oven well enough to place it on a different shelf) and preheat on the highest setting for at least 1 hour. Make 1 pizza at a time unless your peel and oven can accommodate both pizzas. Shape the dough ball on a counter as described on page 168, and transfer it to a peel or an inverted sheet pan that has been dusted with flour.

2. Spread half of the onion slices over the surface of the dough. Sprinkle half of the cheese over the onion slices, then scatter half each of the nuts and the

rosemary over the top. Drizzle 1 tablespoon of the olive oil over the top, spiraling it out from the center.

3. Carefully slide the pizza from the peel onto the baking stone. It should take 7 to 9 minutes to bake. When it is done, the crust should be puffy and slightly charred on the edge and thinner in the center, and the cheese should be golden. The underside of the crust should be brown and crisp, not white and soft. If the underside is not ready when the top is finished, lower the shelf for the next pizza.

4. Remove the finished pizza from the oven and serve it whole (usually 1 pizza per person), or let it cool for about 2 minutes before slicing and serving. Repeat with the remaining ingredients to make the second pizza.

FIRST-GENERATION
NEO-NEAPOLITAN PIZZA

There are two archetypes in the first-generation family of neo-Neapolitan pizzas: regular sauce and mozzarella (sauce and mutz from this point on) and white pizza with clams. Of course, many other pizzas, many topping variations, and many types of white pizza without clams are out there, but these are the two without which the world would be a less joyful place. Every red pizza, no matter the toppings on it, is pretty much a descendant of the sauce and mutz, so let's start with it.

SAUCE AND MUTZ PIZZA

Here is a recipe for making a sauce and mutz pizza in the Sally's, Frank Pepe's, Totonno's, Tacconelli's, John's, Grimaldi's, and DiFara's tradition. A selection of variations follow.

There are two philosophies regarding the order in which the toppings are applied. While most pizzerias lay down the sauce first and then the cheese, as do I, there is good reason (and some precedent) to reverse that order and lay all the mozzarella down first, then carefully ladle on the sauce and top with a small sprinkle of grated aged cheese. When the mutz goes down first, it will melt but not caramelize, and the sauce, because it is exposed to the hot air, will evaporate somewhat and intensify. The result is almost lavalike, with an intense tomato flavor burst and nice molten cheese underneath. When the sauce goes down first and the cheese is placed on top, the mutz caramelizes to a rich gold and its flavor intensifies. It will not be as molten as when it is underneath, however. Each method makes a delicious pizza, so you will want to try them both and decide which works best in your oven and to your taste.

Makes two 12-inch pizzas

2 Neo-Neapolitan Pizza Dough balls, 10 ounces each
   (page 112)

Unbleached high-gluten or bread flour, cornmeal, or semolina
   flour for dusting peel

6 ounces full-fat low-moisture mozzarella cheese, coarsely
   grated or shredded

1/4 cup freshly grated Parmigiano-Reggiano, pecorino
   Romano, Asiago, or other dry aged cheese

2 ounces fresh mozzarella cheese *(fior di latte)*, sliced or
   coarsely shredded

1 cup Crushed Tomato Sauce (page 142)

1 teaspoon dried or chopped fresh oregano

8 fresh basil leaves

1. Place a baking stone on the middle shelf of the oven (unless you know your oven well enough to place it on a different shelf) and preheat on the highest setting for at least 1 hour. Make 1 pizza at a time unless your peel and oven can accommodate both pizzas. Shape the dough ball using the toss-and-spin method on page 167, stretching it to a diameter of about 12 inches. The dough should be very thin, about 1/8 inch thick, nearly translucent, and slightly thicker toward the edge. Transfer the dough to a peel or an inverted sheet pan that has been dusted with flour.

2. In a bowl, stir together the 3 cheeses. Spread 1/2 cup of the tomato sauce over the surface of the dough, leaving a 1/4-inch border uncovered. Distribute half of the cheese blend evenly over the pizza. Sprinkle half of the oregano over the cheese.

3. Carefully slide the pizza from the peel onto the baking stone. It should take 10 to 12 minutes to bake. When it is done, the crust should be crisp and slightly charred on the edge and the cheese should be fully melted and just beginning to caramelize to a rich gold. The underside of the crust should be brown and crisp, not white and soft. If the underside is not ready when the top is finished, lower the shelf for the next pizza.

4. While the pizza is baking, stack the basil leaves, roll them up lengthwise, and cut thinly crosswise to create shreds (known as a chiffonade cut). Remove the finished pizza from the oven and immediately sprinkle half of the basil over the top. Let the pizza cool for about 3 minutes before slicing and serving. Repeat with the remaining ingredients to make the second pizza.

Sauce and Mutz Garnish and Topping Options

Pizzerias have come up with dozens of ways to embellish a sauce and mutz pizza. Here are some ideas and tips to make classic first-generation neo-Neapolitan pizza variations:

FRESH GREENS: Bright greens such as arugula, Italian parsley, and spinach can be substituted for the fresh basil; use the same chiffonade cut described for the basil.

ANCHOVIES: Place anchovy fillets under the cheese, not on top. The flavor will melt into the pizza, and they will have a creamy texture, rather than be tough and chewy.

PEPPERONI AND OTHER CURED MEATS: If you like your pizza oily, slice the pepperoni or other meat and place the pieces on top. But to intensify flavor and reduce greasiness, grill, panfry, or boil the slices in advance to melt out much of the fat. The meat will still crisp up on top of the pizza, but it will not release any fat. If you don't want it to be crisp, bake it under the mutz.

VEGETABLES: Lightly sauté bell peppers, onions, mushrooms, and other vegetables before you place them on top of the pizza. This will keep them from burning and being overly chewy. Raw vegetables should go under the mutz to prevent burning. Roasted Eggplant, Tomato, and Lemon Topping (page 159) and Sweet-and-Sour Onion Marmalade (page 151) are two good premade vegetable additions that can go on the top.

GARLIC OIL: Using garlic-infused oil imparts more garlic taste than putting raw garlic on the pizza before it bakes. You can either use the oil left over from making caramelized garlic (page 149), or press or mince 12 garlic cloves and add them to 1/2 cup extra virgin olive oil that has been heated on the stove just to warm it up a bit, 100°F to 110°F. Cover and leave at room temperature for at least 1 hour to steep before using. Strain out some of the garlic from the oil, and sprinkle the strained garlic either under or over the mutz. Save the remaining garlic and oil to drizzle over the pizza after it comes out of the oven. Refrigerate any unused garlic oil; it will keep for up to 1 week. Raw garlic carries bacteria, which can lead to the growth of toxins if left out of the refrigerator for long stretches. Rather than replenish your oil when it runs low, make a fresh batch.

CARAMELIZED GARLIC CLOVES OR PURÉE (page 149): Place the whole cloves under the mutz, not on top. Puréed caramelized garlic can go on top of or under the cheese.

SEAFOOD: Toss uncooked shrimp, clams, and other seafood in Herb Oil (page 147) and bake them on top. You can also season cooked shrimp with the oil, but slip them under the mutz.

FRESH TOMATOES: During tomato season, slice your best-tasting variety about 1/4 inch thick, toss the slices in Herb Oil (page 147), and lay them on top of the pizza. They will have more eye appeal if garnished with chiffonade-cut fresh basil just after the pizza comes out of the oven.

WHITE CLAM PIZZA

Frank Pepe Pizzeria Napoletana (aka Pepe's) in New Haven is generally credited with inventing this pizza. Pepe's clam topping is a family secret, and I never attempt to pry a recipe away from a reluctant creator, although I do try my best to emulate. The challenge is to see if I can do it as well. Here's how I make my clam pizza, in tribute to the flawless version made at Pepe's.

When making this pizza, look for freshly shucked medium-sized whole clams, such as manila, cherrystone, or littlenecks. You can also shuck them yourself or steam them open. An easier method, however, is to use either canned whole baby clams or another canned product called cocktail clams, which are large pieces of tender clam meat that can be used whole or cut in half. (With these canned products, just drain the clams well and save the juice for soups or to add to tomato-juice cocktails. I like to drink it with a shot of Tabasco.) I do not suggest using chopped clams, even fresh ones, unless that is all you can find, as they tend to toughen during the bake. They are mainly valve meat, and what you want is belly meat.

Makes one 12-inch pizza

1/4 cup Herb Oil (page 147)

1 tablespoon freshly squeezed lemon juice

5 ounces clam meat (see recipe introduction)

1 Neo-Neapolitan Pizza Dough ball, 10 ounces (page 112)

Unbleached high-gluten or bread flour, cornmeal, or semolina
   flour for dusting peel

1/2 cup shredded full-fat low-moisture mozzarella cheese

1/2 cup freshly grated Parmigiano-Regianno, pecorino
   Romano, Asiago, or other dry aged cheese

1/8 teaspoon salt, or to taste

1/8 teaspoon freshly ground black pepper, or to taste

2 tablespoons chopped fresh flat-leaf parsley

1. Place a baking stone on the middle shelf of the oven (unless you know your oven well enough to place it on a different shelf) and preheat on the highest setting for at least 1 hour. While the oven is preheating, in a bowl, combine the Herb Oil and lemon juice and stir in the clam meat to coat. Cover and marinate in the refrigerator for 1 hour.

2. Shape the dough ball using the toss-and-spin method on page 167, stretching it to a diameter of about 12 inches. The dough should be very thin, about 1/8 inch thick, nearly translucent, and slightly thicker toward the edge. Transfer the dough to a peel or an inverted sheet pan that has been dusted with flour.

3. In a bowl, stir together the 2 cheeses. Distribute the cheese blend evenly over the surface of the dough. Spread the clam and oil mixture evenly over the cheese. Sprinkle the surface evenly with the salt and pepper.

4. Carefully slide the pizza from the peel onto the baking stone. It should take 10 to 12 minutes to bake. When it is done, the crust should be crisp and slightly charred on the edge and the cheese should be fully melted and just beginning to caramelize to a rich gold. The underside of the crust should be brown and crisp, not white and soft. If the underside is not ready when the top is finished, lower the shelf for the next pizza.

5. Remove the finished pizza from the oven and immediately sprinkle the parsley over the top. Let the pizza cool for about 3 minutes before slicing and serving.

Seafood Variations

You can make other seafood pizzas in the same way. Use raw squid, shrimp, bay scallops (whole), or sea scallops (cut in half), or any combination.

SECOND-GENERATION
NEO-NEAPOLITAN PIZZA

Unless you grew up in one of the major first-generation coal-oven pizza meccas
like New York City or New Haven, your frame of reference for American pie is
probably what I call second generation neo-Neapolitan pizza, whether from one of
the many chains or independent by-the-slice pizzerias across the country. This is
also the style through which pizza has achieved worldwide, cross-cultural popularity.
These pizzas aren't always baked in a wood- or coal-fired oven; the doughs are
often tenderized and enriched to accommodate our high-protein flours; and they
are sometimes even fermented by sourdough wild yeast. But regardless of the
mechanics, these pizzas satisfy the masses simply by being crust with some variation
of sauce and/or cheese on top. As with any food products, there are some pizzerias
that achieve a higher degree of excellence than others, but when all is said and
done, this is the category that established pizza as the new American pie.

NEW YORK–STYLE SAUCE
AND CHEESE PIZZA

Any of the neo-Neapolitan toppings apply to this style of pizza, which is the
foundation for the pizza-by-the slice pizzas now found across the country.
One distinguishing characteristic is that the dough is not stretched quite as
thin as the first-generation neo-Neapolitan pizzas, and it is usually slightly
underbaked when it first emerges from the oven, causing the slices to sag at
the tip, or nose. The nose is then either flipped back onto the top of the slice,
or two slices are stacked on top of each other and then folded down the middle to make something like a pizza sandwich. (Remember when Tony Manero,
aka John Travolta, chomped away on his double-decker in an early scene in
Saturday Night Fever?). To crisp the crust, you can put a cooled slice back into
the oven for a few minutes, just until the cheese melts again.

The dough balls for this pizza are scaled to about 12 ounces, slightly bigger than in the other dough recipes. They are stretched to the same diameter
as the other neo-Neapolitans, however, to create the slightly thicker crust that
is traditional for the style.

Makes one 12-inch pizza

1 New York–Style Pizza Dough ball, 12 ounces (page 114)

Unbleached high-gluten or bread flour, cornmeal, or semolina
flour for dusting peel

1/4 pound full-fat or low-fat low-moisture mozzarella cheese,
coarsely grated

1/4 cup freshly grated Parmigiano-Reggiano, pecorino
Romano, Asiago, or other dry aged cheese

1/4 cup coarsely grated medium-sharp Cheddar or
provolone cheese

1/4 teaspoon dried oregano or 1/2 teaspoon chopped fresh
oregano leaves

1/4 teaspoon dried basil or 1/2 teaspoon chopped fresh
basil leaves

1/8 teaspoon freshly ground black pepper

1/2 teaspoon granulated garlic powder (optional)

2/3 cup All-Purpose *Marinara* Pizza Sauce (page 143)

1. Place a baking stone on the middle shelf of the oven (unless you know your
   oven well enough to place it on a different shelf) and preheat on the highest
   setting for at least 1 hour. Shape the dough ball using the toss-and-spin method
   on page 167, stretching it to a diameter of about 12 inches. The dough should
   be about 1/4 inch thick and slightly thicker toward the edge. Transfer the dough
   to a peel or an inverted sheet pan that has been dusted with flour.

2. In a bowl, stir together the 3 cheeses, oregano, basil, pepper, and garlic powder.
   Spread the tomato sauce evenly over the surface of the dough, leaving a 1/4-inch
   border uncovered. Spread the cheese mixture evenly over the pizza.

3. Carefully slide the pizza from the peel onto the baking stone. It should take
   about 12 minutes to bake. When it is done, the crust should be crisp and
   slightly charred on the edge and the cheese should be fully melted and just
   beginning to caramelize to a rich gold. The underside of the crust should be
   brown and crisp, not white and soft.

5. Remove the finished pizza from the oven and let it cool for about 3 minutes
   before slicing and serving. If you want a "snappier" crust, let the pizza cool
   completely, then return individual slices to the hot oven for recrisping.

NEW YORK–STYLE WHITE PIZZA

This is my version of a white pizza I had at Ray's in New York City (yes, on Prince Street, not any of the other Ray's). It uses a white sauce instead of tomato sauce, and is generously topped with seasoned ricotta cheese. For a more adventurous version, substitute an equal amount of any pesto (pages 144 and 145) for the ricotta cheese, or add streaks of pesto, to taste, on top of the ricotta topping.

Makes one 12-inch pizza

1 New York–Style Pizza Dough ball, 12 ounces (page 114)

Unbleached high-gluten or bread flour, cornmeal, or semolina
    flour for dusting peel

1 1/2 cups ricotta cheese

1/4 teaspoon salt

1/4 teaspoon dried or chopped fresh thyme

1/8 teaspoon coarsely ground black pepper

1/2 cup White Sauce (page 155)

1 tablespoon chopped fresh flat-leaf parsley

1. Place a baking stone on the middle shelf of the oven (unless you know your oven well enough to place it on a different shelf) and preheat on the highest setting for at least 1 hour. Shape the dough ball using the toss-and-spin method on page 167, stretching it to a diameter of about 12 inches. The dough should be about 1/4 inch thick and slightly thicker toward the edge. Transfer the dough to a peel or an inverted sheet pan that has been dusted with flour.

2. In a bowl, stir together the ricotta, salt, thyme, and pepper. Spread the White Sauce over the surface of the dough, leaving a 1/4-inch border uncovered. Spread the ricotta mixture evenly over the White Sauce.

3. Carefully slide the pizza from the peel onto the baking stone. It should take about 12 minutes to bake. When it is done, the crust should be crisp and slightly charred on the edge and the cheese should be bubbling and just beginning to caramelize. The underside of the crust should be brown and crisp, not white and soft.

4. Remove the finished pizza from the oven and garnish it immediately with the parsley. Let the pizza cool for about 3 minutes before slicing and serving. If you want a "snappier" crust, let the pizza cool completely, then return individual slices to the hot oven for recrisping.

PEPPERONI *PIZZA AMERICANA*

This recipe brings together the elements of the classic Saturday night home-delivered pizza in a different, yet familiar, way. There are now so many creative pizza variations available at any neighborhood pizzeria or from the freezer section of any supermarket that we have pretty much seen it all. Yet pepperoni still wins the pizza-topping popularity contests. Just as popular is a crust made from the classic *Americana* dough. Here, these two time-honored stars are given center stage, but the pepperoni is presented in a new way. Instead of slicing the pepperoni into thin disks, as most pizzerias do, I cut matchstick-sized strips. The thicker cut, along with the precooking step, brings out more flavor.

There are many types of Italian salami that are as good as or superior to pepperoni (see page 166); feel free to substitute one of them, the spicier and more garlicky the better.

Makes two 10- to 12-inch pizzas

1 tablespoon olive oil

6 ounces pepperoni or favorite Italian salami, cut into matchstick strips

4 cloves garlic, slivered

2 *Americana* Pizza Dough balls, 10 ounces each (page 116)

Unbleached high-gluten or bread flour, cornmeal, or semolina flour for dusting peel

1 cup coarsely shredded full-fat low-moisture mozzarella or Monterey Jack cheese

1/2 cup coarsely shredded medium-sharp Cheddar, provolone, Swiss, or Gouda cheese

1/2 cup freshly grated Parmigiano-Reggiano, pecorino Romano, Asiago, or other dry aged cheese

20 fresh basil leaves

3/4 cup All-Purpose *Marinara* Pizza Sauce (page 143)

1. Place a baking stone on the middle shelf of the oven (unless you know your oven well enough to place it on a different shelf) and preheat on the highest setting for at least 1 hour.

2. While the oven is heating, in a frying pan, combine the olive oil and pepperoni pieces over medium heat and sauté for 4 to 5 minutes, or just until the pepperoni begins to crisp up. Add the garlic and cook for another 2 minutes, or until softened but not browned. Remove from the heat and pour the contents of the pan into a sieve or colander resting over a bowl. Set the pepperoni and garlic mixture aside. You can stir the oil collected in the bowl into the tomato sauce for additional flavor, or you can discard it.

3. Make 1 pizza at a time unless your peel and oven can accommodate both pizzas. Shape the dough ball using the toss-and-spin method on page 167, stretching it to a diameter of 10 or 12 inches and slightly thicker toward the edge. A 12-inch diameter yields a thinner, crispier crust, while a 10-inch diameter is a little thicker and more breadlike. The choice is yours. Transfer the dough to a peel or an inverted sheet pan that has been dusted with flour.

4. In a bowl, stir together the 3 cheeses. Stack 5 of the basil leaves, roll them up lengthwise, and cut thinly crosswise to create shreds (known as a chiffonade cut). Stir the basil shreds into the cheese mixture. Spread half of the sauce over the surface of the dough, leaving a 1/4-inch border uncovered. Scatter half of the crisped pepperoni strips evenly over the surface. Then distribute half of the cheese mixture over the pepperoni, covering the surface evenly.

5. Carefully slide the pizza from the peel onto the baking stone. It should take 10 to 12 minutes to bake. When it is done, the crust should be crisp and slightly charred on the edge and the cheese should be fully melted and just beginning to caramelize to a rich gold. The underside of the crust should be brown and crisp, not white and soft. If the underside is not ready when the top is finished, lower the shelf for the next pizza.

6. While the pizza is baking, stack 5 more basil leaves and cut them in the same manner. Remove the finished pizza from the oven and immediately sprinkle the basil over the top. Let the pizza cool for about 3 minutes before slicing and serving. Repeat with the remaining ingredients to make the second pizza.

THREE CHEESE PIZZA WITH ROASTED EGGPLANT, TOMATO, AND LEMON

A sourdough crust has its own charm and, for all practical purposes, it can be made with any of the topping variations found on other pizzas. That said, the Cheese Board in Berkeley, California, has sourdough pizza down to an art form, and the topping style there is very specific—always vegetarian, unsauced, and with an emphasis on the bold flavors of the cheeses they use. The following is my own version of a Berkeley-style sourdough pizza, inspired by the radical creativity I found on Shattuck Avenue during my visits to the Cheese Board. Use it as a springboard to create your own variations.

Makes two 10-inch pizzas

2 Sourdough Pizza Dough balls, 10 ounces each (page 122)

Unbleached high-gluten or bread flour, cornmeal, or semolina flour for dusting peel

1 cup shredded Gruyère, Gouda, Bel Paese, or other favorite good melting cheese

2 cups Roasted Eggplant, Tomato, and Lemon Topping (page 159)

1/2 cup crumbled feta cheese

1/4 cup freshly grated Parmigiano-Reggiano, pecorino Romano, Asiago, or other dry aged cheese

1. Place a baking stone on the middle shelf of the oven (unless you know your oven well enough to place it on a different shelf) and preheat on the highest setting for at least 1 hour. Make 1 pizza at a time unless your peel and oven can accommodate both pizzas. Shape each dough ball using the toss-and-spin method on page 167, stretching it to a diameter of about 10 inches. If the dough begins to resist extension and springs back, lay it on a lightly floured counter, cover it with a kitchen towel or plastic wrap, and move on to the other ball; after a 5-minute rest, the dough should be relaxed enough to continue shaping. Each disk should be about 10 inches in diameter and 1/4 inch thick. Transfer one to a peel or an inverted sheet pan that has been dusted with flour.

2. Distribute half of the shredded cheese over the surface of the dough. Spread half of the Roasted Eggplant, Tomato, and Lemon topping over the pizza. Sprinkle half each of the feta and the grated aged cheese over the top.

3. Carefully slide the pizza from the peel onto the baking stone. It should take 9 to 11 minutes to bake. When it is done, the crust should be puffy and slightly charred on the edge and thinner in the center, the cheese will be bubbling, and the other ingredients will be golden brown. The underside of the crust should be brown and crisp, not white and soft. If the underside is not ready when the top is finished, lower the shelf for the next pizza.

4. Remove the finished pizza from the oven and let it cool for about 3 minutes before slicing and serving. Repeat with the remaining ingredients to make the second pizza.

THIRD-GENERATION NEO-NEAPOLITAN PIZZA

The *pogacha* I discovered in Bellevue, Washington, which its makers described as a Croatian pizza, was actually a creative Pacific Northwest version of what people in most of the rest of the country call "California pizza." In other words, when the pizzas get fancy, when the toppings take a bit of advance preparation, even when you put a Croatian name to it, California gets the credit or the blame. Whether deserved or not, *California-style* has become the common term for the third generation of neo-Neapolitan pizza in America. While many purists think this genre is a little over the top, it provides a framework and precedent for letting our imaginations run free. When the principles of balance, unity, focus, and flow are honored, you will discover California-style pizza flavors that are quite extraordinary.

The following recipes are some of my own attempts to break into the realm of the extraordinary. They are inspired by visits to the newest generation of gourmet pizzerias around the country and, of course, in California. I am including only a handful of topping ideas, ones that I particularly like, in the hope that they will give you ideas and inspiration for creating your own California pizzas. If you find that you like this push-the-envelope approach to pizza making, I recommend *The California Pizza Kitchen Cookbook*, by Larry Flax and Rick Rosenfield, as well as the books of James McNair and Wolfgang Puck.

Even though I am calling these pizzas third generation neo-Neapolitan, which means that you can make them with any type of dough, I believe that the *Napoletana* dough, made with a little whole-grain flour, is the best choice, albeit with two exceptions, my smoked salmon and Greek salad pizzas. This use represents the neo-Neapolitan concept coming full circle, back to its *Napoletana* roots, yet with a distinctly American twist. If, however, you prefer the flavor, texture, or ease of handling of one of the other doughs, use it instead.

If you decide to create your own toppings for a *Napoletana* crust, remember that the dough can be tricky to handle because of the low gluten content, so it is important to limit the quantity of toppings. In other words, the less-is-more rule applies. Use ingredient components that have great flavor bursts and deliver them on a crust that makes the entire experience truly memorable. That, in a nutshell, is the essence of California-style gourmet pizza.

CANDIED FIGS, PECANS, ANDOUILLE, AND GOAT CHEESE PIZZA

Makes two 9-inch pizzas

1/2 cup water

1/2 cup sugar

8 ripe figs, quartered through stem end

1/2 cup pecan or walnut halves

3 tablespoons olive or vegetable oil

1/2 pound andouille sausage or any other favorite smoked
   sausage, cut into 1/4-inch-thick slices

2 *Napoletana* Pizza Dough balls made with whole-grain
   variation, 6 ounces each (page 109)

Unbleached all-purpose flour, cornmeal, or semolina flour for
   dusting peel

1/4 pound fresh goat cheese, crumbled

Salt and freshly ground black pepper

1. Place a baking stone on the middle shelf of the oven (unless you know your
   oven well enough to place it on a different shelf) and preheat on the highest
   setting for at least 1 hour.

2. While the oven is heating, in a saucepan, bring the water and sugar to a boil.
   Lower the heat to a simmer and cook for about 3 minutes, or until the liquid
   is reduced to a medium-thick syrupy consistency. Remove from the heat and
   drop in the figs and the pecans. Toss to coat with the syrup and set aside to
   cool completely.

3. In a frying pan, heat 1 tablespoon of the oil over medium heat. Add the
   sausage slices and sauté for about 5 minutes, or until the slices begin to release
   their fat and just begin to brown or crisp on the edges. Using a slotted spoon,
   transfer the sausage slices to a paper towel to drain.

4. Make 1 pizza at a time unless your peel and oven can accommodate both pizzas. Shape the dough ball on a counter as described on page 168, and transfer it to a peel or an inverted sheet pan that has been dusted with flour.

5. Gently brush the surface of the dough with 1 tablespoon of the olive oil. Distribute half of the goat cheese evenly over the surface. Top evenly with half of the sausage slices. Then spread half of the fig-pecan mixture over the top.

6. Carefully slide the pizza from the peel onto the baking stone. It should take 7 to 9 minutes to bake. When it is done, the crust should be puffy and slightly charred on the edge and thinner in the center, the cheese will be bubbling, and the other ingredients will be golden brown. The underside of the crust should be brown and crisp, not white and soft. If the underside is not ready when the top is finished, lower the shelf for the next pizza.

7. Remove the finished pizza from the oven and season to taste with salt and pepper. Serve the pizza whole (usually 1 pizza per person), or let it cool for about 2 minutes before slicing and serving. Repeat with the remaining ingredients to make the second pizza.

ONION MARMALADE, WALNUTS, AND BLUE CHEESE PIZZA

Makes two 9-inch pizzas

2 *Napoletana* Pizza Dough balls made with whole-grain variation, 6 ounces each (page 109)

Unbleached all-purpose flour, cornmeal, or semolina flour for dusting peel

1 cup Sweet-and-Sour Onion Marmalade (page 151)

3/4 cup coarsely chopped walnuts

1/4 pound Danish blue or other firm blue cheese, crumbled

1. Place a baking stone on the middle shelf of the oven (unless you know your oven well enough to place it on a different shelf) and preheat on the highest setting for at least 1 hour. Make 1 pizza at a time unless your peel and oven can accommodate both pizzas. Shape the dough ball on a counter as described on page 168, and transfer it to a peel or an inverted sheet pan that has been dusted with flour.

2. Spread half of the onion marmalade over the surface of the dough. Top evenly with half of the walnuts and then half of the blue cheese.

3. Carefully slide the pizza from the peel onto the baking stone. It should take 7 to 9 minutes to bake. When it is done, the crust should be puffy and slightly charred on the edge and thinner in the center, and the cheese will be melted but not caramelized. The underside of the crust should be brown and crisp, not white and soft. If the underside is not ready when the top is finished, lower the shelf for the next pizza.

4. Remove the finished pizza from the oven and serve it whole (usually 1 pizza per person), or let it cool for about 2 minutes before slicing and serving. Repeat with the remaining ingredients to make the second pizza.

SMOKED EGGPLANT PIZZA

Makes two 9-inch pizzas

2 *Napoletana* Pizza Dough balls made with whole-grain
  variation, 6 ounces each (page 109)

Unbleached all-purpose flour, cornmeal, or semolina flour for
  dusting peel

1/2 cup Smoked Eggplant Purée (page 150) or store-bought
  baba ghanouj or eggplant salad

1 cup freshly grated Parmigiano-Reggiano, pecorino Romano,
  Asiago, or other dry aged cheese

2 plum tomatoes, cut into 1/4-inch-thick slices

1/4 cup Herb Oil (page 147)

1. Place a baking stone on the middle shelf of the oven (unless you know your
   oven well enough to place it on a different shelf) and preheat on the highest
   setting for at least 1 hour. Make 1 pizza at a time unless your peel and oven
   can accommodate both pizzas. Shape the dough ball on a counter as described
   on page 168, and transfer it to a peel or an inverted sheet pan that has been
   dusted with flour.

2. Spread 1/4 cup of the eggplant purée over the surface of the dough, leaving a
   1/4-inch border uncovered. Sprinkle half of the grated cheese over the eggplant.
   Dip the slices from 1 tomato into the Herb Oil and fan them over the surface
   of the pizza.

3. Carefully slide the pizza from the peel onto the baking stone. It should take
   7 to 9 minutes to bake. When it is done, the crust should be puffy and slightly
   charred on the edge and thinner in the center, and the cheese will be golden
   brown. The underside of the crust should be brown and crisp, not white and
   soft. If the underside is not ready when the top is finished, lower the shelf for
   the next pizza.

4. Remove the finished pizza from the oven and drizzle some of the Herb Oil
   over the surface, spiraling it out from the center. Serve the pizza whole (usually
   1 pizza per person), or let it cool for about 2 minutes before slicing and serving. Repeat with the remaining ingredients to make the second pizza.

CREAM CHEESE AND CRAB PIZZA

Makes two 9-inch pizzas

2 *Napoletana* Pizza Dough balls made with whole-grain
variation, 6 ounces each (page 109)

Unbleached all-purpose flour, cornmeal, or semolina flour for
dusting peel

1 cup Crab and Cream Cheese Topping (page 156)

2 tablespoons capers

1 onion, any kind, cut into thin strips

Tabasco or other hot-pepper sauce

8 fresh chives, snipped with scissors into small bits

1. Place a baking stone on the middle shelf of the oven (unless you know your
   oven well enough to place it on a different shelf) and preheat on the highest
   setting for at least 1 hour. Make 1 pizza at a time unless your peel and oven
   can accommodate both pizzas. Shape the dough ball on a counter as described
   on page 168, and transfer it to a peel or an inverted sheet pan that has been
   dusted with flour.

2. Spread 1/2 cup of the crab topping over the surface of the dough. Distribute
   1 tablespoon of the capers evenly over the surface. Top with half of the onion
   strips.

3. Carefully slide the pizza from the peel onto the baking stone. It should take
   7 to 9 minutes to bake. When it is done, the crust should be puffy and
   slightly charred on the edge and thinner in the center, and the topping will be
   bubbling and molten. The underside of the crust should be brown and crisp,
   not white and soft. If the underside is not ready when the top is finished,
   lower the shelf for the next pizza.

4. Remove the finished pizza from the oven and immediately sprinkle it with a
   few drops of hot sauce to taste and half of the chives. Serve the pizza whole
   (usually 1 pizza per person), or let it cool for about 2 minutes before slicing
   and serving. Repeat with the remaining ingredients to make the second pizza.

SMOKED SALMON, DILL SAUCE, AND ONION PIZZA

Makes two 12-inch pizzas

2 New York-Style Pizza Dough balls, 12 ounces each
  (page 114)

Unbleached high-gluten or bread flour, cornmeal, or semolina
  flour for dusting peel

2 tablespoons olive oil

1/2 cup Dill and Chive Sauce (page 157)

1 Vidalia, Walla Walla, Maui, or other sweet onion, cut into
  thin strips

2 tomatoes, thinly sliced

1/4 pound smoked salmon, thinly sliced

2 lemons, each cut into 7 wedges

1/4 teaspoon freshly ground black pepper, or to taste

Dill sprigs

1. Place a baking stone on the middle shelf of the oven (unless you know your
   oven well enough to place it on a different shelf) and preheat on the highest
   setting for at least 1 hour. Make 1 pizza at a time unless your peel and oven
   can accommodate both pizzas. Shape the dough ball using the toss-and-spin
   method on page 168, stretching it to a diameter of about 12 inches. The
   dough should be about 1/4 inch thick and slightly thicker toward the edge.
   Transfer the dough to a peel or an inverted sheet pan that has been dusted
   with flour.

2. Gently brush 1 tablespoon of the olive oil over the surface of the dough, and
   then prick the surface all over with a fork. Carefully slide the dough from the
   peel onto the baking stone and bake for 6 to 8 minutes. If it puffs up while
   baking, quickly pop the bubbles with a fork to deflate. When the crust is
   golden brown, remove it from the oven.

3. While the crust is still hot, spread half of the dill sauce over the surface. Cover
   with half of the onion strips, and then fan the slices from 1 tomato over the

onion strips. Cover the tomatoes with half of the smoked salmon slices. Squeeze 1 wedge of lemon evenly over the top. Sprinkle the top with $1/8$ teaspoon of the pepper, or to taste. Garnish with a few dill sprigs.

4. Cut the pizza into 6 slices. Place 1 lemon wedge on each slice, and serve immediately while the crust is still warm. Repeat with the remaining ingredients to make the second pizza.

FOLDED GREEK SALAD PIZZA

Makes 2 folded pizzas

GREEK DRESSING

$1/2$ cup extra virgin olive oil

3 tablespoons red wine vinegar

3 tablespoons freshly squeezed lemon juice

7 Greek olives, pitted

2 tablespoons brine from the Greek olives

2 cloves garlic

$1/3$ cup crumbled feta cheese

1 scallion, coarsely chopped

$1/8$ teaspoon freshly ground black pepper

$1/8$ teaspoon dried oregano

2 Neo-Neapolitan Pizza Dough balls, 10 ounces each (page 112)

Unbleached high-gluten or bread flour, cornmeal, or semolina flour for dusting peel

1 cup shredded or coarsely grated full-fat or low-fat low-moisture mozzarella cheese

TOSSED SALAD

1 head iceberg or green leaf lettuce, torn or cut into small pieces

1 English or other sweet cucumber, peeled and cut into $1/2$-inch cubes

2 tomatoes, chopped into small pieces

1 small Vidalia, Walla Walla, Maui, or other sweet onion,
  cut into thin strips

12 Greek olives, pitted

1/2 cup crumbled feta cheese

6 peperoncini (mild pickled peppers), stemmed and coarsely
  chopped

1. Place a baking stone on the middle shelf of the oven (unless you know your oven well enough to place it on a different shelf) and preheat on the highest setting for at least 1 hour.

2. While the oven is heating, make the dressing: Combine all the ingredients in a blender and process until smooth.

3. Make 1 pizza at a time unless your peel and oven can accommodate both pizzas. Shape the dough ball using the toss-and-spin method on page 167, stretching it to a diameter of about 12 inches. The dough should be very thin, about 1/8 inch thick, nearly translucent, and slightly thicker toward the edge. Transfer the dough to a peel or an inverted sheet pan that has been dusted with flour.

4. Gently brush a small amount of the dressing over the surface of the dough. Spread 1/2 cup of the grated cheese evenly over the top. Carefully slide the dough from the peel onto the baking stone and bake for 7 to 9 minutes. If it puffs up while baking, quickly pop the bubbles with a fork to deflate. When the edge of the crust is golden brown and the cheese is melted, remove it from the oven.

5. While the crust is baking, in a large bowl, combine all the salad ingredients. Drizzle with the dressing (reserve a little to brush on the second crust before it goes into the oven) and toss to coat all the ingredients. When the crust is finished baking, remove it from the oven and immediately cover one-half of it generously with salad. Fold the uncovered half over the salad, press down, and transfer to a platter.

6. Serve with a knife and fork while the crust is still warm. Repeat with the remaining ingredients to make the second pizza. Serve the extra salad on the side.

ROMAN-STYLE PIZZA

The defining characteristic of most pizza in Rome is the cracker-thin crust. The product of assiduous rolling and stretching, the crusts are also more uniform from center to edge than those in the *Napoletana* style. Even though the toppings are typically restrained, that first snap of the crust under the tooth unleashes an explosion of flavor, mingling with the smell of the hearth deck.

Then there is the wondrous *pizza al taglio* (cut pizza, or pizza by the slice), a cross between focaccia and standard pizza, both in shape and in thickness. It goes by a variety of names, including *pizza al metro* (by the meter)—an apt description since this plank-shaped pizza can be up to six or seven feet in length. It is sold by weight: you spread your hands to indicate the size you want, and a section is cut off the pizza and placed on a scale. No matter how much you buy, it always seems that you should have ordered more. I first saw it being made at Antico Forno, a venerable bakery in the picturesque Campo dei Fiori in Rome. The staff was selling the long, narrow pizzas as fast as they came out of the oven, and a new one seemed to emerge every three to five minutes.

In New York City, several new pizzerias have started making plank-style pizza, and I expect to see more and more of it across the country. Sullivan Street Bakery in Greenwich Village, where Jim Lahey and his team of bakers are constantly experimenting with new topping ideas, makes the best version I've had in the States.

PIZZA ALLA ROMANA CON SALUMI

In Rome, the toppings are often thinly sliced cured meats or anchovies, laid on the top as soon as the pizza emerges from the oven. I like to crisp the meat slices in a frying pan to bring out more flavor and to rid them of some of their fat. This prevents them from burning and also from making the pizza greasy. Garnished with shredded fresh arugula and basil, this pizza is a favorite of mine; you can also use any of the *Napoletana* topping combinations with this dough.

Makes two 12- to 14-inch pizzas

4 ounces of any favorite Italian *salumi* (see page 166), sliced into very thin circles or strips

2 Roman Pizza Dough balls, 6 ounces each (page 110)

Unbleached all-purpose flour, cornmeal, or semolina flour for dusting peel

1 cup All-Purpose *Marinara* Pizza Sauce (page 143) or Crushed Tomato Sauce (page 142)

6 ounces fresh mozzarella cheese *(fior di latte)*, shredded

1/4 cup freshly grated pecorino Romano, Parmigiano-Reggiano, Asiago, or other dry aged cheese

8 large basil leaves

8 arugula leaves

1. Place a baking stone on the middle shelf of the oven (unless you know your oven well enough to place it on a different shelf) and preheat on the highest setting for at least 1 hour.

2. While the oven is heating, cook the *salumi* pieces in a dry sauté pan over medium-high heat until they just begin to crisp, 3 to 5 minutes. Using a slotted spoon, transfer the meat to a paper towel to drain the fat.

3. Make 1 pizza at a time, since the size of each is large. About 30 minutes before you plan to bake the first pizza, lightly dust the counter with flour and use a rolling pin to roll 1 of the dough balls, from the center to the edges, into a flat

circle about 8 inches in diameter. Dust the top of the dough with flour if
needed to prevent the pin from sticking. Dust the top of the dough with more
flour, cover it with a kitchen towel, and let it rest for 15 minutes. Then, hand
stretch the dough into as wide a circle as possible using your knuckles as
described in the toss-and-spin method on page 167. When the dough resists
stretching and begins to spring back, stop stretching it. Lightly dust the
counter with more flour, lay the stretched dough on the counter, and again
lightly dust the top of the dough with more flour. Let it rest uncovered for
3 to 5 minutes. To complete the shaping, use the rolling pin and roll from the
center to the edge in all directions, continuing over the edge of the dough to
flatten it. The dough should be about 14 inches in diameter and cracker thin,
about $1/16$ inch. Using a pastry blade, transfer the dough to a peel or an
inverted sheet pan that has been dusted with flour.

4. Spread $1/2$ cup of the tomato sauce over the surface of the dough, leaving a
   $1/4$-inch border uncovered. Arrange half of the mozzarella over the top of the
   sauce and sprinkle with half of the grated aged cheese.

5. Carefully slide the pizza from the peel onto the baking stone. It should take
   7 to 9 minutes to bake. When it is done, the crust should be puffy and slightly
   charred on the edge and thinner in the center, and the cheese should be fully
   melted and just beginning to brown in spots. The underside of the crust
   should be brown and crisp, not white and soft. If the underside is not ready
   when the top is finished, lower the shelf for the next pizza.

6. Remove the finished pizza from the oven and immediately take half of the
   basil and arugula leaves, roll them up together lengthwise, and cut thinly
   crosswise to create shreds (known as a chiffonade cut). Sprinkle these over
   the top of the pizza. Then distribute half of the crisp *salumi* pieces over the
   top. Slice and serve. Repeat with the remaining ingredients to make the
   second pizza.

PIZZA AL TAGLIO, ROSSA E BIANCA

With this recipe, you can prepare the two types of this pizza on offer at Antico Forno: *pizza bianca* (topped with olive oil) and *pizza rossa* (topped with red sauce). Because a home oven and baking stone cannot accommodate a seven-foot-long strip of dough, this recipe yields mini versions, with strips only as long as your baking stone is wide. It will probably take a little practice before you are able to slide a strip off the peel onto the stone with ease, but within a few tries you should be experiencing on a smaller scale the reason for the buzz that surrounds this addictive product.

Makes three 14 by 4-inch pizzas
3 pounds *Pizza al Taglio* Dough (page 137)
2 cups unbleached all-purpose or bread flour
1 cup extra virgin olive oil
All-Purpose *Marinara* Pizza Sauce (page 143) for red pizza
Coarse sea salt or kosher salt for white pizza

1. Place a baking stone on the middle shelf of the oven (unless you know your oven well enough to place it on a different shelf) and preheat on the highest setting for at least 1 hour.

2. Put the flour and olive oil into separate bowls and place them near your work counter. Toss a large handful of the flour onto the counter and spread it to cover an area 1 foot square. Dip a plastic bowl scraper into the water and, working gently, use it to scrape the dough from the bowl onto the floured counter. (If you don't have a plastic scraper, wet your hands and use them to scoop the dough onto the counter.) Sprinkle a little flour over the top of the dough, and gently lift and tug the dough into a sheet about 12 inches wide and 6 inches long. Be gentle with the dough so as to degas it as little as possible. To keep the dough from sticking to the counter, slide a pastry blade or the plastic scraper under it, and continue sprinkling flour under and on top of the dough as needed.

3. Generously dust a peel or an inverted sheet pan with flour. Using the pastry blade, and beginning from the left side, cut off a lengthwise strip from the

dough about 4 inches wide. Slip the pastry blade or plastic bowl scraper under the strip and slide it away from the dough sheet. This piece, which is 6 inches long and 4 inches wide, will be your first pizza. Dip your fingers into the oil and dimple the entire surface of the dough strip, degassing it without flattening it completely. It should now not only be a little flatter, but also a little longer and wider. Wipe and dry your fingers clean, dip your hands in the flour, and slip them under the strip of dough. Lift and move the dough onto the peel, stretching it out to the width of the peel, or stretching it on a diagonal to get additional length. If using a sheet pan, stretch it either to the length of the pan, or diagonally from corner to corner. While a length of 14 inches is possible, be sure the dough is no longer than the width of the stone on which you plan to bake it. Also, make sure there is enough flour under the dough for it to slide freely on the peel. Test it by jiggling the peel.

4. *For a red pizza,* dip a pastry brush in the tomato sauce and gently brush the top of the dough with a thin layer of the sauce. *For a white pizza,* dip a pastry brush in the olive oil and brush it down the center, letting the oil flow into the dimples. Be careful not to get the peel wet with the sauce or oil, or the dough will stick when you attempt to load it into the oven.

5. Carefully slide the pizza onto the baking stone. Use short motions, not long strokes, with the peel slanted slightly downward toward the stone. The dough should slide onto the stone across the width of the oven. Immediately close the oven door. The pizza should take 10 to 12 minutes to bake. It will puff up and expand as it bakes and is ready when the edge turns golden brown and the bottom is golden and crisp.

6. Remove the finished pizza from the oven to a cooling rack. If you are making a white pizza, you can drizzle or brush more oil over the top, followed by a few grains of coarse sea salt. The red pizza is ready to eat without additional sauce, although you can brush on a little more sauce if you like. Let the pizza cool for about 5 minutes before cutting and serving.

7. Repeat the process with the remaining dough to make more pizzas. If you do not want to use all of the dough, return the unused portion to an oiled bowl, cover it, and refrigerate. It will be useable for another 2 days.

Variations

For the white pizza, you can substitute Herb Oil (page 147) for the olive oil. You can also sprinkle fresh rosemary leaves on the pizza after you brush it with either the olive oil or Herb Oil. For the red pizza, you can top the finished pizza with a light sprinkle of grated dry aged cheese. Other toppings can be used as well, such as the specialty toppings on pages 146 to 159 or the topping for Potato Rosemary Focaccia on page 235. Indeed, almost any pizza or focaccia topping can be used on these plank-style pizzas. It is best to make a few red or white versions first until you get the hang of it, since more elaborately laden pizzas are difficult to load into the oven.

GRILLED PIZZA

Grilled pizzas, when done correctly, are the greatest thing since pizza itself. The smoky flavor and crisp snap of the crust, created by the intense heat of charcoal cooking, is hard to beat. However, there are a few key concepts and tricks you need to know to pull off grilled pizzas at the highest level. Some of these are my own discoveries and some I learned directly from George Germon of Al Forno, the god-father of the genre.

First, the nature of the dough is critical to success. It must be tacky, though not sticky, because it must be stretched very thin and yet be easy to handle. Also, for the best flavor, you must coat the dough balls with olive oil. At Al Forno, the balls rest in a pan with about a quarter inch of oil. Since my dough recipe uses zippered storage bags to hold the individual dough balls, I drizzle some olive oil into the bag with each piece of dough.

Second, you must set up a *mise en place* system. In other words, you need to assemble all your tools and ingredients, get your grill or grills set up properly, and plan your grilling method, that is, your system. Here are the ingredient and equipment basics.

Dough: The recipe for the dough is on page 128 and is easy to make. Plan on 1 pizza per person if pizza is the main course. This is probably more pizza than you will need, but you will want to have that many dough balls available, depending on what else you are serving. If pizza is just one of many dishes, then figure 1 dough ball for every 2 or 3 people. Even if you have leftovers, you will be happy you do.

Tomatoes: These can be fresh or canned. If fresh, figure on 1 large tomato per average-sized pizza. Use whatever is the best-tasting seasonal tomato available. To peel the tomatoes, dip them in boiling water for about 30 seconds, transfer them to cold water, and then peel off the skin. Dice them into chunky pieces and toss them in a bowl with 1 tablespoon olive oil and 1 clove garlic, minced, per tomato. Season to taste with salt and freshly ground black pepper. You can also add chopped fresh basil to the mix, about 2 leaves per tomato, if you like.

If tomatoes are out of season, use good-quality canned tomatoes. Plan on one 28-ounce can whole tomatoes for every 3 or 4 pizzas. For each can, drain off the juice (save the juice for making sauces and soups) and cut the tomatoes into chunky pieces, continuing to drain off and collect the juice as you work. In a bowl, toss the tomato pieces with 3 tablespoons olive oil and 3 cloves garlic, minced. Season to taste with salt and freshly ground black pepper (some brands are saltier than others, and you may not need to add any salt). A little chopped fresh basil is optional. Keep the tomatoes in the refrigerator until you are ready to grill. You can also use the Crushed Tomato Sauce on page 142.

Cheese: You will need a few types of cheese. The first is a good melting cheese like full-fat low-moisture mozzarella, fresh mozzarella, Monterey Jack, or even Cheddar or Gouda. The cheese should be grated or shredded. A flavorful dry aged cheese is also important, such Parmigiano-Reggiano, Asiago, pecorino Romana, or *grana padano.* Finally, have a fresh, creamy cheese on hand, such as fresh goat cheese, Boursin (herbed cream cheese), mascarpone, or something from the *stracchino* family of cheeses. Regular American cream cheese will also work in a pinch. Gorgonzola or other blue cheeses can be used in small portions as well.

Assorted Specialty Toppings: The list on page 222 details my favorite topping combinations. These are all made up of "flavor burst" ingredients, which means that they deliver a big taste in small quantities. You do not need to use all of the toppings every time, of course. Choose the ones you want to use and have them ready by grill time.

One or Two Grills: George Germon does not advocate two grills, so I'll take the blame, but I have found that a two-grill system works well, and one of the grills can even be gas-fired (this is where I get into trouble with George). I use a kettle grill heated with good-quality hardwood lump charcoal as my primary grill, and then I use my gas-fired grill for the finish. The official Al Forno method calls for one grill with a graduated slope of charcoal. On one side, the grill is very hot, with the coals only a few inches from the grate, while the other side contains only a few coals, enough for low heat, with the coals much farther from the grate. You can even place a brick in the center and build the coals only on one side, leaving the other side nearly empty.

My method is to use the kettle grill as the hot grill for the first phase, and to use the gas grill, which cannot achieve the necessary heat nor impart true charcoal flavor, only for the second phase. I have found that plenty of charcoal flavor is infused into the crust during the first phase, thus compensating for the gas grill finish. However, in the best of all possible worlds, which means that you have a grill large enough to handle the load, you will achieve the finest results if both sides of the dough are grilled over charcoal.

Use real hardwood lump charcoal, not briquettes. George is partial to maple charcoal, now available at many markets; he feels it imparts a subtle, not-too-smoky flavor, and does not burn as hot as mesquite or hickory. The critical point, however, is to use true hardwood charcoal; fussing over the type of hardwood falls into the realm of fine-tuning.

The Setup

Once you have your dough and topping ingredients ready, start the charcoal using either a charcoal chimney or other preferred method, avoiding lighter fluid if possible. Use enough charcoal to create either one bed of hot coals 3 to 5 inches from the grate if using the two-grill system, or a graduated slope of coals if using the one-grill system. After one or two sessions, you will know exactly how much charcoal you will need.

If using the two-grill system, set the grills next to each other. Place one worktable on either side of the grill or grills. I use an L-shaped setup, but a straight-line setup will also work. On the table closest to the hot side of the charcoal grill, leave enough space to roll out the dough, either directly on the table or on another suitable surface. Have on hand flour for dusting the rolling surface, a good rolling pin or 3/4-inch dowel, kitchen towels or plastic wrap for covering the dough, and a small bowl of olive oil and a basting brush for applying it.

On the table closest to the cooler side of the charcoal grill, or to the second grill, arrange all your toppings, including the tomatoes and cheese. Have a small cutting board and a sharp knife on hand for cutting herbs. You will also need a large metal spatula and some ladles, spoons, and tongs for applying the toppings. Squeeze bottles are excellent for any purées you might be using. A complete list of the tools and other items for both tables appears below. It looks like a large list, and it is, but once you have everything in its place, the operation will go smoothly and quickly.

Checklist for Grilling Worktables

HOT SIDE	COOL SIDE
1 or 2 sheet pans	1 or 2 long metal spatulas
Metal or wooden peel	Tongs, spoons, and ladles
6 1/2-ounce dough balls, including at least 2 extra in case of mishaps	All topping ingredients
	Cooking mitts or pot holders
Rolling pin or 3/4-inch dowel	Chef's knife and small board for cutting herbs
Large kitchen towel or plastic wrap	Large cutting board for landing the pizzas
Nonstick cooking spray	1 or more serving platters
Surface for rolling out dough	Roller-style pizza cutter or large knife for cutting pizzas
Bowl of flour for dusting	
Small bowl of olive oil and a basting brush	
Pastry blade	
Plastic bowl scraper	
Cooking mitts or pot holders	
2 clean kitchen towels or rags, one wet and one dry, for cleaning your hands and surfaces	
Grill tongs for moving coals	

How to Grill a Pizza

1. Two hours before grilling, pour 2 tablespoons olive oil per dough ball into a sheet pan. Remove the dough balls from the refrigerator and from the plastic bags. Roll them in the oil and let them sit in the pan, uncovered, at room temperature. (If the dough is coming directly from the freezer, allow 4 hours. If the temperature of the room is unusually warm, adjust accordingly.)

2. Set up your grill or grills and worktables as described.

3. About 15 minutes before you begin grilling the pizzas, use your palm to press each dough ball into a rough circle about 4 inches in diameter, or as far as it will comfortably go without springing back. If space is limited, you can stack the oiled dough pieces, but check them from time to time to make sure they are not sticking to one another, and separate them if they are.

4. Take a second sheet pan and turn it upside down. Brush 2 tablespoons olive oil on the back side of the pan. When you are ready to make your first pizza, take 1 round of dough and place it on the oiled pan. Press it with your hand to flatten it further. It should slide on the surface and spread out. You can continue to press it; you can use a rolling pin or dowel to extend it; or you can pick it up and stretch it as you would a regular pizza dough on the knuckles of your hand (see page 168, shaping on a counter, for instructions on this technique). Stretch the dough until it is a thin circle or oblong about $1/8$ inch thick—almost, but not quite, paper-thin. It does not have to be perfectly round; it can even be rectangular if that is how the dough takes itself. If the final shape is too big to fit on your grilling surface, trim some of it off with a pizza cutter. (Save the scraps and combine them with other scraps to make another ball of dough.) If the thickness of the dough is uneven, use the rolling pin to even it out. The dough should be 12 to 15 inches in diameter.

5. When the dough is ready for the grill, lay it on the back of the oiled sheet pan or on an oiled metal or wooden peel. Mist the grill with cooking spray to assure that nothing will stick. Carefully slide the dough onto the grill over the hot coals. To do this successfully, jiggle the sheet pan or peel with short vibratory strokes to insure that the dough slides to the proper location and lays flat. Within 30 to 60 seconds, the surface of the dough will begin to bubble. Using a metal spatula, peel, or tongs, lift the dough and peek under to make sure that it is not burning. If it is, remove it immediately to a cooler spot on the grill or to the cooler grill. (The coals may be too hot, in which case you should wait for them to cool before proceeding.)

6. When you see the dough begin to char, remove it from the hot side with either a peel, a spatula, or tongs, and flip it over, charred side up, onto either the cooler side of the grill or onto the second grill. Immediately brush the surface with olive oil and begin putting on the toppings.

7. The grated cheeses go on first. This includes the mozzarella-style cheeses and any grated aged cheeses. You do not need as much cheese as you would put on an oven pizza—perhaps half the amount, but it must go on first, directly onto the dough.

8. Tomatoes go on next. Working quickly, use a spoon or tongs to place pieces of tomato over the surface. Try not to scoop up any tomato juice, just the tomato

meat. If using tomato sauce, use a ladle held just above the surface so that the ladle does not disrupt the cheese.

9. Next, place the dollops, dots, squirts, and sprinkles of the other toppings. The toppings do not need to cover the entire surface, but rather appear strategically in 6 to 8 spots.

10. If using a gas grill, you can close the lid at this point. If using a charcoal grill, you can use the lid, but make sure all the vent holes are open, or you can finish the pizza without the lid. (Again, if you grill both sides of the dough on the same charcoal grill, be sure to find the coolest spot on the grill to place the dough when you flip it, as you will need a few minutes for the toppings to cook and the cheese to melt.) It will take 3 to 6 minutes for the pizza to finish grilling, depending on the heat source.

11. Mince or chiffonade-cut the garnishes while the pizza finishes on the grill. If time permits, return to the unbaked dough pieces and begin to prepare the next pizza.

12. To determine if the pizza is ready to come off the grill, look for two signs: the cheese should be melted, and the underside should have brown spots or slight charring. If the dough appears to be burning, remove it immediately from the heat. When you know that the pizza is done, transfer it with a peel or metal spatula (I sometimes use 2 metal spatulas, one in each hand, for stability) from the grill to the cutting board on the second table. Immediately garnish the pizza and, if using, drizzle a small amount of Spicy Oil (page 148) over the top (or offer the oil in small pitchers at the dining table).

13. You may cut the pizza on the board or serve it whole (pieces can be torn off or cut off with a pizza cutter or large knife at the dining table). In either case, transfer the pizza to a platter and serve immediately. Then begin making the next pizza.

You will become fairly proficient by the second or third time you make grilled pizzas, developing your own rhythm and timing. At that point, your friends, who will be amazed by these extraordinary pies, will begin calling you the grill maestro supreme. However, to become exceptionally good at this technique requires a lot of practice. George Germon insists that what distinguishes Al Forno's grilled pizzas from everyone else's is the years of experience

Topping Combinations

Here are some of my favorite topping combinations. They should encourage you to experiment to create your own topping ideas. Remember, do not overload your pizza, or the crust will dry out or burn before the toppings cook.

Mozzarella and Parmigiano-Reggiano blend and fresh or oven-roasted tomato slices, followed by small dollops of Smoked Eggplant Purée (page 150) and mascarpone or fresh goat cheese, then a few caramelized garlic cloves (page 149) and a sprinkle of toasted pine nuts. Garnish with a sprinkle of fresh basil or arugula and drizzle with Spicy Oil (page 148).

The same as above, but replace the eggplant purée with Butternut Squash Purée (page 154), and replace the caramelized garlic with streaks of Sweet-and-Sour Onion Marmalade (page 151). Garnish with a sprinkle of minced fresh thyme and flat-leaf parsley in place of the basil.

Mozzarella, Gruyère or Gouda, and Parmesan blend, strips or small chunks of smoked turkey or rotisserie-cooked chicken, dots of blue cheese, streaks of Sweet-and-Sour Onion Marmalade (page 151), and a sprinkle of toasted walnuts or pecans. Garnish with scallions, chives, or arugula.

The same as above, except substitute precooked smoked or cured sausage pieces, such as andouille or *chaurice*, for the chicken.

The same as above, except substitute well-seasoned grilled shrimp or scallops for the sausage. Garnish with a sprinkle of minced flat-leaf parsley and a drizzle of Spicy Oil (page 148).

Mozzarella and Parmesan blend, grilled or sautéed wild mushrooms or portobello strips (page 152), grilled red and gold bell pepper strips, a few whole spinach or arugula leaves, and dollops of Butternut Squash Purée (page 154) and mascarpone. Garnish with a drizzle of Spicy Oil (page 148).

at the technique. I've watched George's protégé, Brian Kingsford, cook many times, and he told me it took him about six years before he felt as if he had mastered the grill. You will get better at grilling pizza over time, but, believe me, you will still wow your friends even during your novice period.

Piadina

You can also make a *piadina*, a folded Italian sandwich, using this same technique. Proceed as for grilled pizza, but after you flip over the dough, top it with sandwich fillings such as slices of cheese, marinated grilled vegetables, and slices of meat or poultry. After about 2 minutes, fold the dough in half to make a sandwich. Continue grilling for another minute or two, then flip the sandwich over and grill the other side for about 2 minutes, or until it is lightly charred. Serve piping hot.

CHICAGO DEEP-DISH PIZZA AND STUFFED PIZZA

Admittedly, I was not totally won over by the deep-dish and stuffed pizzas of Chicago. But if the happy crowds I saw there are any indication, thousands of people clearly feel as strongly about the pizzas at Lou Malnatti's, Gino's East, Giordano's, Pizzeria Uno, and Pizzeria Due as I do about the pizzas at Pizzeria Bianco, Da Michele, and Frank Pepe's. It is instead a question of category preference: I just happen to be a thin-crust, neo-Neapolitan kind of guy. Still, I have discovered that every once in a while I'm in the mood for the full-bodied adventure of deep-dish, and I have developed recipes for the Chicago model to satisfy that craving.

I am including a basic recipe with topping variations that works for both the classic deep-dish pizza and its cousin, the stuffed pizza, which includes a top crust hidden just below a second layer of toppings. The latter is more like a pie than like conventional pizza, loaded as it is with lavalike fillings. A slice is a meal. The crusts for both the classic and the stuffed pizzas are prebaked before the toppings are added. A baking stone will bake the pizzas more evenly but is not essential.

A typical restaurant deep-dish pizza is 14 inches in diameter, though you can get them smaller. Since most home cooks do not have a 14-inch pan, I have given instructions for baking the pizzas in regular 10-inch cake pans, but if you have a larger pan, you can use the same total amount of dough, rolling it out into one 20-inch disk; the same topping amounts can also be used. Add about 5 minutes to the baking time for a 14-inch pie.

CLASSIC DEEP-DISH PIZZA

Makes two 10-inch pizzas

**2 Chicago Deep-Dish Pizza Dough balls, 18 ounces each
(page 130)**

**2 1/2 cups coarsely shredded full-fat or low-fat low-moisture
mozzarella cheese**

4 cups Crushed Tomato Sauce (page 142)

**1/2 cup freshly grated Parmigiano-Reggiano, pecorino
Romano, Asiago, or other dry aged cheese**

1. Place a baking stone, if using, on the middle shelf of the oven (unless you know your oven well enough to place it on a different shelf) and preheat to 400°F. If you do not have a baking stone, position 1 oven shelf in the center of the oven and a second in the lowest position.

2. Oil two 10-inch round cake pans. Roll out each dough ball with a rolling pin, working from the center outward, into a disk about 14 inches in diameter. If the dough resists rolling or becomes too springy and elastic, cover it with a towel and let it rest for 5 minutes before resuming. Lay a finished disk over a prepared pan, lower it gently into the pan, and then press the dough snuggly into the bottom, corners, and then up the sides. Ideally, the dough will drape slightly over the rim; crimp the overhang to form a thick edge around the top of the rim. Prick the entire surface with a fork to minimize bubbling in the oven.

3. If you like a thin crust, bake immediately. If you prefer a thicker crust, cover the dough-lined pans with a kitchen towel and let sit at room temperature for 30 to 60 minutes. Bake the crusts on the middle shelf of the oven for 3 to 4 minutes to set them. The rim of the dough will slide back down into the pan somewhat, but this is normal and will form the edge.

4. Place each crust in its pan on the counter and let cool for at least 5 minutes. Evenly spread the mozzarella cheese in the bottom, then ladle in the tomato sauce to fill the pans. Sprinkle the grated aged cheese evenly over the top of the sauce.

5. Place the pans in the oven on the baking stone or, if not using a stone, on the lowest oven shelf. Immediately reduce the heat to 375°F and bake for 15 minutes. Then, if baking on a stone, rotate the pan 180 degrees. If baking directly on the shelf, move the pans to the middle shelf and rotate them 180 degrees. In either case, continue to bake for 20 to 25 minutes longer, or until the edges of the crust are a deep brown (but not burned) and the cheese is golden.

6. Remove the pizzas from the oven and place on a cooling rack for 5 minutes. Remove the pizzas from the pans by loosening the crust with a metal spatula and then gently sliding the spatula under the pizza to lift it out. Serve the pizzas on a cutting board, or cut and serve directly from the pan.

Deep-Dish Toppings

RICOTTA AND CHEESE: Cut the quantity of mozzarella cheese in the master recipe to 1 1/2 cups and stir it together 1 1/2 cups cups ricotta cheese or full-fat or low-fat small-curd cottage cheese. Add 2 eggs, beaten, and 1 teaspoon salt and stir until all the ingredients are evenly distributed. Fill the prebaked shells with the cheese mixture and ladle the tomato sauce over the cheese to fill the shell. Omit the grated aged cheese, if desired. Bake as directed.

ITALIAN SAUSAGE: This is the most popular deep-dish topping in restaurants. You can make it two different ways. For my favorite method, shape 2/3 pound Italian pork sausage meat (removed from the casing) into 2 patties the diameter of the deep-dish pans. Layer the mozzarella cheese, the tomato sauce, and the dry aged cheese in the pan as directed, then lay the patty over the top like a lid. Brush the patty with olive oil and bake as directed. The sausage will have taken on a dark, rich color when the pizza is ready.

For the second method, which is less fatty, fry 2/3 pound Italian sausage meat in a frying pan over medium heat, stirring to break up any lumps, for about 5 minutes, or until lightly browned. Transfer the contents of the pan to a sieve placed over a bowl to drain off the fat. Layer the mozzarella cheese and the tomato sauce in the pan, scatter the cooked sausage over the top, and then finish with the grated aged cheese. Bake as directed.

You can substitute ground beef, lamb, chicken, or turkey seasoned with salt and pepper (about 1/2 teaspoon salt and 1/8 teaspoon coarsely ground black pepper) and fresh or granulated garlic powder to taste for the sausage in either method.

SPINACH: In a bowl, stir together 12 ounces thawed, frozen chopped spinach, squeezed dry, with 2 1/2 cups shredded full-fat or low-fat low-moisture mozzarella cheese. Season to taste with minced fresh garlic or granulated garlic powder to taste, if desired. Substitute this mixture for the mozzarella cheese in the master recipe and then continue as directed.

VEGETABLE: In a bowl, stir together 2 cups lightly sautéed chopped vegetables such as onion, bell pepper, mushroom, zucchini or yellow squash, kale, or chard and the grated aged cheese. Layer the mozzarella cheese and the tomato sauce in the pan and top with the vegetable-cheese mixture. Bake as directed.

OTHER OPTIONS: Add olives, anchovies, onions, peperoncini (pickled peppers), pesto (page 144), or other cheeses, including cream cheese, sour cream, or mascarpone, to taste, to the classic recipe or any of the variations.

Stuffed Pizza

To make this popular variation of the Chicago pie, you will need an additional 6-ounce Chicago Deep-Dish Pizza Dough ball or the same amount of any of the following doughs for each 10-inch stuffed pizza you plan to make: Neo-Neapolitan (page 112), New York–Style (page 114), or *Americana* (page 116). (You will need 12 ounces of dough if making a 14-inch stuffed pizza.) Using a rolling pin, roll out the additional dough to the diameter of the deep-dish pan. Dust the counter and the dough as needed to prevent it from sticking; allow the dough to rest for 5 minutes if it is too springy to hold its shape. Layer 1 1/4 cups mozzarella cheese (or the spinach topping variation), 1 1/4 cups tomato sauce, and any other toppings you wish in the prebaked crust. Lay the round of dough evenly over the top of the pan. Press it into the topping, allowing the edge of the dough to drape over the rim of the pan (it will cover the top edge of the prebaked crust and then sink down into the pan). Cut a pair of 1-inch slits in the top for vents. Ladle about 3/4 cup of the tomato sauce over the top dough, filling the pan. Top with the grated aged cheese. Bake as directed for Classic Deep-Dish Pizza.

SARDINIAN *CARTA DI MUSICA* PIZZA

In my world, there are two types of Sardinian pizza. One is the kind typically served on the island, basically pizza made in the style of Naples, which lies just across the Tyrrhenian Sea. The other is crisp, like a cracker bread. Both entered my world as a result of my visit to Arcodoro & Pomodoro, a wonderful Italian restaurant in Dallas, where I ate a Sardinian riff on Neapolitan pizza and also first saw *carta di musica*, Sardinia's everyday bread.

As soon as I tried the *carta di musica*, I thought about using it for making pizza. Later, when I read about well-known chef Mario Batali launching a pizzeria in New York that would do just that, I knew I would have to eat there. But when I showed up at Batali's stylish Otto Enoteca, the crusts were a variation of griddled *Napoletana*-style dough. "The *carta di musica* crusts weren't strong enough to support the toppings I had in mind," he told me. "They were too brittle, so we came up with our own unique concept."

Since the home kitchen can be a lot more forgiving than the restaurant setting, I forged ahead with my notion and came up with two variations. The first bakes the *carta di musica* only until it is a soft flatbread, while the second crisps it to cracker consistency in a second visit to the oven. Both methods make an ultrathin crust, but the second version produces a supercrispy, highly fragile base. I can see why it would not be practical in a restaurant situation, although it works quite well at home. Even the soft version ultimately makes a crisp pizza because it gets rebaked when the toppings are applied. Only you can be the arbiter as to which is best. However, both methods should yield the thinnest, crispiest pizza crust you will find anywhere.

Any pizza-topping combinations used elsewhere in the book can be used on these crusts as long as you don't overload them. The following two pizzas are tributes to the Sardinian passion for bold flavors.

PIZZA ALLA PESCATORA

Pescatora means "fisherman's style." Even though Sardinia is an island, much of the cuisine is more land based than sea, with a wonderful array of local cheeses, olive oil, and meats, mainly lamb. But given the long coastlines, I couldn't resist making the following pizza, which evokes the island mystique about as well as anything I can imagine.

Makes two 10 by 7-inch pizzas

12 mussels, scrubbed

12 manila or cherrystone clams

8 shrimp, peeled and deveined, or bay scallops

1/4 cup extra virgin olive oil

2 *carta di musica* crusts, either soft or crisp (page 132)

1 1/2 cups Crushed Tomato Sauce (page 142)

4 cloves garlic, cut into slivers or thin slices

2 teaspoons capers

1/8 teaspoon freshly ground black pepper

2 tablespoons chopped fresh flat-leaf parsley

1/4 cup freshly grated Parmigiano-Reggiano, pecorino
   Romano, Asiago, or other dry aged cheese (optional)

1. Place a baking stone on the middle shelf of the oven (unless you know your oven well enough to place it on a different shelf) and preheat to 450°F for at least 1 hour.

2. While the oven is heating, place the mussels and clams in a dry cast-iron frying pan, cover tightly, and place over medium-high heat. Cook for about 4 minutes, or just until the shells open. Remove the mussels and clams, discarding any that do not open, and set aside to cool. Leave them in their shells. Next, sauté the shrimp in 2 tablespoons of olive oil over medium-high heat until just cooked, about 2 minutes. Transfer the shrimp to a bowl to cool and reserve the pan juices.

3. Make 1 pizza at a time unless your peel and oven can accommodate both pizzas. Set 1 crust, rough surface up, on a peel or inverted sheet pan. (You do not need to dust the peel with flour because the baked crust will not stick.) Spread 3/4 cup of the tomato sauce over the surface of the crust, leaving a 1/4-inch border uncovered. Sprinkle half each of the garlic and capers over the top. Place 4 of the shrimp around the top of the pizza, and do the same with 6 each of the mussels and clams in their shells. Drizzle 1 tablespoon of the olive oil over the surface, spiraling it out from the center. Sprinkle with half of the black pepper and drizzle with half of the reserved pan juices.

4. Carefully slide the pizza onto the baking stone and bake for about 6 minutes, or until the mussel and clam shells are very hot. Remove the finished pizza from the oven and place on a serving platter. Immediately sprinkle half each of the parsley and the cheese over the top. To eat, break off sections by hand. Repeat with the remaining ingredients to make the second pizza.

PIZZA CON LE SARDE

Sardines may rise and fall in popularity, but they never completely disappear from the culinary landscape. If you are not a sardine person, you may substitute 8 anchovy fillets, or 8 shrimp, peeled and deveined and lightly sautéed in garlic and olive oil.

Makes two 10 by 7-inch pizzas

2 *carta di musica* crusts, either soft or crisp (page 132)

1/2 cup Crushed Tomato Sauce (page 142)

4 high-quality sardines

6 ounces fresh mozzarella, either *mozzarella di bufala* or *fior di latte*, or full-fat low-moisture mozzarella cheese, cut into thin strips

12 caramelized garlic cloves (page 149)

16 Kalamata or favorite brine- or salt-cured black olives

2 tablespoons extra virgin olive oil

8 fresh basil leaves

1. Place a baking stone on the middle shelf of the oven (unless you know your oven well enough to place it on a different shelf) and preheat to 450°F for at least 1 hour. Make 1 pizza at a time unless your peel and oven can accommodate both pizzas. Set 1 crust, rough surface up, on a peel or inverted sheet pan. (You do not need to dust the peel with flour because the baked crust will not stick.)

2. Spread 1/4 cup of the tomato sauce over the surface of the crust, leaving a 1/4-inch border uncovered. Cut 2 sardines crosswise to yield 4 pieces each and distribute the pieces evenly over the crust. Arrange half of the cheese strips evenly over the surface, and then top with 6 garlic cloves and 8 olives. Drizzle 1 tablespoon of the olive oil over the surface, spiraling it out from the center.

3. Carefully slide the pizza onto the baking stone and bake for about 6 minutes, or until the cheese melts. While the pizza is baking, stack the basil leaves, roll them up lengthwise, and cut thinly crosswise to create shreds (known as a chiffonade cut). Remove the finished pizza from the oven and place on a serving platter. Immediately sprinkle half of the basil over the top. Let the pizza cool for 3 minutes before serving. To eat, break off sections by hand. Repeat with the remaining ingredients to make the second pizza.

FOCACCIA

Much of the focaccia I encountered in Italy was simple, with little or no embellishment other than a dusting of salt or seeds or a single topping such as olives, *marinara* sauce, pancetta, sautéed leeks, or roasted peppers. But focaccia is like pizza—actually it is just pizza under a different name—which means that there are countless variations to explore, all wonderful. Carol Field writes about many of them in her excellent cookbooks, should you desire to explore the full range of this pizza relative.

Unlike pizza, which cooks quickly, focaccia spends a while in the oven. For this reason, most cheeses cannot be put on it until the last few minutes of baking. The exceptions are some creamy cheeses, such as Gorgonzola, which can stand up to the long bake.

Sun-dried tomatoes and other dried products have a tendency to burn if laid on the surface. To protect them, you must either mix them into the dough, or dimple them into the surface and cover them with something else later, such as caramelized onions. Caramelized garlic (page 149) is delicious on focaccia, too, but usually only in concert with other ingredients like sausage slices or potatoes.

As with pizza, the best toppings are wasted if the dough underneath is not excellent. This is the reason I suggest making your first focaccia with just plain olive oil (or Herb Oil) and a sprinkling of salt, in the classic style of Genoa. When you have mastered the dough, then the realm of topping options begins to unfold like a good novel.

FOCACCIA ALLA GENOVESE

An important distinguishing characteristic of focaccia is the dimpled surface; the dimples collect olive oil and contribute to the flavor. After you have transferred the dough to the pan, the dimpling occurs in three stages, as described below. The method for shaping and baking focaccia dough is the same for most focaccia recipes, so the variations that follow refer back to it.

Makes one 12 by 17-inch focaccia

Focaccia Dough (page 136)

1/4 cup plus 2 tablespoons olive oil or Herb Oil (page 147)

1/2 teaspoon coarse sea salt or kosher salt

To shape and dimple the dough:

1. Line a 12 by 17-inch sheet pan with baking parchment or with a silicone nonstick baking pan liner (Silpat). Drizzle the 2 tablespoons olive oil onto the parchment or liner and spread it over the surface. Dip a plastic bowl scraper into water and, working gently, use it to scrape the dough from the bowl into the prepared pan. (If you don't have a plastic scraper, wet your hands and use them to scoop the dough into the pan.) Be gentle with the dough so as to degas it as little as possible.

2. Drizzle the 1/4 cup olive oil over the surface of the dough. Using only your fingertips, press down on the dough, creating dimples and pockets all over the surface for the oil to fill. Do not press the dough outward toward the edges of the pan; instead, simply press downward at only a slight angle toward the edges. The dough will spread on its own; any attempt to force it toward the pan edges will tear it and cause uneven sections. The dough will probably fill the pan a little more than half full before it begins to become elastic and spring back toward the center. When this occurs, stop pressing and let the dough relax at room temperature for about 15 minutes. Do not worry if some or much of the oil slides off the top of the dough; it will all be absorbed eventually. The pan of dough does not need to be covered, as the oil will protect it from developing a skin.

3. Repeat the dimpling process, beginning at the center and gradually working out toward the edges of the pan. This time the dough will nearly fill the pan. Try to keep the dough somewhat even across the top. Again, let the dough relax at room temperature for about 15 minutes.

4. Repeat the dimpling. This time the dough should fill the entire pan (if it does not quite fill the corners, don't worry, it will when it rises). Do not degas the dough any more than necessary as you spread it to fill the pan. Let the dough rise at room temperature for 2 to 3 hours, or until it fills the pan.

To bake and cool the focaccia:

5. Preheat the oven to 500°F. Just before baking, sprinkle the salt over the top of the dough. Place the sheet pan on the middle shelf of the oven, lower the temperature to 450°F, and bake for 20 minutes. Rotate the pan 180 degrees and continue baking for 10 to 20 minutes longer, or until both the top and underside are golden brown and slightly crisp.

6. Just before the focaccia is ready, place a cooling rack inside or over a sheet pan (to catch any dripping oil). Remove the finished focaccia from the oven and, using a metal spatula or pastry blade, loosen it from the sides of the pan. Slip the spatula or pastry blade between the focaccia and the parchment or baking liner and lift up the edge of the focaccia. Then jiggle the focaccia out of the pan onto the rack, leaving the parchment or baking liner in the pan. Pour any oil left in the pan over the top of the focaccia.

7. Let the focaccia cool for at least 20 minutes before cutting and serving.

POTATO ROSEMARY FOCACCIA

This focaccia variation, which goes under the name *focaccia con patate e rosmarino* in Tuscany and "potato pizza" in New York City, is beginning to emerge as the most popular topping among the new generation of focaccia fanciers. It is their benchmark in much the same way that the *pizza Margherita* is the benchmark for pizza and the baguette is for bread. When you make it, you'll understand why.

Makes one 12 by 17-inch focaccia
Focaccia Dough (page 136)
1/4 cup plus 2 tablespoons olive oil
8 new potatoes or 1 1/2 pounds Yukon Gold potatoes
1 large white or yellow onion, cut into thin strips (optional)
Leaves from 1 rosemary sprig
1 cup Herb Oil (page 147)
1/2 teaspoon coarse sea salt or kosher salt
1/2 teaspoon freshly ground black pepper, or to taste

1. Shape and dimple the dough in a 12 by 17-inch sheet pan as described on pages 233 to 234, using the 2 tablespoons olive oil for preparing the pan and the 1/4 cup olive oil for dimpling the dough. Let the dough rise at room temperature for 2 to 3 hours, or until it fills the pan.

2. While the dough is rising in the pan, prepare the potatoes. If using new potatoes, place them in a saucepan with water to cover, bring to a boil, and boil for about 10 minutes, or until they can be easily pierced with a fork. Drain, let cool (or plunge them in cold water to speed the process), and cut into 1/4-inch-thick slices. If using regular-sized Yukon Gold potatoes, slice them paper-thin using a food processor, a mandoline, or a chef's knife. In a bowl, combine the sliced potatoes, onion, and rosemary. Pour in the Herb Oil and toss gently to coat.

3. Preheat the oven to 500°F. When the focaccia is fully risen and ready to bake, remove the potatoes from the oil, shaking off the excess oil, and spread the slices over the surface of the dough, either randomly or stacked like dominoes.

Place the sheet pan on the middle shelf of the oven, bake for 5 minutes, and then lower the temperature to 400°F. Bake for 15 minutes, then rotate the pan 180 degrees. Continue to bake for 20 to 25 minutes longer, or until the dough and the potatoes are golden around the edges.

4. Remove the finished focaccia from the oven and immediately transfer it to a cooling rack as described on page 234. Drizzle any oil remaining in the pan, as well as any remaining Herb Oil, to taste, over the potatoes. Season with the salt and pepper, then let cool for at least 20 minutes before cutting and serving.

FOCACCIA WITH ONION MARMALADE, BLUE CHEESE, AND WALNUTS

Here is my all-time favorite focaccia. The Ligurian version usually calls for creamy Gorgonzola, but I prefer a firmer cheese, such as Danish blue or some of the domestic brands, because they are easier to crumble and distribute over the top. While the firmer cheese still melts, it does not completely puddle and disappear into the onion marmalade like the softer Gorgonzola.

Makes one 12 by 17-inch focaccia

Focaccia Dough (page 136)

1/4 cup plus 2 tablespoons olive oil

1 1/2 cups Sweet-and-Sour Onion Marmalade (page 151)

1/4 pound blue cheese (see recipe introduction), crumbled or
  cut into 1/2-inch pieces

1 cup coarsely chopped walnuts

1. Shape and dimple the dough in a 12 by 17-inch sheet pan as described on pages 233 to 234, using the 2 tablespoons olive oil for preparing the pan and the 1/4 cup olive oil for dimpling the dough. Let the dough rise at room temperature for 2 to 3 hours, or until it fills the pan.

2. Preheat the oven to 500°F. When the focaccia is fully risen and ready to bake, gently spread the onion marmalade evenly over the surface. Evenly distribute the blue cheese over the onion marmalade and scatter the walnuts over the top.

3. Place the sheet pan on the middle shelf of the oven, lower the temperature to 450°F, and bake for 20 minutes. Rotate the pan 180 degrees and continue baking for 20 to 25 minutes longer, or until the dough is golden on the bottom and the top.

4. Remove the finished focaccia from the oven and immediately transfer it to a cooling rack as described on page 234. Drizzle any oil remaining in the pan over the top. Let cool for at least 20 minutes before cutting and serving.

RAISIN FOCACCIA

You have never tasted raisin bread this good—wonderful for breakfast or for dessert. You can use different liquids to plump the raisins, such as a liqueur, wine, or even plain water, but I like to use orange or grape juice concentrate. For a little extra flavor, substitute 1/4 cup orange liqueur or brandy for an equal amount of the fruit juice concentrate. You can also use sweetened dried cranberries, dried currants, or other dried fruits in place of the raisins, or put together a combination you like. Because the soaked raisins and additional flour add weight to the dough, you need only a half batch of the basic recipe to fill the pan. Nor will the dough rise as high as plain focaccia dough because of all the fruit, but the taste will still be superb.

Makes one 12 by 17-inch focaccia

2 cups dark or golden raisins

1/2 cup warm water

1/2 cup orange or grape juice concentrate, heated until warm

1/2 recipe Focaccia Dough (page 136), prepared through the resting step

1 cup (4 1/2 ounces) unbleached bread flour, or as needed

1/4 cup plus 2 tablespoons olive oil

1/4 cup coarse sugar, raw sugar, or brown sugar

1. In a bowl combine the raisins, water, and orange juice concentrate and leave the raisins to plump for 1 hour.

2. Begin making the Focaccia Dough as directed. After the 5-minute rest, add the raisins and any liquid remaining in the bowl at the same time the olive oil called for in the dough recipe is added. Continue mixing, slowly adding the additional 1 cup flour, until the dough clears the sides of the bowl. Add more flour if needed until the dough achieves the described texture. The raisins will expel some of their liquid as you mix, so monitor the addition of the flour closely. Form the dough into a ball and refrigerate overnight as directed. The next day, the dough should have nearly doubled in size. Allow it to sit at room temperature for about 2 hours before making the focaccia.

3. Shape and dimple the dough in a 12 by 17-inch sheet pan as described on pages 233 to 234, using the 2 tablespoons olive oil for preparing the pan and the 1/4 cup olive oil for dimpling the dough. Let the dough rise at room temperature for 2 to 3 hours, or until it fills the pan about three-fourths full.

4. Preheat the oven to 500°F. Just before baking, sprinkle the sugar over the top of the dough. Place the sheet pan on the middle shelf of the oven, lower the temperature to 450°F, and bake for 20 minutes. Rotate the pan 180 degrees and continue baking for 20 to 25 minutes longer, or until the dough is golden and slightly crisp on the bottom and the top.

5. Remove the finished focaccia from the oven and immediately transfer it to a cooling rack as described on page 234. Drizzle any oil remaining in the pan over the top. Let cool for at least 20 minutes before cutting and serving.

GRAPE FOCACCIA

I have had a number of versions of this double-layered focaccia, which is more properly called *schiacciata* because it hails from Tuscany, not Liguria. Regardless of the place of origin, it's like the ultimate grape jelly sandwich. The following recipe, which is my variation of Carol Field's version in *Focaccia: Simple Breads from the Italian Oven*, has wonderful licorice tones from the aniseed and anise liqueur. If possible, use 10-inch springform pans. Their tall sides hold in the juice and accommodate the double-decked layers. Cake pans will also work. If you do not like the flavor of anise, you can omit the aniseed and substitute orange liqueur or water for the anise liqueur.

Makes two 10-inch round focaccias

Focaccia Dough (page 136), with substitution noted below

1/2 cup sambuca or other anise liqueur

2 teaspoons aniseed

1/4 cup olive oil

3 pounds seedless red, black, or green grapes, or any
combination

1/4 cup coarse sugar, raw sugar, or brown sugar

1/2 cup granulated sugar

1/4 cup water

1. Make the Focaccia Dough as directed, substituting 1/4 cup of the anise liqueur for 1/4 cup of the water in the recipe and working in the aniseed when you have nearly finished mixing the dough.

2. The next day, sprinkle some flour on the counter. Dip a plastic bowl scraper into water and, working gently, use it to scrape the dough from the bowl onto the floured counter. (If you don't have a plastic scraper, wet your hands and use them to scoop the dough onto the counter.) Be gentle with the dough so as to degas it as little as possible. Divide the dough into 4 equal pieces. Using 1 tablespoon of the olive oil for each pan, oil two 10-inch springform pans. Lay 1 piece of dough in each prepared pan, then brush the top of each piece with 1 tablespoon oil. Shape and dimple the dough as described in step 2 on

page 233. If the dough does not spread to fill the pans, let it relax for 5 or 10 minutes and then dimple it again.

3. Divide the grapes into 4 equal portions. Spread 1 portion on top of each pan of dimpled dough. Sprinkle 1 tablespoon of the coarse sugar over the grapes in each pan, then gently press the grapes into the dough. Oil your palm and use it to press the remaining 2 pieces of dough into disks on the floured counter, brushing the disks with oil if necessary to keep them from sticking to your hand. Let the pieces rest for a few minutes and then press again. Repeat the pressing and resting until the disks are each at least 10 inches in diameter. Lay these dough pieces over the grapes in each pan, and crimp the edges of the top and bottom dough layers to seal. Top each second layer with 1 of the remaining grape portions. Sprinkle the remaining 2 tablespoons coarse sugar evenly over the tops, and then gently press the grapes into the dough. Cover the pans with a kitchen towel or plastic wrap and let the focaccias rise at room temperature for about 45 minutes. The dough will not double in size, but it will increase in size by about 25 percent or so.

4. Preheat the oven to 450°F. Place the pans on the middle shelf of the oven, lower the temperature to 375°F, and bake for 25 minutes. Rotate the pans 180 degrees and continue baking for about 15 minutes, or until the tops and undersides are golden brown and slightly crisp.

5. While the focaccias are baking, in a small saucepan, combine the granulated sugar and water and bring to a boil over high heat. Lower the heat to medium and cook for about 5 minutes, or until the liquid is reduced to a thick, syrupy consistency. Add the remaining 1/4 cup anise liqueur and boil for 1 minute longer, then remove from the heat.

6. When the focaccias appear nearly done—the grapes will look shriveled and the edges of the dough will be golden—brush the top of each focaccia generously with the syrup and continue baking for 5 minutes longer, or until the tops are golden. Remove the finished focaccias from the oven to a cooling rack. Let cool for 5 minutes, then invert each pan onto a plate to unmold the focaccia. Turn each focaccia right side up on a cooling rack and let cool for at least 20 minutes before cutting and serving.

FOCACCIA COL FORMAGGIO DI RECCO

This Ligurian specialty does not conform to the common notion of focaccia. It's more like the best quesadilla you've ever tasted. It comes from the town of Recco and is similar to a Macedonian pita (see page 245), though it lacks the multiple layers of the latter. In Recco, cooks fill the focaccia with *stracchino*, a fresh, creamy cultured cheese made from cow's milk. Italian *stracchino* is hard to find in the United States, but the more accessible *mozzarella di bufala*, though made by a different process, is a good substitute, as is *fior di latte*, cow's milk mozzarella. However, the mozzarella should be mixed with some type of fresh cream cheese to approximate *stracchino* more closely. *Robiola* and *crescenza* are other creamy Italian cheeses that have the good melting properties that this focaccia needs. Though not on the table in Recco, even a young Brie or Camembert without the rind would work. Yet the easiest and best substitute for *stracchino* is probably mascarpone, a full-fat Italian cream cheese that is widely available and melts into a decadent puddle. I've made *focaccia col formaggio* with all of these cheeses; I've even used plain old American cream cheese whipped with a little sour cream and had respectable results.

The most amazing thing about *focaccia col formaggio*, whether of Recco or a pretender, is the sheer simplicity that translates into such total satisfaction. We think of pizza as a simple food of dough, sauce, and cheese. But pizza, with its fermentation and baking requirements, is rocket science when compared to *focaccia col formaggio*. This extraordinary focaccia requires only a conventional oven, the simplest of doughs (flour, water, and a pinch of salt), and the most basic of young cheeses. Aging or manipulating of any of the ingredients is out of the question. I'm sure that there is a lesson in that, but the implications of it frighten me, a man in love with not only the process, but also the very concept, the metaphor, of fermentation.

The best way to roll out this simple dough is with a $1/2$- or $3/4$-inch wooden dowel, rather than a rolling pin. The dowel allows you to exert enough pressure to overpower the gluten and extend the dough to its fullest diameter; with a regular rolling pin, you cannot get that kind leverage. Also, as you become more proficient at making this focaccia, you may want to dispense with the pan and bake it directly on a stone, as you would a *Napoletana* pizza. Many places in Recco do it this way.

Makes two 10- to 12-inch round focaccias

4 *focaccia col formaggio* dough balls, 1 1/2 ounces each
(page 138)

1/2 pound *stracchino* cheese or a blend of cheeses (see recipe
introduction)

Salt and freshly ground black pepper

1/4 cup extra virgin olive oil

1. Place a baking stone on the middle shelf of the oven (unless you know your oven well enough to place it on a different shelf) and preheat to 500°F. If you do not have a stone, position a shelf in the lower third, but not on the bottom rung, of the oven. Lightly oil two 10-inch cake pans or two 12-inch pizza pans with olive oil.

2. Place the 4 dough balls on a floured counter. Working with 1 at a time, and using a dowel or rolling pin, roll them out into flat disks, dusting the dough with flour as needed to prevent sticking. The pieces will probably extend only about 4 inches before springing back. Cover them with a kitchen towel and let rest for 5 minutes.

3. Roll out the pieces again, working from the center to the edges, extending them as much as possible before they resist and shrink back. If using a dowel, you should be able to roll each piece into a paper-thin circle 10 to 12 inches in diameter; if using a pin, the circle will be a bit thicker and 8 to 10 inches in diameter. Use only as much flour as you need to keep the dough from sticking to the dowel and counter. Cover the dough pieces and let them rest for at least another 5 minutes.

4. Regardless of the rolling method, lift 1 disk and gently hand stretch it to a full 12 inches in diameter. Work from the edge, not the center, and use the back of your hands and your knuckles to stretch the dough gradually into a larger and larger disk, as described in the toss-and-spin method on page 167. It should stretch to a thin, translucent sheet, like onionskin paper. Lay the stretched dough on 1 prepared pan and straighten it out so that it lays flat and covers the side walls. Repeat with another piece of dough and line the second pan in the same manner.

5. Divide the cheese into 2 equal portions, one for each pan. Using a tablespoon, drop the cheese in 8 dollops evenly over the dough in each pan. Sprinkle a pinch of salt and pepper over the cheese dollops. Then, stretch out the remaining 2 pieces of dough in the same way. Lay 1 dough piece over the top of each pan, matching up the edges of the top and bottom layers and pressing them together to seal. Using a small knife, cut 5 small slits in the top of each focaccia for vents. Drizzle 2 tablespoons of the olive oil over the top of each focaccia, and then sprinkle the top with a pinch of salt.

6. Place 1 focaccia either on the stone or on the lower oven shelf. Bake for about 10 minutes, or until the top crust develops a number of golden brown streaks or patches. Remove the finished focaccia from the oven and immediately remove it from the pan with a spatula, first inverting it onto a plate and then turning it right side up on a cutting board. Using a large knife, cut the focaccia into a cross-hatch pattern, 2 cuts in each direction, to form 9 pieces. Serve immediately. Bake and serve the second focaccia in the same way.

PITA

Here is a translation of the definition of *pita* in *The Dictionary of Common Modern Greek:* "1. A food or sweet made with phyllo dough and with different ingredients, which is baked in an oven; pita can be made with cheese *(tiropita),* spinach *(spanako-pita),* pumpkin or squash *(kolokithopita),* or meat *(kreatopita).*" This first definition continues, explaining that pita is also used as a slang term for "to flatten someone or something," as in "I made him into pita," or "A trailer truck fell onto my car and made it into pita." A second definition follows: "A type of unleavened bread, flat and usually round."

Many Americans are familiar with the most famous member of the pita family, *spanakopita,* but few are aware of the many variations that exist. I was fortunate enough to come under the tutelage of Antigone (Ann) and Soterios (Sam) Tsimikas and their daughter, Evdoxia (Yvonne). The Tsimikas family owns a restaurant and pizzeria in Cranston, Rhode Island. Antigone still makes the traditional pitas that she learned in her village of Megaro in the Macedonian region of northern Greece near Epirus, the most famous pita region. Evdoxia has become somewhat of a historian and anthropologist of her heritage. They served as my pita mentors and showed me how to make the following pies.

The main difference between the Greek pita and Ligurian *focaccia col formaggio* is the number of layers of dough. Most pitas are multileaf pies with various fillings. They can be made with commercial phyllo dough, as is usual in Greek American homes, but the authentic village method is to make a thin dough in the same manner as the dough for *focaccia col formaggio.* Since hand-rolled dough is not normally made as thin as commercial phyllo dough, many Middle Eastern and Greek markets now carry a product called village phyllo, which is a slightly thicker leaf *(phyllo* means "leaf"), similar to the hand rolled version. In other words, if you can find a source for village phyllo, you can make the following pitas—and even *focaccia col formaggio*—without making the dough.

PRASOPITA

This leek–filled pie is the first pita that Antigone and Evdoxia taught me. It is
traditionally baked in a large round pan, like a big cake pan, but can also be
made in a sheet pan if you are using store-bought, rectangular village phyllo.
The following steps are for a round pita made with hand-rolled dough. This is
a labor-intensive project—it takes time to roll out all the layers—but you cannot buy anything like these hand-rolled pitas. Antigone is picky about her feta,
preferring a high-quality creamy style, in the tradition of her village. The pita
will work with a crumbly feta, though the filling will not be as smooth.

Makes one 14-inch pita

2 bunches thin leeks (about 6 leeks total), including tender
    green tops, finely chopped

2 eggs

1 pound creamy feta cheese

3/4 cup ricotta cheese

3/4 cup small-curd full-fat cottage cheese

1/8 teaspoon freshly ground black pepper, or to taste

20 pita dough balls, 11/2 ounces each (page 138)

1/2 cup unsalted butter, melted, or olive oil

1. Put the leeks into a sauté pan, cover, place over medium heat, and steam the
   leeks in their own moisture for about 5 minutes, or until tender. Remove from
   the heat, uncover the pan, and set aside to cool for at least 15 minutes.

2. In a bowl, combine the eggs and the 3 cheeses and stir until smooth. Add the
   cooled leeks, mix well, and season with the pepper. (The feta should provide
   enough salt.)

3. Preheat the oven to 375°F. Brush the bottom and sides of a 14-inch cake pan
   with a little of the butter. Place the dough balls on a floured counter and flatten them with your palm. Working with 1 ball at a time, and using a dowel or
   rolling pin, roll them out as far as they will go without springing back. The

pieces will probably extend only about 4 inches. Cover them with a kitchen towel and let them relax for 10 to 15 minutes.

4. Roll and stretch out 1 piece of dough into a paper-thin disk 14 inches in diameter, using the process described in steps 3 and 4 on page 243. Lay the stretched dough flat on the bottom of the pan and brush the surface with a little butter. Repeat with 9 more dough pieces, brushing each one with butter, for a total of 10 layers.

5. Spoon half of the leek-cheese filling into the pan on top of the dough layers, spreading it into an even layer. Roll out 2 more pieces of dough in the same manner and lay them on top of the filling, brushing each one with butter after you place it in the pan. Spoon the remaining filling on top, again spreading it into an even layer.

6. Roll out the remaining 8 pieces of dough in the same manner, but make them a little larger, so that they will extend beyond the pan rim. Add them to the pan one at a time, brushing the top of each one with butter. After you brush the top layer with butter, crinkle it so that it is wrinkled rather than smooth. Crimp the overhanging dough into an edge, or lip, and tuck the edge inside the rim of the pan.

7. Place the pan on the middle shelf of the oven and bake for 40 to 50 minutes, or until the top layer is a rich golden brown. Remove the pan from the oven to a cooling rack. Let the pita cool for 5 minutes before cutting it into wedges. Serve hot.

Filling Variations

Spanakopita

There are many versions of this classic spinach pie, but this is the way Antigone Tsimikas learned to make it in her village.

1 pound baby spinach, coarsely chopped
1 small bunch scallions, including tender green tops,
  finely chopped
2 eggs
1 pound creamy feta cheese
3/4 cup ricotta cheese
3/4 cup full-fat small-curd cottage cheese
2 tablespoons finely chopped fresh dill
1/8 teaspoon freshly ground black pepper, or to taste

1. Put the spinach and scallions into a sauté pan, cover, place over medium heat, and steam the vegetables in their own moisture for about 5 minutes, or until tender. Remove from the heat, uncover the pan, and set aside to cool for at least 15 minutes.

2. In a bowl, combine the eggs and the 3 cheeses and stir until smooth. Add the cooled vegetables and dill, mix well, and season with the pepper. (The feta should provide enough salt.) Proceed as directed for *Prasopita*.

Tssouknidopita

Mature nettles have stinging needlelike hairs that make them nearly impossible to handle, but baby nettles have a delicate, wonderful flavor and are not prickly. Look for them in specialty produce markets or farmers' markets. Substitute 1 pound baby nettle leaves for the spinach in the *Spanakopita* recipe and proceed as directed.

Kolokithopita

Butternut squash is the best, but sweet pumpkin and even acorn or other golden squash varieties can be used in this rich autumn pita. In the absence of a fresh squash, use a 1-pound can of pumpkin purée.

1 medium-to-large butternut squash
1 tablespoon sugar, or to taste
2 tablespoons unsalted butter, melted
1/4 teaspoon salt, or to taste
1/8 teaspoon freshly ground black pepper, or to taste

1. Preheat the oven to 375°F. Place the squash on a sheet pan and bake for about 45 minutes, or until tender when pierced with a knife. Remove from the oven and let cool for 15 minutes.

2. Cut the squash in half and scrape out and discard the seeds. Scoop out the flesh, measure out 2 cups, and place in a bowl. Add the sugar and butter and stir until the mixture breaks down into a coarse purée. Season with the salt and pepper. Proceed as directed for *Prasopita*.

Tiropita

This Greek cheese pita is closest to the *focaccia col formaggio*. I think of it as the missing link between Greece and Liguria. In fact, this filling could be used in the *focaccia col formaggio* in place of the Recco version, for what we could then call a Greek *pissa*.

4 eggs
1 pound creamy feta cheese
3/4 cup ricotta cheese
3/4 cup small-curd, full-fat cottage cheese

In a bowl, combine the eggs and the cheeses and stir until smooth. Proceed as directed for *Prasopita*.

Acknowledgments

Searching for perfect pizza really has become an American pastime, right up there with baseball and going to the movies, so I'm thrilled to have been able to give voice to one such adventure. But this book could never have happened without four things: extraordinary *pizzaioli*, fellow pizza hunters, dedicated recipe testers, and an amazing editorial team. There have been so many people who have been part of this book that I risk leaving out some, so I ask in advance for your forgiveness if I have somehow omitted thanking you, especially those whom Susan and I met while on the road who offered suggestions of great pizzerias or pizza-making tips.

I would love to list every pizzeria that we heard about or visited, especially since, for literary reasons, many didn't make it into the narrative. However, rather than risk offending those who may be inadvertently omitted, let me give you the web address of one of my favorite sites, www.pizzatherapy.com, run by Albert Grande. He's done a fabulous job compiling favorite pizzerias by region, along with comments from, well, from people like you. For food fanatics at the deepest level, I suggest visiting www.chowhound.com, originated by Jim Leff; the various message boards have some great, though highly picky, commentaries on pizza as well as on just about every type of food imaginable. This site will lead you to others, many of which magically are born just when you may need them. One of my favorites is www.fat-guy.com, chronicling the adventures of one of the truly great pizza hunters (and all-around food hunters) I've ever read, Steven A. Shaw, aka the Fat Guy (his writings can also be found at www.egullet.com, another exciting web-zine for serious food fanatics).

I also want to thank Marc Botts of *Pizza Today* magazine (www.pizzatoday.com), and Tom Boyles of *Pizza Marketing Quarterly*, both of whom were very helpful in my research. Also thanks to Tom Lehman, for his excellent technical columns.

Special thanks to Gerard Ruggieri of Atwood World Travel for organizing our tour of Italy.

To the many pizza hunters, *pizzaioli*, colleagues, and friends who helped in many ways, thank you all: John Ash, Mario Batali, Rick and Deann Bayless, Linda Beaulieu, Ed Behr, Andy and Rachel Berliner, Chris and Marco Bianco, Gary Bimonte, the Bisso brothers, Howard Brownstein, Pasquale Bruno Jr. (*The Great Chicago-Style Pizza Cookbook*), Rosario Buonassisi (*Pizza: From Its Italian Origins to the Modern Table*), Howie Buten, Alan, Katherine, and Rose Cahn, Linda Carucci, Brad Cassidy, Paul Castelucci Jr., Gail Ciampa, Michele Condurro, Flo Consiglio, Domenico DeMarco, Francesco Farris, Carol Field, Margaret Fox, Jeff and Alyson Frank, Peter, Robin, Joe, and Steve Friedman, Mark Furstenburg, Chris and Gary Garafano, Francee Garcia, Steve Garner, George Germon, Michael Goldfarb, Philip, Colleen, and Elizabeth Goodrich, Dr. Phyllis Greenwald, Ruth Gresser, Norma and Sherman Hillelson, June Jacobs, Kate Jansen, Pamela Sheldon Johns (*Pizza Napoletana!*), Paul Kamuf, Robert Kedzlie, Kathleen Kennedy, Johanne Killeen, Brian Kingsford, Roxanne Klein, Joel, Becca, Quinn, and Cloe Kostman, Ed Ladou, Jim Lahey, Paula Lambert, Sarah Lagrotteria, Bonnie Tandy Lebang, David Lebovitz, Ellen Liberman, Ron Manville, Morimoto Masaharu, Alfonso Mattozzi, Angela Miller, Emily Wise Miller, Tracy O'Grady, Jonathan Osler, Antonio Pace, Mial Parker, Tamar Peltz, Buncky and Marcantonio Pezzini, Paige Poulos, Walter and Carmella Potenza, Ria Ramsey, Christopher Reinhart, Fred and Patty Reinhart, Harry Reinhart, Phyllis Reinhart, Rudy Reinhart, Hal Robinson, David Rosengarten, Vincent Rossi, William Rubel, Andy and Marla Ryan, Jose Salguerio, Cindy Salvato, Sante Salvoni, Fred Scarpulla, Ursula Schulz, Dennis Schwakopf, Art Smith, Paul Starkman, Jeffrey Steingarten, Vince Tacconelli, Greg Tompkins, the entire Tsimikas family, Bill Twieg, Steven Uhr, Bill and Suzie Van Wyck, Alice Waters, Joanne Weir, Frankie Whitman, Leah and Sarah Whitman-Salkin, Faith Willinger, John Woolley, all the culinary managers at the Sur la Table, Central Market, and other cooking schools around the country where I taught and then hunted (or hunted and then taught), and all the restaurateurs and *pizzaioli* who invited us into their passionate pizza world.

Many thanks to the over 100 recipe testers, many of whom are members of the Bread Baker's List, a wonderful e-group of serious baking enthusiasts (www.bread-bakers.com), who taught me as much as I taught them about making pizza at home: Dena Allbee, Nancy Allen, Bill Almond, Pedro Arellano III, Valda Baily, Dave Barrett, Kevin Bell, Ken Bird, Don Bischoff, Mary Blender, Kathy Bluestone, Dan Bolyard, Bonni Lee Brown, Nora Brown, Robert Scott Campbell, Rich Cardillo, Harold Chapman, Taimi Clark, Jim Clayton, Alan Connell, Chris Dalrymple, Carolyn Dandalides, Leigh Davisson, Cindy DeCesare, Robert Dempsey, Kathy Destadio, Maija Dixon, Reggie Dwork, Barbara Edwards, Jill Farrimond, Brad Feagins, Ellen Fenster, Natalie Fine, Carol Fisher, Sue M. Ford, Marsha Fouks, Sue Freeman, Lorna Friedlein, Wil Gatliff, Dave Glaze, Seth Godin, Ann Gunnett, Dan Haggarty, Ann Hamilton, Donna Handley, Charles Harrison, Nico Harrison, Dulcey Heller, Ross Hendrickson, Michael Hofstetter, Uma Iyer, Alan Jackson, Lis Jackson, David Jimenez, Phyllis Johnpoll, Keith Johnson, Anjali Joshi, Karen Keogh, Jazzbel and Irena Key, Rose Kish, Pat Kleinberg, Dan and Elizabeth Klinger, Jane Koca, Bob Koontz, Sandy Krause, Helen Lacey, Cheryl Lamberty, Bob Leonard Jr., Sandra Levine, Karen Lichti, Gloria Linnell, Jay Lofstead, Rachael Lohr, Roz Macy, Charlene Magee, Ted Manka, Joanie Martin, Ann McCann, Yvonne McCarthy, Ben McGehee, Joe Mielke, Melissa Miller, Rosemary Moore, Beth Muroff, M.L. Myers, Erin Nesmith, Eve Ng, Patrick O'Brien, Ed Okie, Mary O'Neill, Michelle Ossiander, Jeffrey Palmer, Lynne Paschetag, Ronna Payne, Art Perrin, Suzanne Pickett, Janis Pretzlav, Ilene Rachford, Linda Rawson, Herman Reinhart, Roxanne Rieske, Pat Robb, Wendy Robinson, Debby Rogers, JoAnn Ruppert, Georgia Sabourin, Joanne Sawyer, Carolyn Schaffner, Barbara Schmitt, Dan Schwarz, Richard Scotty, Steve Shelton, Liz Simpson, Amy Smereck, Jim Souter, Pat Stewart, Mark and Vanessa Strobel, Amy Stromberg, Larry Tannenbaum, Adam Tenner, Robby Thompson, Andreas Wagner, Kyle Warendorf, William Welch, Evie Werthmann, Barbara Westfield, Marlene White, Allan Wirth, Larry Wright, Rita Yaezel, and Michael Zusman.

To my colleagues at Johnson & Wales University, who provided the scheduling flexibility and resources I needed to manage writing, teaching, and pizza hunting, especially Dr. John Yena, Dr. John Bowen, Karl Guggenmos, Paul McVety, Martha Crawford, Pam Peters, Kevin Duffy, Steve Shipley, Ciril Hitz, and librarian Barbara

Janson. And to my students, the future culinary stars of America, especially those who helped with the final tweaking of the recipes.

Thanks to my agent Pam Bernstein.

And thanks to the brilliant editorial team at Ten Speed Press, headed by my editor, Aaron Wehner, and art director Nancy Austin, as well as to publisher Kirsty Melville and editorial director Lorena Jones. I loved the collaborative process that transformed my words into better words, then a beautiful design, and ultimately this book, of which I am very proud. A special thanks to Sharon Silva for her inspired copyediting, as well as to proofreader Jasmine Star and indexer Ken DellaPenta. My gratitude to photographer Maren Caruso, who imaginatively brought aspects of the hunt to life, and to the folks at Pizzetta 211 for letting us shoot in their wonderful pizzeria. And an overdue thanks to Dennis Hayes, Gonzalo Ferreyra, and Mark Anderson, as well as to my publicist, Lisa Regul.

And finally, to my wife, Susan, who not only went on many of the pizza hunts and brought a discerning palate to the quest, but also endured the endless marathon writing and testing sessions. As always, she was there for me from start to finish.

Index